THE PORT OF MILWAUKEE

The Port of

MILWAUKEE

An Economic Review

ERIC SCHENKER

With the collaboration of

John Weicher and John Wilson

The University of Wisconsin Press

Madison, Milwaukee, and London, 1967

Published by the University of Wisconsin Press
Madison, Milwaukee, and London
U.S.A.: Box 1379, Madison, Wisconsin 53701;
U.K.: 26–28 Hallam Street, London, W.1

Printed in the United States of America
by North Central Publishing Co., St. Paul, Minnesota

Library of Congress Catalog Card Number 67-13553

FOREWORD

THE mid-continent region of North America is heavily dependent on world trade. Agricultural surpluses are disposed of in world markets; Midwestern industry depends substantially on sales abroad; and many human and industrial needs of the Midwest area require imports from Canada, Latin America, and all the continents.

Yet, despite such basic reliance on world trade, the region has tended not fully to appreciate its own critical stake in the world marketing and distribution process. Historians theorize that such insularity may have developed because, for the past hundred years, the energies of our people looked westerly across a developing continent and concentrated on railroads and highways rather than on the sea lanes of the world. Whatever the reasons, it would be safe to say that the average Midwestern industrial city, be it a lake port or an inland trading center, has had a much lower level of interest or perception in these matters, than does a San Francisco, a New Orleans, a Baltimore, or a New York.

Dr. Eric Schenker's able study helps to fill a void, not only in the literature of the mid-continent, but in public understanding. It is necessary that the people of Milwaukee, of Wisconsin, and of the whole mid-continent comprehend the economic issues involved; the incalculable value of a seaway to the market places of the world; and the commercial opportunities and earning power that derive from ships, port operations, and cargo distribution.

Dr. Schenker reminds us that literally Milwaukee was a port before it was a city, and he ably documents the rising role of the port in the local economy. He finds that a public port has been a prudent investment for the people of Milwaukee as well as an economic stimulator of major importance. He has drawn together a volume of data not heretofore assembled and thus provides a new frame of reference for readers and researchers. The bibliography appended to his study is in itself a valuable service and a new reference source for the area.

The mid-continental area, including Milwaukee and the state of Wisconsin, must gradually shed its traditional insularity as it develops the new maritime potentials of the "Fourth Seacoast." In the process a new maturity will develop concerning the interlocked world in which we live and trade. A new public appreciation of the forces at work will stimulate discussion, and a new body of research and literature will emerge from the process. The great value of Dr. Schenker's work is that it analyzes and anticipates these forces, blazing a trail that others will follow.

HARRY C. BROCKEL
Port Director, Port of Milwaukee

February 28, 1966

ACKNOWLEDGMENTS

THIS publication was supported by the research phase of the University of Wisconsin Urban Program under a grant from the Ford Foundation. The authors gratefully acknowledge the financial aid provided by this program.

Many persons have freely and generously supplied much of the information incorporated in the text. Invaluable was the assistance from Mr. Harry C. Brockel, Port Director of the Port of Milwaukee, and his staff, who so willingly offered their services. To him and all the others, a word of thanks.

Special thanks are due to Mrs. Beatrice Goldberg and Miss Marian Pierce, whose patience and sacrifice in typing this manuscript will never be forgotten. Our gratitude also goes to our student helpers, Mr. Paul Naus and Mr. Michael Blasinski. In conclusion, I wish to express my gratitude to my wife, Virginia Schenker, for her numberless contributions.

ERIC SCHENKER

CONTENTS

FIGURES

TABLES

THE PORT OF MILWAUKEE

1

INTRODUCTION

THE economic importance of ports and shipping facilities is not a new topic of interest to economists. The most famous chapter in the most famous work in economics, "That the Division of Labour is Limited by the Extent of the Market," is almost entirely concerned with "water-carriage." Adam Smith regarded it as the most important and practically the only way in which "the extent of the market" was widened; he compared the costs of land and water transport between London and Edinburgh, to the great disadvantage of the former, and he noted a strong correlation between the development of civilization and the development of shipping, either foreign (the countries around the Mediterranean) or domestic (Egypt and the Nile). "What goods could bear the expense of land-carriage between London and Calcutta?" [1]

After this beginning, the field of port economics might have appeared to be headed for extensive investigation and study. In the next century, however, the railroad was invented, and ever since then, it has occupied the central place in transportation economics. Texts on the subject often devote more space to railroads than to all other modes of carriage put together.[2] The view is widely held among both scholars and laymen that the railroad alone made possible the rapid westward expansion of the

1. Adam Smith, *The Wealth of Nations*, pp. 17–21.
2. For example, D. Philip Locklin devotes twenty-two chapters solely to railroads in *Economics of Transportation*, four chapters to highways and trucking, two each to water and air transport, and one to pipelines.

1

United States [3] and that railroads greatly helped Prussia to achieve unification of Germany under its leadership.[4]

It is ironic that water transport, the most important form of carriage for three thousand years, should have lost its unquestioned supremacy just as economic science was being developed; this coincidence has meant that port economics have been neglected by economists and left to the study of engineers, geographers, and commercial shippers. Fortunately, in recent years the pendulum has begun to swing in the other direction, and economists have begun to follow the trail first blazed by Smith. One major reason for renewed interest in the field, in this country, has been the St. Lawrence Seaway, the great waterway connecting the Great Lakes with the Atlantic Ocean and permitting direct water shipping between the ports of the world and the heart of North America. Controversy over the Seaway has continued for half a century, long before, during, and after its construction; the question was and is basically an economic one, and in the debate all sides relied primarily on economic arguments to support their position.

Even with renewed academic interest in port economics, much if not most of the growing body of literature on the subject has been written in response to the demands of government and business for information on a specific problem of one particular port or region; little has been done to measure the total economic impact of any port on its local, regional, and national economy. The few studies that have investigated this impact strongly suggest that it has been seriously underestimated by casual observers and that much further research, including refinements in the methods of measuring port-created economic benefits, should have high priority.[5]

3. The best-known scholarly exposition of this view is Leland Hamilton Jenks, "Railroads as an Economic Force in American Development," *Journal of Economic History*, IV (May, 1944), 1–20.

4. Clapham, *Economic Development of France and Germany, 1815 to 1914*, pp. 150–55, 345–48.

5. A major study by the port and city of New Orleans reached the conclusion that seventy cents of every dollar of New Orleans income was traced directly or indirectly to port operations and foreign trade. The New Orleans study found that 100,000 jobs were a direct consequence of port activities, foreign trade, and allied fields.

The University of Virginia, through its Population and Economic Research Bureau, recently made a study of employment, wages, and business activity stimulated by the commerce of the ports of Virginia. This research was completed in 1964, and was based on an intensive study of the period 1953–63.

Another major study, by the Port of New York Authority (1956), found that

The purpose of this study is to describe and measure the economic impact of the Port of Milwaukee, Wisconsin. Milwaukee is one of the nation's largest cities and major manufacturing centers; the city ranked eleventh in population in 1960, with 741,000, and the Standard Metropolitan Statistical Area (SMSA), including Milwaukee and Waukesha counties, ranked seventeenth, with 1,194,000 people. There were 2,355 manufacturing establishments in the area in 1963, employing 194,756 people and producing $2,224,346,000 in value added by manufacturing, the thirteenth highest value figure among all SMSA's in the nation. Major manufacturing activities include machinery, transportation equipment, primary and fabricated metal products, leather and leather goods, and food and kindred products.[6] It is the most important commercial center for the heavily populated southeastern Wisconsin region, particularly in retail trade, transportation, and communication; its wholesaling trade includes the entire state of Wisconsin, the Upper Peninsula of Michigan, and parts of Iowa and Minnesota.

As a port, Milwaukee handled over 6,380,000 short tons of traffic in 1964 (the latest year for which statistics are available), including over 970,000 tons of exports and imports. A number of other Great Lakes harbors handled more tonnage, but most of these were virtually one-commodity ports, deriving the bulk of their tonnage from interlake shipments of iron ore, coal, or limestone. Only four lake ports handled more overseas trade — Chicago, Detroit, Toledo, and Duluth.

In addition to its sheer tonnage volume, Milwaukee has many features that make it of special interest to economists: it is one of the most diversified lake ports; its tonnage has remained remarkably stable for fifty years, while the individual commodities comprising it have fluctuated sharply; its railroad car ferries give it special economic advantages; the components of its overseas traffic highlight the port's relationships with

3,120,000 persons living in the New York–New Jersey port district owed their livelihood to the handling of waterborne commerce in the Port of New York. The study, published under the title *The Port and the Community*, found that 430,000 jobs were created by port commerce directly. Assuming two jobs in support of each job in direct employment, the study concluded that 1,300,000 jobs in the New York metropolitan area were directly or indirectly related to port activity. With the usual allowance for dependencies, one out of four persons in the periphery of the Port of New York is "directly or indirectly dependent for his livelihood on the commerce of this great bi-state harbor."

6. Milwaukee is irrevocably connected in the public mind with brewing, but it should be noted that only once (1889) was brewing the most important industry in the community.

the federal government; and it participates in the only important passenger route on the Great Lakes.

Milwaukee was the first Great Lakes port in the United States to establish a public port authority. Since the Rivers and Harbors Act of 1919 declared "that water terminals are essential to all cities and towns located upon harbors or navigable waterways and that at least one public terminal should exist, constructed, owned, and regulated by the municipality, or other public agency of the State and open to the use of all on equal terms," [7] public administration of some or all port facilities has become as common in United States ports as in those of the rest of the world. Milwaukee had established its first port agency in 1909 and in 1920 created a permanent body, the Board of Harbor Commissioners, to construct and administer municipal port facilities. Federal, state, and local governments all have legitimate concerns with port development, ranging from national defense interests to the economic fact that port facilities serve large tributary areas beyond the immediate municipality in which they are located, and often beyond state boundaries. Governmental authority, particularly the power of condemnation, has appeared almost essential for developing harbor facilities and connecting them with important land transport routes.

Milwaukee's port is both public and private. The harbor consists of an "inner harbor," along the banks of the three rivers which meet in Milwaukee, and an "outer harbor," along the lake front north and south of the river mouth. The inner harbor is primarily composed of privately owned facilities, which are used almost exclusively for the handling of bulk commodities (grain, coal, salt, and building materials), although the city-owned Municipal Open Dock (also for bulk commodities) and Car Ferry Terminal (leased by the Chesapeake & Ohio Railway) are located in the inner harbor. The city also created and operates a mooring basin for ships on the Kinnickinnic River. The outer harbor is entirely municipally owned; facilities include two piers for handling general cargo, the high-value goods which are often shipped in small quantities and must be loaded and unloaded by human labor; however, the terminals on these piers have been leased to private terminal operators. There is a municipal passenger pier leased to the commercial ships carrying tourists across Lake Michigan, a special pier for tanker ships bringing petroleum to the private marine terminals of the city, and an extensive city-owned railroad track system serving the harbor facilities and connecting with the major commercial railroads serving Milwaukee and Wisconsin. Public

7. Act March 2, 1919, c. 95, § 1, 40 Stat. 1286; 33 U.S.C.A., § 551.

and private facilities at Milwaukee are not usually competitive with each other. The interlake general cargo traffic, prominent in the port before World War I, had virtually disappeared when the city opened its first general cargo terminal in 1933. There is one private car ferry terminal, owned by the Grand Trunk Western; the Chesapeake & Ohio and Grand Trunk ferries connect with different ports on the eastern shore of the lake, and the two railroads have always had separate facilities, even before the municipal terminal opened in 1929.

There has been no full-dress study of the Port of Milwaukee's economic importance. Engineering consultants who planned the public port facilities offered incidental insights into the economics of the port, and the publications of the Board of Harbor Commissioners have chronicled the historical development of port commerce and facilities. The only scholarly investigation of the port that has been found is *The Port of Milwaukee*, by Edward Hamming. This book contains a large amount of useful information on the port, some of which has been drawn upon in this study, but Hamming viewed the port from the standpoint of a geographer and was content to indicate the existence of certain economic benefits derived by the city; he did not attempt to measure them quantitatively. Moreover, the book was written in 1953, and the impact of the St. Lawrence Seaway has changed the port's geography as well as its economy.

Basic data for the present study have been developed from a number of sources. The chapters dealing with port traffic have made use of the shipping statistics published by the U.S. Army Corps of Engineers and the Census Bureau. The records of the Milwaukee Board of Harbor Commissioners and its staff have also been drawn upon. Statistical measures of economic benefits from various port activities have been developed in a number of ways; most important have been the pioneering study of the Delaware River Port Authority in 1953, measuring the revenues produced by port handling of shipping cargo, and a 1963 export origin study by the Department of Commerce. A recent study of imports handled through the Port of Chicago (*Import Traffic of Chicago and Its Hinterland*, by Edwin H. Draine) has been useful in preparing Chapter 6, measuring the territorial extent of Milwaukee's hinterland. However, much of the study, particularly in regard to governmental financing of the port facilities, has been developed from primary data, and the unique nature of a large fraction of the port's traffic has necessitated developing measurement techniques for some economic benefits of which no previous estimates have been made.

The present study is almost solely concerned with the Port of Milwaukee. In Chapters 2 and 3, however, the port has been placed in the context of the Great Lakes system, particularly in reference to the impact of the St. Lawrence Seaway and overseas trade. Chapters 4 and 5 discuss the domestic and foreign traffic of the port, respectively, and Chapter 6 analyzes the effectiveness of the port in developing its potential overseas traffic. Milwaukee's foreign shipping has been intimately connected with the policies of the federal government, and the interrelationships of the port and the government are investigated in Chapter 7. The port's relations with the local government are similarly analyzed in Chapter 8, with particular reference to the costs and benefits of local government activity. All of these chapters are also concerned with the economic benefits derived by the community from the port; Chapter 9 presents statistical estimates of the magnitudes of some of these benefits and describes the nature of others which cannot be quantitatively estimated with any degree of precision. The summary in Chapter 10 is followed by a brief discussion of possible policy recommendations for future port activities.

2

EXPORTS OF THE GREAT LAKES AREA

THE most significant factor affecting Midwest foreign trade in the last ten years has been the Great Lakes–St. Lawrence Seaway. Actually opened on April 15, 1959,[1] after five years of construction, the Seaway climaxed over a half century of public discussion and political consideration. The Seaway project consists of a 27-foot deepwater dimension to the Great Lakes–St. Lawrence system, with companion locks and appropriate channel and harbor clearances. With its completion, the Great Lakes ports will be accessible to approximately 70 per cent of the world's merchant ships (but less than 50 per cent by fleet-carrying capacity).

It is still far too early to estimate the total impact of the Seaway on the foreign trade routes of the United States. Improvements in the harbors of some Great Lakes ports have not been completed by the U.S. Army Corps of Engineers. More important, trade routes do not adjust overnight. The habits of shippers change only gradually, and accurate information about the relative advantages of the Seaway has been lacking. The relative rate structures of alternative means of transportation also have to adjust to the new competition of the Seaway, and this process is still going on; it can be expected to continue for some time.

Despite all these factors, however, the opening of the Seaway has already brought about a significant shift in the foreign trade transport routes in the country. This is shown in Table 2-1, summarizing the relative shares of United States exports shipped from each of this country's four coasts in recent years. The change in the traffic pattern between 1958 and 1959 is marked. The relative share of exports for Great Lakes

1. The Seaway went into operation officially on June 26, 1959.

7

TABLE 2-1
SHIPPING WEIGHT AND VALUE OF U.S. WATERBORNE EXPORTS, 1951-63, BY AREA OF ORIGIN

Year	United States Weight (1,000's of short tons)	United States Value (millions of dollars)	Atlantic coast Weight (%)	Atlantic coast Value (%)	Gulf coast Weight (%)	Gulf coast Value (%)	Pacific coast Weight (%)	Pacific coast Value (%)	Great Lakes Weight (%)	Great Lakes Value (%)
1951	115,689	10,113	47	61	19	25	13	11	20.4	2.9
1952	102,687	9,024	41	58	23	26	13	13	22.4	3.2
1953	81,848	7,829	34	62	25	23	14	12	27.1	3.6
1954	80,083	8,539	39	60	24	23	14	13	23.2	3.5
1955	114,311	9,459	49	63	20	22	12	12	19.3	3.4
1956	148,126	11,485	50	60	22	25	11	12	16.9	3.2
1957	167,816	13,267	50	57	24	27	11	13	14.6	3.2
1958	116,565	10,948	48	59	24	26	12	12	15.0	3.2
1959	110,342	10,776	38	56	29	27	14	12	18.6	5.3
1960	127,151	13,406	37	53	30	28	16	13	18.1	4.8
1961	128,697	13,913	35	53	31	28	16	13	17.9	5.7
1962	135,294	13,987	35.2	53.5	32.6	27.1	13.6	12.1	18.6	6.4
1963	157,638	15,101	36.4	52.1	30.4	27.3	15.2	15.2	18.0	6.7

Source: U.S. Bureau of the Census, *United States Foreign Waterborne Commerce, Great Lakes Area, Annual Reports, 1951-63.*

ports increased by over 25 per cent measured by weight and by almost 67 per cent measured by value. Moreover, while the relative share measured by weight has declined slightly since 1959, measured by value it has shown a further significant increase, rebounding from the slump in 1960.

Table 2-1 shows that, even with the Seaway, Great Lakes exports are a smaller fraction of the total tonnage than they were as recently as

TABLE 2-2
SHIPPING WEIGHT OF U.S. WATERBORNE EXPORTS,
1951–63, EXCLUDING BITUMINOUS COAL

Year	United States (1,000's of short tons)	Great Lakes (%)
1951	65,494	11.4
1952	60,894	12.8
1953	51,173	13.7
1954	50,081	12.2
1955	64,172	12.5
1956	81,099	10.7
1957	92,077	9.2
1958	65,921	10.2
1959	72,260	12.9
1960	86,622	12.3
1961	93,355	13.6
1962	96,107	15.0
1963	110,985	14.2

Source: U.S. Bureau of the Census, *United States Foreign Waterborne Commerce, Great Lakes Area*, Annual Reports, 1951–63.

1955, but this fact should not be overemphasized. As the relative figures for weight and for value indicate, Great Lakes exports are largely commodities of large bulk and low value. Analysis of the commodities entering into foreign trade shows that bituminous coal is annually the largest single commodity, by weight, for both the Great Lakes and the rest of the nation. Great Lakes exports of bituminous coal have ranged from a high of 16,187,000 short tons in 1951 to a low of 9,955,000 short tons in 1962; for the rest of the nation, exports have varied from 14,157,000 short tons in 1953 to 57,568,000 in 1957. If this highly volatile component of our export trade is excluded, the downward trend of the Great Lakes share largely disappears, as illustrated in Table 2-2. It is worth noting that the increase in the Great Lakes relative share of exports between 1958 and 1959 is still about the same — just over 25 per cent.

Bituminous coal may justifiably be discounted in measuring the effect of the Seaway on trade patterns because an overwhelming share of the coal exported via the Great Lakes goes to Canada. Table 2-3, even

TABLE 2-3

BITUMINOUS COAL SHIPMENTS, LAKE ERIE PORTS TO CANADA,
1954, 1958–63
(Thousands of short tons)

Port	1954	1958	1959	1960	1961	1962	1963
Toledo	3,403	3,932	4,909	4,844	5,923	6,052	5,783
Sandusky	1,462	1,497	1,859	1,602	703	621	738
Ashtabula	1,789	1,503	1,764	1,632	1,401	1,304	2,364
Fairport	595	448	313	179	222	230	273
Erie	806	464	286	194	243	380	371
Lorain	1,151	533	242	648	338	238	230
Buffalo	340	127	207	101	0	0	0
Conneaut	293	253	43	162	161	230	565
Huron	17	21	0	27	7	0	2
Cleveland	27	0	0	26	81	60	0
Total	9,883	8,778	9,623	9,415	9,079	9,115	10,326
Total, all Great Lakes ports	12,370	10,563	11,070	10,739	10,312	9,955	12,628
% Lake Erie ports of total Great Lakes ports	80	83	87	88	88	91	82

Source: U.S. Army Corps of Engineers, *Waterborne Commerce of the United States*, Annual Reports, 1954, 1958, 1959, 1963; U.S. Bureau of the Census, *United States Foreign Waterborne Commerce*, Annual Reviews, 1960, 1961, 1962, 1963.

though it concerns only that coal shipped from the Lake Erie ports to Canada, brings this out clearly.

As Table 2-1 shows, the choice of a different unit of measurement will yield a strikingly different pattern of foreign trade. Which unit should be used depends upon the purposes of the study. In estimating the income generated by a port, the value figures are preferable. As will be indicated in Chapter 9, different kinds of commodities generate different amounts of revenue per ton; "general cargo" — the high value, small bulk com-

TABLE 2-4

GENERAL CARGO EXPORTS, MAJOR GREAT LAKES PORTS,
1958–63

(Thousands of short tons)

Port	1958	1959	1960	1961	1962	1963
Buffalo	42	21	24	30	51	20
Chicago	106	414	345	348	490	653
Cleveland	45	62	81	60	55	81
Detroit	33	98	305	141	290	317
Duluth	1	21	46	85	166	308
Milwaukee	44	124	107	153	159	165
Toledo	11	31	33	76	51	68
Total	282	771	941	893	1,262	1,612

Source: U.S. Army Corps of Engineers, *Waterborne Commerce of the United States, Annual Reports, 1958–63.*

modities which require special handling in shipping — generates a much greater revenue per ton than do the bulk commodities, such as bituminous coal. The Atlantic coast ports, as Table 2-1 suggests, ship a far greater proportion of the nation's general cargo exports than of its bulk commodities.

GENERAL CARGO EXPORTS

In a recent study, *The Impact of the St. Lawrence Seaway on the Upper Midwest,* Professor Krueger estimated general cargo exports in 1960 as 7,814,000 short tons for the seven leading Atlantic coast ports, as compared to 1,149,000 for seven Great Lakes ports.[2] While Professor Krueger's definition of Great Lakes general cargo exports is not entirely suitable for this study,[3] redefinition changes the results only in detail. The definition of "general cargo" given by the Bureau of the Census is used in Table 2-4.[4] The figures exclude grains, soybeans, flaxseed and oil seeds, unmanufactured cotton, coal, coke, bulk petroleum products, limestone, sand and gravel, sulphur, mineral ores and concentrates, and

2. Krueger, *Impact of the St. Lawrence Seaway,* pp. 10–15.

3. *Ibid.,* p. 15: "General cargo totals were derived from individual port commodity statistics by taking total export traffic in the port and subtracting major bulk items (grains, soybeans, petroleum and gasoline, iron ore)." Professor Krueger also excludes exports to Canada, apparently because these would not be affected by the Seaway.

4. U.S. Bureau of the Census, *Domestic Movements of Selected Commodities in United States Waterborne Foreign Trade,* p. 3.

TABLE 2-5

TOTAL MANUFACTURING EXPORTS, BY REGIONS AND STATES,
1960 AND 1963, WITH PERCENTAGE CHANGE

Geographic region and state	Total estimated manufactured exports (millions of dollars)		% change
	1960	1963	
Total value at port	16,092.5	18,298.8	14
Total value f.o.b., Prod. Plant	14,343.2	16,277.4	13
NEW ENGLAND	921.0	1,091.9	19
Maine	37.8	41.7	10
New Hampshire	45.8	40.0	−12
Vermont	25.0	34.5	38
Massachusetts	401.2	526.2	31
Rhode Island	52.4	59.2	13
Connecticut	358.7	390.3	9
MIDDLE ATLANTIC	3,092.4	3,526.4	14
New York	1,228.4	1,447.0	18
New Jersey	777.7	841.7	8
Pennsylvania	1,086.3	1,237.7	14
EAST NORTH CENTRAL	4,173.8	4,918.6	18
Ohio	1,218.6	1,419.7	17
Indiana	390.2	471.9	21
Illinois	1,261.6	1,440.5	14
Michigan	918.0	1,086.3	18
Wisconsin	385.4	500.2	30
WEST NORTH CENTRAL	672.8	804.7	20
Minnesota	146.6	193.7	32
Iowa	218.9	239.6	9
Missouri	175.1	204.6	17
North Dakota	1.1	1.6	46
South Dakota	5.8	7.9	35
Nebraska	34.3	40.3	18
Kansas	91.0	117.1	29
SOUTH ATLANTIC	1,626.4	1,816.7	10
Delaware	22.8	28.2	23
Maryland	213.2	224.9	5
District of Columbia	6.5	8.1	24
Virginia	335.3	367.8	10
West Virginia	140.4	154.1	10
North Carolina	438.2	482.8	10
South Carolina	103.9	115.1	11
Georgia	205.4	208.1	1
Florida	160.8	227.6	42

TABLE 2-5 (*continued*)

Geographic region and state	Total estimated manufactured exports (millions of dollars)		% change
	1960	1963	
EAST SOUTH CENTRAL	517.3	592.3	14
Kentucky	151.3	167.3	11
Tennessee	187.7	188.1	—
Alabama	102.6	135.1	32
Mississippi	75.7	101.9	34
WEST SOUTH CENTRAL	1,225.6	1,357.7	11
Arkansas	66.5	84.4	27
Louisiana	258.5	283.2	10
Oklahoma	73.8	91.0	23
Texas	826.8	899.1	9
MOUNTAIN	180.8	227.4	26
Montana	7.4	16.3	120
Idaho	11.4	15.5	36
Wyoming	0.9	1.4	55
Colorado	59.7	72.9	22
New Mexico	20.0	20.7	3
Arizona	29.4	46.8	59
Utah	47.2	47.9	2
Nevada	4.9	6.0	22
PACIFIC	1,931.5	1,939.2	—
Washington	478.0	300.9	−37
Oregon	76.5	88.4	16
California	1,334.0	1,494.2	12
Alaska	25.7	37.6	15
Hawaii	17.3	18.2	11

Source: U.S. Bureau of the Census, *Survey of the Origin of Exports of Manufactured Products, 1963.*
Figures have been rounded.

all Department of Defense, special category, and low value shipments.[5] Table 2-4 illustrates that general cargo exports increased by 177 per cent in 1959 as an immediate result of the opening of the Seaway and subsequently increased again by 106 per cent between 1959 and 1963. Despite this total increase of 572 per cent over the 1958 total, Great Lakes gen-

5. These figures differ from those used by Professor Krueger primarily in that those in Table 2-4 include wheat flour and animal feeds and exclude scrap iron, flaxseed, and ores and concentrates, for Canada as well as overseas. There are some other, relatively minor, differences.

eral cargo exports are still small when compared with those of the east coast.

The paucity of general cargo traffic at the Great Lakes ports stands out even more clearly when exports via the ports of the region are compared with its manufactures of export commodities. A Department of Commerce study in 1963 (see Table 2-5), estimated the value of exports manufactured in each state, making such a comparison possible.[6] The 1963 exports manufactured in the Midwest may be most easily compared with the 1963 exports shipped via the Great Lakes ports, as assembled by the Chicago Association of Commerce and Industry research and statistics division. For the purpose of this comparison, Midwest states include Ohio, Indiana, Illinois, Michigan, Wisconsin, Minnesota, Iowa, Missouri, the Dakotas, Kansas, Nebraska, and Kentucky.[7]

The value of the Midwest's manufactured exports was $5,890,700,000 in 1963; the value of manufactured exports shipped via the Great Lakes ports was $456,212,955 in 1963. Great Lakes ports, in other words, shipped about 7.7 per cent of the exports produced in the Great Lakes area. By contrast, the ports on the Delaware River (primarily Philadelphia) shipped $357,191,069 worth of manufactured exports in 1963, while their hinterland of Pennsylvania, Delaware, and half of New Jersey produced $1,668,000,000 worth of such exports. Philadelphia's share was about 21.4 per cent, almost three times that of the Great Lakes ports.

THE HINTERLAND

This comparison, striking as it is, understates the situation; it is surely too favorable to the Great Lakes. On the one hand, Philadelphia is about halfway between the two major general cargo ports of the east coast (and of the nation), New York and Baltimore. Its cost advantages in its assumed hinterland are likely to be very small. Furthermore, the western part of Pennsylvania, including Pittsburgh, is in fact in the hinterland of the Great Lakes ports; Pittsburgh itself also lies in the hinterland of Cleveland. Including this heavy-industry area in the Philadelphia hinterland drastically overestimates that port's potential exports.

On the other hand, the hinterlands of the Great Lakes ports are understated in the above enumeration. This is obvious in the case of Erie,

6. U.S. Department of Commerce, *Value of Exports of Manufactured Products, with Estimates by Region and State, and by Major Product Group*: 1960; 1963.

7. The reasons for choosing this definition of "Midwest" and for the subsequent modifications of it are given in detail in Chapter 6; these states roughly correspond to the areas in which the Great Lakes ports have shipping cost advantages over other ports.

Buffalo, Oswego, and the other Great Lakes ports in New York and Pennsylvania; these ports surely draw traffic primarily from their own states. If the $10,779,000 of exports from these ports are excluded from the estimates, then about 7.06 per cent of the remaining Great Lakes area's export production is shipped via Great Lakes ports. But, as stated above, the Pittsburgh area actually lies in the Cleveland hinterland, rather than in that of Erie. Cleveland also is the cheapest port of export for nearly all of West Virginia. The hinterlands of various other Great Lakes ports include the northern half of Tennessee, if not more, and much of Colorado (including Denver), Wyoming, and Montana. If we allow for these areas, by adding the value of manufactured exports for all of West Virginia and half of Pennsylvania, Tennessee, Colorado, Wyoming, and Montana, the total production in the Great Lakes area is $6,793,200,000, of which the area's ports ship about 6.7 per cent.[8]

Whichever hinterland is used in the measurements, the point is the same. There are several reasons for the predominance of east coast ports in this country's general cargo exports. Most obvious is the seasonal nature of shipping via the Great Lakes; the St. Lawrence Seaway is only open between eight and nine months of the year. A rough allowance for this factor can easily be made, however, by assuming that these exports are produced at an even flow during the year. On this basis, at least two-thirds of the area's exports would be ready for shipment during the Seaway shipping season, or between $3,827,133,332 and $4,528,800,000, according to the 1963 Commerce Department study. But the Great Lakes ports are still shipping only between 10.07 and 11.92 per cent of this potential traffic.

Rather than enter into a detailed discussion of other factors tending to limit the area's shipment of exports, it is convenient to defer consideration of them to Chapter 6, where they will be discussed in connection with the Port of Milwaukee. However, before then, we shall analyze the other side of Great Lakes foreign trade, imports; and then summarize the total foreign trade of the region.

---

8. As stated in n. 7, justification for including these areas in the ports' hinterlands are given in Chapter 6.

3

IMPORTS OF THE GREAT LAKES AREA

THE import traffic of the Great Lakes ports shows a somewhat similar pattern to their exports. Table 3-1 summarizes the relative shares of imports received via each of the country's coasts; according to this table, the Great Lakes ports receive a consistently larger share of the nation's imports when measured by weight than when measured by value. This is also true of exports, as was shown in Table 2-1, though the disparity is much smaller in the case of imports, indicating that bulk commodities play a smaller role in the area's imports than in its exports.

With the opening of the St. Lawrence Seaway in 1959, Great Lakes imports rose sharply. The region's relative share measured by weight rose by almost 67 per cent from 1958 to 1959, while the relative share measured by value rose by 25 per cent. This is exactly the reverse of the increases registered by exports in the first year of Seaway operation (see page 9). The inference to be drawn from this contrast is that the Seaway provided a greater stimulus to general cargo *exports* than to bulk commodities, and to bulk rather than general cargo *imports*.

That this was indeed the case is shown by the comparison of bituminous coal exports with imports of iron ore and concentrates in Table 3-2. Bituminous coal, as mentioned in the previous chapter, is the largest single commodity, measured by weight, in Great Lakes exports, while iron ore holds the same position in the region's imports.

All of the iron ore imports in these years came from Canada, just as most of the bituminous coal exports went to Canada (see Table 2-3). Iron ore imports, however, were stimulated by the Seaway; since the Canadian ore comes largely from Labrador, it is not an interlake traffic.

16

TABLE 3-1

SHIPPING WEIGHT AND VALUE OF U.S. WATERBORNE IMPORTS, 1951–63, BY AREA OF DESTINATION

Year	United States Weight (1,000's of short tons)	United States Value (millions of dollars)	Atlantic coast Weight (%)	Atlantic coast Value (%)	Gulf coast Weight (%)	Gulf coast Value (%)	Pacific coast Weight (%)	Pacific coast Value (%)	Great Lakes Weight (%)	Great Lakes Value (%)
1951	107,791	8,473	78	75	11	13	5	10	6.3	2.7
1952	115,043	8,153	77	74	11	14	5	9	6.2	3.5
1953	127,992	8,298	74	73	12	13	8	9	5.8	4.1
1954	129,289	7,665	75	73	14	14	6	10	4.6	3.3
1955	152,918	8,351	75	74	12	13	6	11	5.7	3.1
1956	174,130	9,289	73	73	12	13	8	11	6.2	3.2
1957	186,189	9,667	72	72	13	12	10	12	5.4	3.3
1958	189,227	9,628	71	71	15	12	9	13	4.2	3.3
1959	213,408	11,612	69	70	14	12	10	14	7.0	4.1
1960	211,138	11,144	68	70	14	12	12	14	6.1	4.1
1961	199,902	10,644	67	70	14	12	13	14	6.0	4.4
1962	222,533	12,211	66	69	14	12	12	14	7.0	4.8
1963	227,221	12,838	68	68	13	12	11	15	7.9	5.2

Source: U.S. Bureau of the Census, *United States Foreign Waterborne Commerce, Great Lakes Area,* Annual Reports, 1951–63.

TABLE 3-2

BITUMINOUS COAL EXPORTS AND IRON ORE IMPORTS,
GREAT LAKES PORTS, 1958–63

(Thousands of short tons)

| Year | Bituminous coal | | Total exports | | Coal % total exports |
	Amount	% Change	Amount	% Change	
1958	10,564	—	17,270	—	61
1959	11,070	5	20,397	18	54
1960	10,739	−3	21,360	5	50
1961	10,312	−4	22,963	8	45
1962	10,659	3	25,165	10	42
1963	13,148	23	28,340	13	46

| Year | Iron ore and concentrates | | Total imports | | Iron ore % total imports |
	Amount	% Change	Amount	% Change	
1958	4,191	—	7,884	—	53
1959	9,621	130	14,709	87	65
1960	8,133	−15	12,952	−12	63
1961	7,357	−10	11,971	− 8	62
1962	10,193	39	15,622	31	65
1963	12,333	21	18,000	15	69

Source: U.S. Bureau of the Census, *United States Foreign Waterborne Commerce*, Annual Reviews, 1958–63.

In this respect iron ore differs from coal, and the ore imports should be included in evaluating the impact of the Seaway.

The preponderance of iron ore in the import traffic of the Great Lakes should not be taken to mean that general cargo has not also been stimulated by the Seaway, for the region's percentage of imports measured by value has continued to rise. This increase parallels that shown in Table 2-1 for the value of exports, and it indicates that general cargo is looming larger in both the export and import trade of the Great Lakes.

GENERAL CARGO IMPORTS

The trend of general cargo imports since the opening of the Seaway is indicated in Table 3-3 for seven leading Great Lakes ports. These are the same ports whose exports were listed in Table 2-4. The import figures are substantially higher than were those for exports, but the basic pattern is generally similar: a large jump in the first year of Seaway operation is

TABLE 3-3

GENERAL CARGO IMPORTS, MAJOR GREAT LAKES PORTS, 1958–63
(Thousands of short tons)

Port	1958	1959	1960	1961	1962	1963
Buffalo	22	84	44	26	105	81
Chicago	411	676	507	578	662	816
Cleveland	202	195	198	215	423	329
Detroit	143	265	220	324	758	860
Duluth	39	30	44	52	62	67
Milwaukee	88	141	107	114	178	145
Toledo	12	93	88	112	125	196
Total	917	1,484	1,208	1,421	2,313	2,494

Source: U.S. Army Corps of Engineers, *Waterborne Commerce of the United States*, Annual Reports, 1958–63.

followed by a slackening of growth in 1960 and another great surge forward in 1962.

The definition of general cargo used in compiling Table 3-3, as in compiling Table 2-4, is that of the Bureau of the Census.[1] It excludes grains, sugar, bananas, pulpwood, coal, coke, bulk petroleum products, limestone, sand, gravel, mineral ores and concentrates, manganese, chrome, and ferroalloys. Table 3-3 includes imports from Canada, of which a large share is newsprint. This commodity is similar to iron ore in that much of it is shipped from Quebec and eastern Canada and thus makes use of the Seaway proper. However, newsprint was an important import before the Seaway was completed. Removing it from Table 3-3 would change the level of import traffic, but would not greatly affect the trend.[2]

Unfortunately, no study has been made of the final destination of imports within the United States, so that it is not possible to estimate the importance of the Great Lakes ports in bringing imports into their hinterlands. A study of Chicago, however, based on a mail survey of importers, has recently been made by Edwin H. Draine.[3] The Port of Chicago's

1. U.S. Bureau of the Census, *Domestic Movements of Selected Commodities in United States Waterborne Foreign Trade*, p. 3.

2. Newsprint imports ranged from 499,000 short tons in 1958, to 528,000 in 1959, 562,000 in 1960, 492,000 in 1961, 601,000 in 1962, and 612,000 in 1963. In each year Chicago imported a large share of the total: 277,000 in 1958; 279,000 in 1959; 294,000 in 1960; 296,000 in 1961; 281,251 in 1962; and 299,962 in 1963.

3. Draine, *Import Traffic of Chicago*; the survey procedure is described on pp. 15–24.

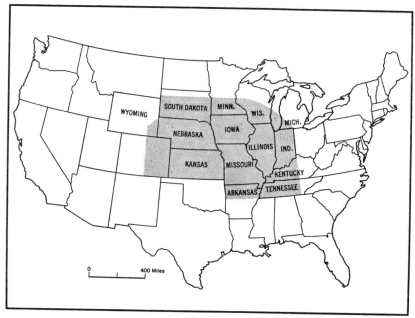

Figure 3-A. Chicago Import Traffic Study Area. *Source*: Draine, *Import Traffic of Chicago*. Map drafted by the University of Wisconsin Cartographic Laboratory.

share of the imports destined for its hinterland is shown in Table 3-4. The "study area" is delineated on the accompanying map (Figure 3-A).

The table clearly shows the predominance of the Atlantic and Gulf coasts even in the areas which are geographically part of the Great Lakes regions. It should be pointed out that Chicago's 21.5 per cent of the total imports is well above the 5 to 6 per cent figure given earlier for the Great Lakes share of its hinterland's exports. The difference is even more pronounced if the "Other Great Lakes" ports total of 9 per cent is added, giving the Great Lakes 30.5 per cent of the study area imports. The significance of this disparity, however, is open to question. It is possible that Chicago, the largest city and the largest port on the Great Lakes, may be a more important shipper into its hinterland than the other Great Lakes ports are into theirs. If this is in fact the situation, then the Great Lakes ports as a group may not play a significantly larger role in the region's import traffic than in its exports. Although Great Lakes traffic remains primarily bulk in nature, the Seaway seems to be narrowing the gap between the weight and value measures of goods shipped, thus demonstrating its notable impetus to general cargo shipping.

TABLE 3-4
PORTS OF ENTRY FOR STUDY AREA IMPORTS, 1959, EXCLUDING IRON ORE
(Thousands of short tons)

Commodity groups	East coast	Chicago	Gulf coast	Other Great Lakes	West coast	By land Canada-Mexico	Total
0. Animals and animal products	64.2	9.1	23.1	3.6	3.0	5.0	108.0
1. Vegetable food products and beverages	431.0	154.2	448.4	189.3	8.0		1,230.9
2. Vegetable products (inedible)	160.3	3.5	14.2	0.4	0.2	1.3	179.9
3. Textile fibers and manufactures	27.5	4.5	32.2	5.3	2.4		71.9
4. Wood and paper	151.3	286.9	84.4	118.2	121.4	663.1	1,425.3
5. Nonmetallic metals*							
6. Metals and maufactures (excluding machinery and vehicles)*	291.9	580.1	274.7	119.8	13.7	216.0	1,496.2
7. Machinery and vehicles	105.7	13.4	5.7	8.3	3.7		136.8
8. Chemicals and related products	55.5	4.2	151.5	0.5		4.3	216.0
9. Miscellaneous	33.8	3.5	1.1	0.2	25.0	1.2	64.8
Total tonnage	1,321.2	1,059.4	1,035.3	445.6	177.4	890.9	4,929.8
% of total	26.8	21.5	21.0	9.0	3.6	18.1	100.0

Source: Draine, *Import Traffic of Chicago*, p. 35.
*Responses to the question covering "ports of entry" were not sufficiently detailed to permit a separate listing in these groups.

TABLE 3-5

SHIPPING WEIGHT OF FOREIGN WATERBORNE COMMERCE OF THE
UNITED STATES, 1951–63, BY AREA OF ORIGIN—DESTINATION

Year	United States (1,000's of short tons)	Atlantic coast (%)	Gulf coast (%)	Pacific coast (%)	Great Lakes (%)
1951	227,881	61	15	9	13.5
1952	221,315	59	17	9	13.7
1953	209,840	58	17	10	14.1
1954	209,372	61	18	9	11.7
1955	267,229	63	16	9	11.5
1956	322,256	62	17	9	11.1
1957	354,005	61	18	10	9.8
1958	305,792	62	19	10	8.3
1959	323,750	58	20	11	10.9
1960	338,289	56	20	13	10.6
1961	328,599	54	21	14	10.6
1962	357,827	54	21	13	11.4
1963	384,859	55	20	13	12.0

Source: U.S. Bureau of the Census, *United States Foreign Waterborne Commerce, Great Lakes Area*, Annual Reports, 1951–63.

TABLE 3-6

VALUE OF FOREIGN WATERBORNE COMMERCE OF THE UNITED
STATES, 1951–63, BY AREA OF ORIGIN—DESTINATION

Year	United States value (millions of dollars)	Atlantic coast (%)	Gulf coast (%)	Pacific coast (%)	Great Lakes (%)
1951	18,586	67	20	10	2.8
1952	17,177	66	20	11	3.3
1953	16,128	68	18	11	3.9
1954	16,204	66	19	11	3.4
1955	17,810	68	17	11	3.2
1956	20,774	65	19	12	3.2
1957	22,934	64	21	12	3.2
1958	20,576	65	20	12	3.3
1959	22,388	63	19	13	4.7
1960	24,550	61	21	14	4.5
1961	24,557	60	21	13	5.1
1962	26,527	61	20	13	5.8
1963	28,232	60	20	14	6.0

Source: U.S. Bureau of the Census, *United States Foreign Waterborne Commerce*, Annual Reviews, 1951–63.

EXPORTS AND IMPORTS

The foregoing discussions of export and import traffic in the Great Lakes ports are summarized in Tables 3-5 and 3-6, showing each coast's share of the total foreign waterborne commerce. The predominantly bulk nature of the Great Lakes traffic is emphasized by the fact that this region is the only one which consistently ships a much larger share of the total when measured by weight than when measured by value. The gap between these two measures has narrowed significantly, however, since 1959, demonstrating the impetus given by the St. Lawrence Seaway to general cargo shipping in particular, as well as to traffic in general.

Tables 3-5 and 3-6 included bituminous coal exports; because coal plays such a large part in the total exports of the Great Lakes and because it was not generally affected by the Seaway, Table 3-7 presents the

TABLE 3-7

GREAT LAKES SHARE OF U.S. FOREIGN WATER-
BORNE COMMERCE, 1951–63, EXCLUDING
BITUMINOUS COAL EXPORTS

Year	United States (1,000's of short tons)	Great Lakes (%)
1951	166,099	8.6
1952	168,296	8.8
1953	170,141	8.6
1954	170,455	7.0
1955	205,258	8.2
1956	240,570	8.1
1957	264,364	7.0
1958	241,525	6.1
1959	272,467	8.9
1960	285,379	8.3
1961	281,301	8.8
1962	306,738	9.8
1963	338,206	9.8

Source: U.S. Bureau of the Census, *United States Foreign Waterborne Commerce, Great Lakes Area*, Annual Reports, 1951–63.

Great Lakes share of total foreign waterborne trade excluding this commodity. The Seaway's impact stands out more clearly in this table.

Table 3-5, which lists foreign waterborne trade by weight, once again emphasizes the dominance of the Atlantic coast ports. However, because of the predominantly bulk nature of Great Lakes traffic, these comparisons, based on weight, between Great Lakes export shipping and the export shipping of other geographic areas certainly overstate the relative position held by the Great Lakes ports. Any such distortion of the comparative position of the Great Lakes ports is clearly evident when Table 3-5 is compared with Table 3-6. In fact, Table 3-6, which shows foreign waterborne commerce by value, tends to underestimate the importance of the Great Lakes relative to other ports. When measured by weight, Great Lakes export shipping was roughly equal to half the Gulf coast total in recent years and almost equal to the Pacific coast total, but, when measured by value, the Great Lakes share was less than half the Pacific coast total and about a fourth of the Gulf coast figure.

The importance of general cargo export traffic has increased significantly in the Great Lakes area as demonstrated by the fact that the value of its foreign waterborne commerce not only has more than tripled in absolute value over the 1951–63 period, but has more than doubled as a percentage of total U.S. value. During the same period, Great Lakes foreign shipping, in terms of weight, has decreased slightly as a percentage of total U.S. exports even though it has increased by 16,000,000 short tons in absolute figures.

Table 3-7, which excludes bituminous coal exports, shows that the Great Lakes share of U.S. foreign waterborne commerce, measured by weight, increased by 19,000,000 short tons during the thirteen-year period and also increased slightly as a percentage of total U.S. overseas shipping.

Finally, Tables 3-6 and 3-7 leave little doubt regarding the Seaway's impetus to Great Lakes foreign commerce. Table 3-6 illustrates that in 1959 Great Lakes ports experienced a 42 per cent increase in foreign trade over 1958 measured in value, and Table 3-7 shows that, by weight, 1959 foreign shipping was 46 per cent above the 1958 figure. Despite these impressive increases, the Atlantic coast ports, and to some extent the Gulf coast ports, retain their dominance in foreign shipping.

4

THE PORT OF MILWAUKEE'S DOMESTIC TRAFFIC

MILWAUKEE was a port before it was a city. In the eighteenth century, the confluence of the Milwaukee, Menomonee, and Kinnickinnic rivers made the site a good location for visiting fur traders, most of them French; in 1795 the Northwest Fur Company established a trading post there, which flourished for some years and developed into a small village, but declined after 1810. John Jacob Astor's American Fur Company established a post in 1818. The fur trade, however, could only prosper in a relatively unpopulated, backwoods area, and it declined after 1820.[1]

VESSEL TRAFFIC

The development of the lead-mining industry in southwestern Wisconsin during the 1830's provided a greater stimulus to Milwaukee's shipping, particularly after 1836 when capitalists from Buffalo, New York, bought a shot tower at Helena and began to develop an eastern market for lead and shot. These commodities were hauled overland to lake ports; Racine is known to have received a two-ton shipment in the same year, and, by 1838 in Milwaukee, "it was a common thing to see oxen hauling wagons laden with lead from Grant and Lafayette counties appear at

1. Bruce, *History of Milwaukee*, Vol. I, chaps. vi-xi, contains a great deal of material on the history of the early fur trade in Milwaukee. Bruce was chairman of the city's original Harbor Commission from 1911 to 1920, and president of the Board of Harbor Commissioners from 1920 to 1949.

Some historians contend that the fur trade declined because of the decrease in fur-bearing animals and the shift of European hat styles and not because of the overpopulation of Milwaukee and environs in 1820.

the wharves after a journey of eight or ten days." [2] By 1842 and 1843 Milwaukee was shipping over a thousand tons annually to Buffalo, but the production of lead declined after 1844.[3] Milwaukee also began shipping grain in 1841. This traffic grew steadily in importance, and by 1862 Milwaukee was the leading wheat center, shipping over fifteen million bushels. It reached a peak of twenty-five million by 1873, then declined, largely due to competition from St. Paul and Minneapolis. Meanwhile, shipment of other grains grew in volume, and Milwaukee surpassed its 1875 record for all grains in 1892, growing steadily to seventy-six million bushels in 1914.[4]

Other commodities also began to play a part in Milwaukee's traffic. Coal receipts soon came to dominate the port's tonnage, first exceeding 1,000,000 tons in 1888 and never falling below that figure after 1891. At first most of the receipts were anthracite, but by 1897 bituminous coal had become more important, and in the 1911–20 decade bituminous receipts accounted for over 3,500,000 tons of the annual average of 4,700,000.[5] At that time coal accounted for 78 per cent of all receipts and 63 per cent of all traffic, which averaged about 6,100,000 and 7,500,000 tons, respectively.

The record of Milwaukee's Great Lakes traffic between 1890 and 1940 can be traced in Table 4-1. The figures include both domestic and Ca-

TABLE 4-1

GREAT LAKES COMMERCE, PORT OF MILWAUKEE, 1890–1940

(Short tons)

Year	Receipts	Shipments	Total	Value
1890	1,706,973	655,149	2,362,122	(figures not
1891	2,155,311	761,167	2,916,478	available)
1892	2,181,730	838,741	3,020,471	"
1893	1,926,604	735,233	2,661,837	"
1894	2,160,706	718,889	2,879,595	"
1895	2,238,404	826,651	3,065,055	"
1896	2,328,196	1,118,301	3,446,497	"
1897	2,656,889	1,093,457	3,750,346	"
1898	2,753,243	1,357,443	4,110,686	"
1899	2,720,097	1,226,423	3,946,520	"

2. Milwaukee *Sentinel*, Sept. 18, 1838, quoted in Bruce, *History of Milwaukee City and County*, I, 78.

3. *Ibid.*, chap. vii.

4. *Ibid.*, chap. xx.

5. Hamming, *The Port of Milwaukee*, pp. 88–89.

TABLE 4-1 (*continued*)

Year	Receipts	Shipments	Total	Value
1900	2,630,348	1,072,892	3,703,240	(figures not
1901	3,031,163	1,006,434	4,037,597	available)
1902	2,579,157	1,014,965	3,594,122	"
1903	3,935,816	1,135,952	5,071,768	"
1904	3,895,255	1,032,912	4,928,167	"
1905	4,197,533	1,256,874	5,454,407	"
1906	5,013,304	1,190,720	6,204,024	"
1907	6,091,333	1,604,669	7,696,002	"
1908	5,027,416	1,314,529	6,341,945	"
1909	5,619,155	1,395,350	7,014,505	54,344,305
1910	6,396,348	1,348,637	7,744,985	86,786,200
1911	6,224,239	1,388,002	7,612,241	119,653,735
1912	6,360,216	1,419,411	7,779,627	129,231,850
1913	7,116,434	1,530,796	8,647,230	140,734,750
1914	6,542,694	1,942,135	8,484,829	152,870,899
1915	6,437,885	1,681,990	8,119,875	150,348,921
1916	6,616,416	1,309,072	7,925,488	267,155,651
1917	5,745,601	1,075,263	6,820,864	309,582,900
1918	5,475,340	1,611,210	7,086,550	362,564,868
1919	5,689,300	1,418,900	7,108,200	320,079,300
1920	4,666,272	1,094,297	5,760,569	216,381,900
1921	4,766,463	1,664,684	6,431,147	201,660,800
1922	4,012,993	1,529,942	5,542,935	281,415,200
1923	6,351,726	1,353,315	7,705,041	415,936,200
1924	5,099,899	1,376,515	6,476,414	349,913,900
1925	5,611,274	1,296,537	6,907,811	450,001,200
1926	6,111,730	1,425,786	7,537,516	411,139,900
1927	6,512,243	1,720,955	8,233,198	466,726,000
1928	6,197,513	1,787,281	7,984,794	514,399,650
1929	6,698,674	1,866,189	8,564,863	486,228,800
1930	6,122,289	1,580,893	7,703,182	380,551,900
1931	4,873,909	1,702,368	6,576,277	255,868,400
1932	4,203,765	1,043,502	5,247,267	167,197,100
1933	4,848,263	1,503,235	6,351,498	210,146,200
1934	4,889,387	1,194,013	6,083,400	238,139,100
1935	4,621,243	1,217,340	5,838,583	270,752,800
1936	5,641,639	1,310,325	6,951,964	302,208,100
1937	5,305,361	1,312,441	6,617,802	325,079,000
1938	4,351,192	1,498,274	5,849,466	239,105,320
1939	5,038,526	1,291,276	6,329,802	304,491,635
1940	5,544,661	1,335,427	6,880,088	348,327,887

Source: U.S. Army Corps of Engineers, *Annual Reports of the Chief Engineers,* 1920–40; Bruce, *History of Milwaukee,* I, 306–7.

nadian tonnage, which until 1933 comprised all of the port's shipping.[6] In this period the peak was reached in 1913, with 8,647,230 short tons. This was the record for both Great Lakes and total tonnage until 1950, when the port handled 8,926,964 tons, of which 28,409 tons was overseas. Most of the traffic was in bulk commodities, such as those already discussed, but Milwaukee also was one of the leading "package freight" or general cargo ports on the Great Lakes. Over 1,700,000 tons of the 1913 traffic were package freight. This service was disrupted and eventually killed by the Panama Canal Act of 1912, which forbade railroads to own domestic water carriers as of July, 1914; they had owned and operated the service between Chicago and Milwaukee on one hand and the Lake Erie ports (including Detroit) on the other. The railroads now became competitors for the package freight business, which in 1916–20 dropped below half the 1911–15 average. Later, competition from trucks hastened the decline of the business, and the federal government delivered the *coup de grâce* in World War II by requisitioning the remaining freighters.[7]

CAR FERRY TRAFFIC

Statistics on Milwaukee's domestic commerce are compiled by the U.S. Army Corps of Engineers. The Engineers distinguish between "vessel" and "car ferry" traffic, a distinction which will be useful in the rest of this analysis. The car ferries are a unique feature of certain Lake Michigan ports, in effect providing direct rail service between the eastern and western shores of the lake. Railroad cars can be loaded directly onto the car ferries on either shore and shipped to the other without break of bulk, avoiding the necessity of switching through the Chicago terminal district with the consequent risk of damage and delay. The car ferries also eliminate the cost of stevedoring at both ports, which has been one of the major obstacles to a revival of the package freight trade.[8]

There are five ports on the western shore of the lake participating in the car ferry traffic, but Milwaukee has by far the largest share. The city is served by two ferries: the Chesapeake & Ohio Railway connects it

6. In other chapters of this study, Milwaukee's trade with Canada since World War II is treated as foreign commerce, in accordance with Census Bureau foreign trade data. There is no point in differentiating between Canadian and domestic Great Lakes traffic for the earlier period, however, since the two were similar in nature and the Canadian usually amounted to less than 2 per cent of the whole. There was no overseas traffic until 1933 and less than 25,000 tons per year from 1933 to 1941.

7. Hamming, *The Port of Milwaukee*, pp. 113–16.

8. *Ibid.*, p. 117.

with Ludington, Michigan, and a subsidiary of the Grand Trunk Western Railway operates a ferry service to Muskegon. The C & O ferry carries a greater volume of traffic. In 1963, it brought 797,131 short tons to Milwaukee, as compared with 278,246 handled by the Grand Trunk Western; eastbound traffic amounted to 819,265 tons to Ludington and 463,365 to Muskegon. In that year, Milwaukee received about 53 per cent of all westbound traffic and originated approximately 42 per cent of the eastbound traffic.[9]

The car ferries are long-established participants in Milwaukee's shipping. The Grand Trunk Western ferry has operated since 1906 (until 1933 it connected Milwaukee with Grand Haven, Michigan), and the Chesapeake & Ohio since 1897.[10] Generally, the ferry traffic has amounted to between 25 and 35 per cent of the port's Great Lakes tonnage, averaging the annual figures for each of the last four decades (see Table 4-2). The average has increased in recent years because of the decline of the tanker and coal trade.

TABLE 4-2

MILWAUKEE'S CAR FERRY AND TOTAL GREAT LAKES TONNAGE,
1921–64

Decade	Car ferry tonnage (annual average) (short tons)	Total Great Lakes tonnage (annual average) (short tons)	Car ferry as % of total Great Lakes
1921–30	2,018,566	7,308,690	28
1931–40	1,578,655	6,272,615	25
1941–50	2,720,108	7,996,082	34
1951–60	2,430,449	8,164,998	30
1961–64*	2,298,190	7,025,620	33

Source: U.S. Army Corps of Engineers, *Waterborne Commerce of the United States*, Annual Reports, 1953–64; U.S. Army Corps of Engineers, *Annual Reports of the Chief of Engineers*, 1921–52.

*Four-year period.

9. U.S. Army Corps of Engineers, *Waterborne Commerce of the United States*, Annual Report, 1963. The Chesapeake & Ohio also operates ferries from Ludington to Manitowoc and Kewaunee. The Ann Arbor Railroad ferry connects Frankfort, Michigan, with Manitowoc, Kewaunee, and Menominee and Manistique in the Upper Peninsula of Michigan.

10. The car ferries were originally a subsidiary of the Flint & Pere Marquette Railroad. In 1901 this road merged with the Chicago & Western Michigan Railroad to form the Pere Marquette Railway. The Pere Marquette merged with the Chesapeake & Ohio in 1947. (Pere Marquette Railway, *Annual Report*, 1901.)

COMMODITIES HANDLED

The car ferries account for Milwaukee's having one of the most diversified trades on the Great Lakes. The contrast between the composition of vessel and car ferry traffic is exemplified in Table 4-3, listing the most recent year for which figures are available. Whereas vessel traffic consists almost entirely of bulk commodities or goods which can be easily loaded or unloaded, such as motor vehicles, the car ferry traffic includes a large quantity of general cargo or what would be classified as general

TABLE 4-3

PORT OF MILWAUKEE, DOMESTIC FREIGHT INTERLAKE TRAFFIC, 1963
(Short tons)

No.	Commodity	Vessel traffic		Car ferry	
		Receipts	Shipments	Receipts	Shipments
	Total	3,564,956	32,661	1,075,377	1,282,660
010	Meat and products, fresh				390
020	Animal oils and fats, edible			501	1,021
033	Condensed and evaporated milk			843	8,684
035	Dried milk			762	7,326
037	Cheese			145	814
039	Dairy products, nec*			1,291	5,142
040	Fish and products, fresh				57
060	Hides and skins, raw			3,548	3,979
065	Leathers and mfrs			3,499	183
100	Corn		9,398	30	100,298
101	Rice				665
102	Barley and rye			790	39,191
103	Wheat			60	7,093
104	Oats			20	12,736
107	Wheat flour			2,261	18,745
108	Grain sorghums			385	7,350
109	Flour, flour-grain prep, nec			8,043	132,183
110	Animal feeds, nec			4,988	146,275
120	Vegetables and prep, fresh			2,313	3,197
123	Vegetables and prep, canned			12,000	28,071
150	Vegetable oils, fats, edible				1,195
180	Sugar			25	842
185	Molasses, sugar prod, edible				1,431
190	Liquors and wines			334	103,131
200	Rubber, crude, and allied gums				
205	Rubber tires and inner tubes			507	188
207	Rubber manufactures, nec			320	
220	Drugs, herbs, roots, crude				330

TABLE 4-3 (*continued*)

No.	Commodity	Vessel traffic		Car ferry	
		Receipts	*Shipments*	*Receipts*	*Shipments*
240	Oils, fats, waxes, veg, crude				1,170
260	Seeds, except oilseeds				85
320	Cotton manufactures			1,173	350
405	Posts, poles, and piling			330	1,545
408	Wood, nonmanufactured, nec			10,919	14,756
413	Lumber and shingles			7,637	84,827
417	Railroad ties			40	
421	Wood manufactures, nec			690	
440	Pulpwood			36,653	12,588
441	Wood pulp			16,124	10,066
445	Paper base stocks, nec			1,492	2,041
450	Standard newsprint paper			98,944	676
475	Paper and mfrs, nec			13,978	13,030
501	Anthracite coal			20,225	14
502	Bituminous coal and lignite	1,628,296		89,879	41
503	Coal-coke briquets, liquid coal			25	7,628
504	Coke, including petroleum coke		5,100	5,355	46,505
507	Gasoline	477,876			
510	Gas oil, distillate fuel oil	271,402	2,481		
513	Kerosene	8,936			
514	Residual fuel oil	89,563	1,656	24	35
519	Lubricating oils and greases			1,705	410
523	Building cement	388,962		64,305	179
526	Stone and mfrs, nec			16,980	
530	Glass and glass products			398	6,081
540	Clays and earths			10,013	424
543	Brick and tile				32
547	Clay products, nec			51	20
548	Gypsum or plaster rock	9,900		25	
551	Limestone, crushed	373,141		37,522	41,049
554	Sand, gravel, crushed rock	60,246			
555	Nonmetallic minerals, mfrs, nec	145,131		142,519	2,393
556	Slag, metal refuse	8,008			
600	Iron ore and concentrates			415	7,654
601	Pig iron	20,646		359	
602	Iron and steel scrap		7,080	3,667	21,621
603	Iron, steel semifinished prod	658		100,652	40,724
605	Ferrous castings and forgings			27,571	2,542
607	Kitchen and hospital utensils			46	39

TABLE 4-3 (*continued*)

No.	Commodity	Vessel traffic		Car ferry	
		Receipts	Shipments	Receipts	Shipments
608	Iron and steel pipe			13,482	19,346
609	Rolled, finished stl mill prod	15,903	6,765	529	909
612	Metal mfrs and parts, nec			4,347	3,296
617	Aluminum ores, concent, scrap				
618	Aluminum metal and alloys			86	1,058
620	Copper ore, concent, scrap			1,953	698
622	Refined copper in crude forms			117	1,647
624	Copper semifabricated forms			105	152
632	Copper alloy forms and scrap			566	384
640	Lead ores, concent, and scrap				330
670	Zinc ore, concent, and scrap			61	
672	Zinc forms			1,170	350
682	Nonfer ores, metls, scrap, nec				50
700	Electrical machinery			12,375	7,966
710	Engines, turbines, parts, nec			17,099	16,064
722	Const, mining mach, parts				4,405
742	Industrial mach, parts, nec			4,276	25,743
770	Agricultural mach, parts		448	1,735	4,200
780	Motor vehicles			6,150	10,804
782	Motor vehicle parts	66,283	667	37,215	300
786	Railway equipment			56,236	146,057
796	Vehicles and parts, nec			370	
827	Sodium hydroxide, caustic soda				1,499
829	Industrial chemicals, nec			8,635	100
846	Chemical specialties, nec			61,008	4,245
848	Pigments, paints, varnishes			8,134	364
851	Other nitrogenous fert, mat			136	509
855	Potash fertilizer materials			298	1,177
859	Fertilizer and materials, nec			837	2,436
860	Miscellaneous chemical prod			5,819	9,234
900	Commodities, nec	5	4	23,571	7,833
930	Waste materials, nec			56,035	61,735
				651	727

		Internal shipments	Local
Total		0	1,283
040	Fish and products, fresh		1,283

Source: U.S. Army Corps of Engineers, *Waterborne Commerce of the United States*, Annual Report, 1963.

nec = not elsewhere classified.

cargo were it shipped in any other way. Using the same Census Bureau definitions of general cargo as Chapters 2 and 3 and also excluding newsprint, it appears that general cargo commodities accounted for about 73 per cent of all car ferry receipts and 76 per cent of all shipments. The U.S. Army Corps of Engineers has not kept statistics on the value of domestic shipments since 1940, but it is certain that the general cargo commodities would be a still higher percentage of the value. For the years 1928–38, the car ferry traffic was valued at $100.86 per ton, about four times the value of vessel traffic.[11] An extremely rough guess at current value can be made by using the ratio of Commerce Department price deflators for 1957 and 1929–38 on the basis of which the current value would be something over $222.01 per ton of car ferry traffic.[12] A better estimation of current value may be achieved by using the Interstate Commerce Commission (ICC) wholesale value per ton at destination figures for 1959. For example, the value for total manufactures and miscellaneous products is $281 per ton, products of agriculture $101, and animals and products $601.[13]

No individual commodities account for an especially large share of the car ferry traffic. The largest single item among receipts is "nonmetallic minerals and manufactures, not elsewhere classified," with 142,519 short tons. However, in the Corps of Engineers statistics this classification includes salt, in order to avoid inadvertent disclosure of the output of individual salt companies. Salt probably does, in fact, account for nearly all of the reported tonnage. The Chesapeake & Ohio ferry had most of this traffic, with 121,410 tons, and salt is produced near its lines in Michigan. The C & O also carried most of the second- and fourth-ranking commodities, iron and steel semifinished products and bituminous coal, respectively, with 94,322 out of 100,652 short tons of semifinished iron and steel and 79,645 out of 89,879 short tons of bituminous coal. These figures, however, are dwarfed by comparison to the 1,628,296 tons of coal brought to Milwaukee by regular vessel. Newsprint, the third-ranking commodity, accounted for the largest share of the Grand Trunk Western's westbound traffic, with 69,164 short tons, though Milwaukee also received 29,780 short tons via the C & O.

11. Hamming, *The Port of Milwaukee*, p. 77.
12. U.S. Department of Commerce, *U.S. Income and Output*, Table VII-2, pp. 220–21.
13. Interstate Commerce Commission, *Freight Revenue and Wholesale Value at Destination of Commodities Transported by Class 1 Line Haul Railroads, 1959.* Other wholesale values per ton at destination are as follows: products of forests, $58, and products of mines, $11.

Grains were the leading commodities in the port's car ferry shipments, with 464,536 short tons. Over three-fourths (363,132 tons) went to Ludington. On the other hand, about two-thirds of the lumber shipments were to Muskegon (53,847 tons).

The car ferries are of particular importance to Milwaukee in several ways. They operate all year around, in contrast to the shortened vessel season of eight to nine months. Secondly, they bring Milwaukee closer to Michigan and eastern cities in terms of both time and distance. For example, it is 368 miles from Milwaukee to Detroit by way of Chicago; by Chesapeake & Ohio car ferry the distance is 358 miles, including the 97-mile car ferry route to Ludington, and by Grand Trunk Western ferry it is only 273 miles, 80 of them across the lake to Muskegon. The ferries take from six to six and one-half hours to make the journey, at an average speed of 16 to 18 miles per hour.[14]

What is perhaps the most important general benefit of the car ferries is a corollary of the fact that they bring Milwaukee closer to the eastern seaboard. By means of the car ferries, Milwaukee is no farther from many east coast cities than is Chicago, in terms of rail miles. Since distance is the basis for many rail rates, in particular "class rates," Milwaukee and Chicago have the same rates to many places on the seaboard. Furthermore, the rates apply whether the traffic is routed via the car ferries or through Chicago, even though in the latter case the actual mileage to Milwaukee is greater. The car ferry service has caused Milwaukee and the other western shore ports with the service to be placed in the official or eastern freight-rate territory, with a different and lower rate structure to the east than to the west. For goods moving at the class rates, the rate is lower from Milwaukee to an eastern city than it would be for goods moving from Madison or Minneapolis, for example, an equal distance into the eastern territory, because part of the rate for the latter movement would be based on the higher rates of the western trunk-line territory. It would be next to impossible to calculate the benefits to Milwaukee industries and the community at large from the rate equalization with Chicago and the lower rates to the east, but the transport cost savings over the years have surely been very large. Similar savings may accrue on every commodity which may move to Milwaukee, both overland and by water, but the car ferries present the most striking and most concrete example.

It is possible that the favorable rail rates induced by the car ferries have exerted some influence on the location of industry. In the words of

14. Hamming, *The Port of Milwaukee,* chap. v.

the Board of Harbor Commissioners, "an industry can have all the advantages of location in Milwaukee; but ratewise, it is in the fortunate position of having the same rate structure as though it had been established in the more central location of Chicago." [15]

Milwaukee's regular vessel traffic may be described more briefly. Table 4-3 presents an analysis of this traffic for 1963. The most significant aspect of Milwaukee's vessel lake traffic is the remarkable imbalance. Receipts by general cargo vessels are about a hundred times its shipments, and this underlines the lack of material resources in the Milwaukee area. Furthermore, only sixteen commodities were received in domestic vessels, and only nine were shipped, but it should be stressed that these few commodities amounted to 3,598,555 short tons, well over half the port's entire 1963 traffic of 6,626,442 short tons. Receipts of bituminous coal and gasoline in turn make up about 60 per cent of the vessel traffic, with 2,106,172 tons. Other petroleum products, crushed limestone, building cement, and "non-metallic minerals" (probably salt), account for most of the rest. About the only commodities which might be considered as general cargo are gypsum, semifinished iron and steel products, kitchen and hospital utensils, and rolled and finished steel mill products, which together totaled only 34,470 tons. Motor vehicles are a somewhat special case; the Wisconsin and Michigan Steamship Company operates an automobile carrier, the "Highway 16," between Muskegon and Milwaukee, and also uses the "Milwaukee Clipper," the last remaining excursion boat on the Great Lakes, for automobile transit. Cement, sand and gravel, and stone are shipped in special self-unloading vessels.

Although it retains its leading position in Milwaukee's shipping, the coal traffic has shown a sharp decline in recent years. According to the 1964 progress report of the chairman of the Board of Harbor Commissioners, lake coal receipts have continuously drifted downward since World War II, reflecting the continual shift away from coal toward natural gas and petroleum. A brief improvement in 1963 coal traffic marked the first reversal of this downward trend since 1948, but the downward drift in lakeborne coal again was manifest in 1964, with coal receipts dropping to the lowest volume in a half century.[16]

A similar but much sharper drop in petroleum receipts has manifested itself since 1962, the first year of operation for the West Shore Pipe Line.

15. Milwaukee, Board of Harbor Commissioners, *Impact of the Milwaukee Port*, p. 12.

16. Milwaukee, Board of Harbor Commissioners, Chairman's *Annual Report— Port Progress in 1964*, p. 5.

According to the 1964 progress report of the chairman of the Board of Harbor Commissioners, the city government consented to the construction of the West Shore Pipe Line in 1961 and permitted its interconnection to the outer harbor petroleum terminals on the premise that expanded petroleum terminals and distribution facilities would be constructed in the city of Milwaukee. As expected, the first three years of petroleum pipeline operation have had a drastic effect on the waterborne commerce in petroleum at Milwaukee. Prior to the pipeline, waterborne petroleum had been developed to the range of 2.5 million tons or more per year. More than six hundred tanker vessels per year regularly called at this port, and petroleum became a major commodity.

Waterborne petroleum dropped from the previous level of approximately 2.5 million tons to a little more than 1 million tons in 1962, the first year of pipeline operation. A further sharp decline occurred in 1963, with petroleum cargoes dropping to approximately 800,000 tons, and they dropped to little more than 600,000 tons in 1964.

To summarize, the impact of the pipeline has been such that marine petroleum deliveries at Milwaukee have dropped from 2.5 million tons to about 600,000 tons in the third year of pipeline operation. Whereas nine marine terminals in Milwaukee relied on tanker delivery in 1961, by 1964 only three terminals were receiving tanker deliveries, and several of those only spasmodically. The 600 tanker deliveries of previous years dropped to approximately 150 in 1964.

The eight petroleum terminals in the public port area continue in operation as distribution terminals, now served by rail, water, highway, and pipeline. The city receives the equivalent of wharfage charges for the product delivered by pipeline. Thus, despite the shift from waterborne to pipeline delivery, the financial return from the outer harbor oil terminals continues comparable to the revenue levels of earlier years.

In the light of the continued decline in coal and petroleum it is not surprising that lake traffic has reached the lowest level since World War II. In its efforts to meet the challenge, the port is trying to develop its foreign traffic through the St. Lawrence Seaway.

5

THE PORT OF MILWAUKEE'S FOREIGN TRAFFIC

OVERSEAS TRADE

MILWAUKEE was the first Great Lakes port to trade directly with Europe — in 1856 a cargo of wheat was loaded at Milwaukee for Liverpool.[1] Service between the Great Lakes and Europe, however, was never put on a scheduled basis in the nineteenth century, and the occasional sailings had virtually ceased by 1880. The modern story of Great Lakes-to-Europe shipping begins in 1933, when the Fjell Line (a Norwegian company) began sailings to Chicago, with Milwaukee, Detroit, Cleveland, and Toronto as regular ports of call. The Oranje Line of Holland began sailings in 1939. Service was suspended during the war, but the two lines resumed sailings afterward and were quickly joined by other European steamship lines.[2]

Since 1946 Milwaukee's overseas trade has grown steadily, reaching its pre-Seaway peak in 1956 at almost 84,000 short tons and more than doubling that total with 177,847 short tons when the Seaway opened in 1959. Table 5-1 shows the growth of the port's overseas shipping since World War II. The continued growth in the number of shipping lines and number of sailings is impressive, particularly when it is remembered that Milwaukee had only two lines connecting it with Europe before the war. In these categories, the opening of the Seaway merely accentuated an already strong trend. Statistics demonstrate, in Tables 5-1, 5-2, 5-3, and Figure 5-A, that the general trend of Milwaukee's overseas shipping

---

1. Gregory, *History of Milwaukee, Wisconsin*, I, 333, quoted in Hamming, *The Port of Milwaukee*, pp. 121–22. Chicago also had its first European sailing in 1856.
2. Hamming, *The Port of Milwaukee*, pp. 122–23.

TABLE 5-1

TWENTY-YEAR GROWTH HISTORY OF OVERSEAS COMMERCE AT
THE PORT OF MILWAUKEE, 1946–65
(Canadian traffic excluded)

Year	Number of services	Number of sailings	Imports (short tons)	Exports (short tons)	Total (short tons)
1946	3	10	460	1,783	2,243
1947	4	33	658	7,127	7,785
1948	4	41	7,999	13,130	21,129
1949	4	64	3,517	12,303	15,820
1950	5	71	7,054	21,355	28,409
1951	6	67	6,370	6,549	12,919
1952	6	104	6,178	12,874	19,052
1953	10	146	10,186	25,155	35,341
1954	9	188	8,596	32,216	40,812
1955	14	211	15,976	50,013	65,989
1956	20	225	34,671	49,268	83,939
1957	24	223	17,455	38,978	56,433
1958	26	261	22,098	44,898	66,996
1959	33	333	42,456	135,391	177,847
1960	40	294	29,930	200,902	230,832
1961	38	368	58,611	626,752	685,363
1962	43	391	44,928	451,256	496,184
1963	46	359	42,075	411,808	453,883
1964	48	439	104,325	539,969	644,294
1965	49	446	150,888	613,524	764,412

Source: Milwaukee, Board of Harbor Commissioners records, compiled by R. K. Jorgensen, Port Traffic Manager, July, 1965.

TABLE 5-2

IMPACT OF IRON AND STEEL SCRAP EXPORTS ON
OVERSEAS COMMERCE, 1958–63
(Short tons)

Year	Total overseas commerce	Iron & steel scrap exports	Imports from overseas	Overseas exports less iron & steel scrap	Total overseas commerce less iron & steel scrap
1958	66,996	0	22,098	44,898	66,996
1959	177,847	10,864	42,456	124,527	166,985
1960	230,832	76,973	29,930	123,929	153,859
1961	685,363	217,975	58,611	408,777	467,388
1962	496,184	27,205	44,928	424,051	468,979
1963	453,883	0	42,075	411,808	453,883

Source: Milwaukee, Board of Harbor Commissioners records, compiled by Jorgensen.

TABLE 5-3

TEN-YEAR RECORD OF GENERAL CARGO RELATIONSHIP
TO TOTAL OVERSEAS TRAFFIC, PORT OF MILWAUKEE,
1955–64

(Short tons)

Year	Total over-seas cargo	General cargo	General cargo % of total
1955	65,989	55,291	83.8
1956	83,939	68,791	82.0
1957	56,433	41,391	73.4
1958	66,996	57,847	86.3
1959	177,847	145,928	82.1
1960	230,832	124,930	54.1
1961	685,363*	178,543	26.1
1962	496,184*	187,802	37.9
1963	453,883*	191,335	42.2
1964	644,294*	294,624	45.7
Total	2,961,760	1,346,482	45.5
10-year average	296,176	134,648	45.5

Source: Milwaukee, Board of Harbor Commissioners records, compiled by Jorgensen; U.S. Army Corps of Engineers, *Waterborne Commerce of the United States,* Annual Reports, 1955–64.

*Total overseas cargo figures for 1961–64 are considerably higher than those reported by the U.S. Army Corps of Engineers. The Milwaukee Board of Harbor Commissioners count all shipments destined for overseas ports, but transshipped via Canada, as overseas cargo. In the Corps of Engineers annual reports most of these transshipments are classified as Canadian tonnage.

industry has been upward over the past years, and projections indicate that it will continue in that direction. In recent years, however, there have been some notable fluctuations in this generally upward trend, especially as regards total overseas import-export cargoes. Export cargoes account for the major part of these fluctuations because, as Table 5-1 illustrates, Milwaukee's overseas import traffic was only a relatively small part of total overseas trade in recent years.

The most notable fluctuations have been the great increase in 1959 and the even greater increase in 1961 which was followed by the subsequent drops in 1962 and 1963. The first of these great increases in overseas commerce can, of course, be explained simply by the opening of the St. Lawrence Seaway which, in itself, gave a great boost to all Great Lakes foreign shipping. This event caused a doubling in Milwau-

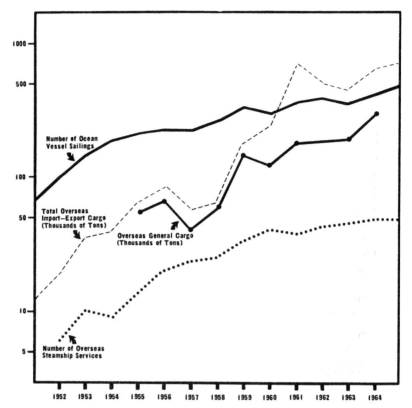

Figure 5-A. Overseas Traffic, Port of Milwaukee, 1951–65. *Source:*
Board of Harbor Commissioners, Traffic Division, City of Milwaukee.

kee's overseas import traffic and tripled overseas exports over the 1958 level.

The 1961 experience, on the other hand, had two important causes. The first of these, which seems to be lasting in duration and which accounts for the greater part of the increase, was nothing more than a general increase in overseas exports of various kinds from the Port of Milwaukee. The second cause and the reason for the subsequent fall in 1962 was the extensive rise in scrap iron and steel exports. In 1961 Milwaukee exported 217,975 tons of iron and steel scrap to Europe and Japan to feed their booming steel industries, an increase of 141,000 short tons over 1960. In 1962, the total fell to 27,205 short tons, a decrease of 190,000 short tons.

This occurrence distorts the figures in Table 5-1 and makes it appear that the port suffered a great setback in 1962 which took four shipping seasons to overcome. However, by dropping the iron and steel scrap figures from the export totals, as is done in Table 5-2, we are able to get a more meaningful picture of the port's growth.

The notable increase in overseas traffic in 1964 is once again due to a general increase in the export of many commodities, coupled this time with a substantial rise in general cargo traffic (103,000 short tons over 1963). Table 5-3 summarizes the growth of overseas general cargo traffic since 1954. The relative fall from 1955, when general cargo equaled 83.8 per cent of Milwaukee's overseas shipping, to 1964, when it equaled 45.7 per cent, was due primarily to diversification of trade and to the additional export capability available after the Seaway opening in 1959. Figure 5-A indicates that general cargo traffic has grown favorably in relation to other measures of growth, and the absolute increase experienced in 1964 highlights the growing importance of this type of commodity.

The steadiest growth, as illustrated in Table 5-1 and Figure 5-A, has been in the number of ocean-going vessels and in the number of overseas steamship services serving the Port of Milwaukee. Even though the growth of the latter items has been more steady, the growth in cargoes over the last fifteen years, though somewhat irregular, has proven relatively greater. This would indicate not only that more and more ships are carrying traffic in and out of Milwaukee each year, but that there is also greater traffic per ship. Whereas Milwaukee may have been only a whistle stop between Chicago and the Atlantic ten years ago, it is now becoming a relatively more important cargo port and is receiving and shipping a greater percentage of each ship's cargo than it did in the past.

FOREIGN SHIPPING

The growth of Milwaukee's foreign shipping is not merely a reflection of overall increases in the trade of the United States. As demonstrated in Table 5-4, Milwaukee's share of total U.S. foreign waterborne commerce has also increased significantly since 1951. The rise has been somewhat irregular, with 1953, a year of unusually high barley and rye imports, and 1961, a year of large scrap iron and steel exports, enjoying the highest percentages of the period. Despite these and other irregularities, the port's share of total foreign commerce has grown quite favorably relative to other Great Lakes ports.

Since 1953, which was both the top year for Milwaukee-Canadian tonnage and the top year, in percentage, for Great Lakes foreign tonnage, Milwaukee-Canadian tonnage has dropped by about 97,000 short

TABLE 5-4

MILWAUKEE'S SHARE OF U.S. FOREIGN WATERBORNE COMMERCE,
1951–63*

	1951	1952	1953	1954	1955
Exports:					
Total U.S.					
(1000's of short tons)	115,689	102,689	80,367	77,601	112,231
Great Lakes %	20.4	22.4	27.4	23.8	19.5
Milwaukee %	0.038	0.032	0.047	0.058	0.045
Imports:					
Total U.S.					
(1000's of short tons)	100,605	107,373	118,969	120,375	141,086
Great Lakes %	6.7	6.6	6.4	4.9	6.2
Milwaukee %	0.213	0.263	0.382	0.295	0.261
Barley & Rye					
% of Milw.'s total	74.7	73.0	82.5	84.2	73.9
Total Commerce:					
Total U.S.					
(1000's of short tons)	216,294	210,062	199,336	197,976	253,317
Great Lakes %	14.1	14.3	14.9	13.3	12.1
Milwaukee %	0.112	0.167	0.249	0.202	0.165
Milwaukee's Canadian					
(1000's of short tons)	229	331	461	359	352
Milwaukee's overseas					
(1000's of short tons)	13	19	34	41	66
Canada's % of Milw.'s total	94.6	94.6	92.9	89.8	84.2
Overseas % of Milw.'s total	5.4	5.4	7.1	10.2	15.8
Barley & Rye					
% of Milw.'s total	66.1	58.9	76.2	74.8	65.1

Source: U.S. Bureau of the Census, *United States Foreign Waterborne Commerce,*
Annual Reviews, 1951–63. U.S. Army Corps of Engineers, *Waterborne Commerce of
the United States*, Annual Reports, 1951–63.

*Figures and percentages will differ very slightly with those presented in Chapter 2 and Chapter 3. Since data presented in *United States Foreign Waterborne Commerce*, Annual Review, are computed on a different basis from data presented in *United States Foreign Waterborne Commerce, Great Lakes Area*, the total figures reflect these differing methods. However, the slight variation will not distort the analysis in any way.

tons, but overseas tonnage is up approximately 270,000 short tons. During the same period, Great Lakes foreign tonnage, as a percentage of total U.S. foreign tonnage, fell by 21 per cent while Milwaukee's fell 27 per cent, but barley and rye imports, which heavily dominated the port's foreign tonnage in earlier years, dropped 80 per cent as a percentage of Milwaukee's total foreign commerce. Over the 1953–62 period, Great

TABLE 5-4 (*continued*)

1956	1957	1958	1959	1960	1961	1962	1963
144,756	165,392	114,624	108,165	122,265	127,523	134,000	156,231
17.0	*14.6*	*15.1*	*18.9*	*17.5*	*18.0*	*18.8*	*18.0*
0.067	*0.032*	*0.045*	*0.154*	*0.181*	*0.456*	*0.364*	*0.264*
159,472	172,286	175,598	200,206	198,757	187,946	210,631	212,485
6.7	*5.8*	*4.4*	*7.3*	*6.5*	*6.4*	*7.4*	*7.9*
0.281	*0.210*	*0.204*	*0.188*	*0.152*	*0.173*	*0.120*	*0.121*
79.7	*72.1*	*66.1*	*48.4*	*54.1*	*60.3*	*26.6*	*40.6*
304,228	337,678	290,222	308,371	321,022	315,469	344,631	368,716
11.6	*10.1*	*8.6*	*11.4*	*10.7*	*11.1*	*11.8*	*12.0*
0.179	*0.123*	*0.141*	*0.176*	*0.164*	*0.287*	*0.214*	*0.181*
460	360	342	365	294	353	418	364
84	56	67	178	231	553	321	304
84.6	*86.5*	*83.6*	*67.2*	*56.0*	*39.0*	*56.6*	*54.6*
15.4	*13.5*	*16.4*	*32.8*	*44.0*	*61.0*	*43.4*	*45.4*
65.6	*62.7*	*57.7*	*33.6*	*31.2*	*20.1*	*9.1*	*15.5*

Lakes imports rose from 6.4 per cent to 7.4 per cent of total U.S. imports, a 15.6 per cent rise. Over the same period Milwaukee's imports, as a percentage of total U.S. imports, fell by 68.6 per cent, but exports showed an increase of 674.5 per cent; at the same time, Great Lakes exports fell from 27.4 per cent to 18.8 per cent of the U.S. total, a decline of nearly one-third.

From 1951 to 1963, the Milwaukee port experienced a 42,000-ton net gain in imports despite a 54,000-ton drop in barley and rye; since 1953, the 202,000-ton drop in total imports is more than accounted for by a 274,000-ton fall in barley and rye imports from Canada. Export tonnage increased to fifteen times the 1951 level by 1963, a net gain of 385,000 tons.

Although Milwaukee's total foreign commerce increased by 62 per cent between 1951 and 1963, the growth would appear much greater if barley and rye shipments from Canada were discounted. By doing this, the growth of 689 per cent in other types of foreign trade becomes apparent. Even since 1953 there has been a 479 per cent growth instead of the 27 per cent decrease that was mentioned above. A great share of this growth in foreign traffic can be attributed to the opening of the St. Lawrence Seaway, which was particularly influential in the growth of overseas trade. Canada's percentage of Milwaukee's foreign commerce averaged about 89 per cent from 1951 to 1958, but dropped to an average of about 55 per cent from 1959 to 1963, and whereas barley and rye accounted for about 66 per cent of the port's commerce in the 1951–58 period, this dropped to an average of less than 25 per cent after the Seaway opening. Generally then, we can see that Milwaukee's foreign commerce has become greatly diversified over the years. In 1961, 61 per cent of the port's foreign commerce was with overseas countries, and in 1962 barley and rye accounted for only 9 per cent of foreign trade. This is certainly a substantial advancement when we remember that only ten years earlier Canada had accounted for 95 per cent of the total, and that in 1953 barley and rye shipments from Canada alone represented 76 per cent of all foreign shipping at the Port of Milwaukee. Recent and current port development projects, which will be outlined in Chapters 7 and 8, indicate that the Port of Milwaukee's foreign commerce will experience further growth and diversification in the future.

Milwaukee's general cargo tonnage also increased both absolutely and relatively in relation to other Great Lakes ports between the opening of the St. Lawrence Seaway and 1961. From 1961 to 1963, although continuing to rise in absolute figures, it has declined relative to other Great Lakes ports, but there are indications that this relative decline will be checked or even reversed in the future.[3] Tonnage figures for the years 1958 to 1963 have previously been given in Table 2-4 and Table 3-3 for exports and imports, respectively; by combining these tables Milwaukee's general cargo traffic can easily be compared with that of the major Great Lakes ports as a whole. Milwaukee's general cargo tonnage in 1958 was approximately 132,000 short tons, which was 11.0 per cent of the seven-port total. After the opening of the Seaway, Milwaukee handled 265,000 short tons in 1959, 214,000 short tons in 1960, 267,000 short tons in 1961, 337,000 short tons in 1962, and 310,000 short tons in 1963; these tonnages were 11.7 per cent, 10.0 per cent, 11.5 per cent, 9.4 per cent, and 7.5 per cent of the total, respectively.

3. Table 5-3 shows a 35 per cent increase in Milwaukee's overseas general cargo traffic between 1963 and 1964, but the impact of this increase on the port's relative standing is not yet available.

Table 3-3, as noted on p. 19, includes imports of newsprint; eliminating this commodity does not change the way in which Milwaukee's general cargo fluctuated relative to the rest of the Great Lakes,[4] but, because newsprint accounted for a larger share of Milwaukee's imports than it did for other ports as a whole, Milwaukee's relative share of general cargo, exclusive of newsprint, is slightly less than it would be with this commodity included. It is clear, however, that only the level of Milwaukee's share is changed by this modification; on either basis, the port still increased its share in 1959, suffered a greater setback in 1960, rebounded almost to the 1959 level in 1961, and then fell substantially in 1962 and 1963.

A more detailed analysis of Milwaukee's foreign trade can be made for the year 1963, using figures published by the Chicago Association of Commerce and Industry.[5] These figures are taken from data prepared by the Foreign Trade Division of the Census Bureau, and, unfortunately, they cannot be completely reconciled with those published by the U.S. Army Corps of Engineers for the same year. According to the latter, Milwaukee's overseas and Canadian traffic combined totaled 668,597 short tons, while the Census Bureau recorded 692,816 short tons, including traffic which was not reported until the winter months of 1963–64 although it had moved earlier during the shipping season. The discrepancy of 24,219 short tons is spread through a number of different commodity classes rather than being isolated in one or two classifications.

Table 5-5 provides a complete list of commodities entering into Milwaukee's foreign waterborne trade, both by value and by tonnage. In sharp contrast to 1961, when iron and steel scrap was the leading export with 217,975 tons or 38 per cent of the total, there were no exports of this commodity in 1963; corn was easily the most important export, with 53 per cent of the total tonnage. Only five other commodities, all of them agricultural products, exceeded the 10,000 ton mark.

When measured by value, no single commodity stands out sharply, although corn, once again, is the leading commodity. The grains and flour group (Commodity Nos. 100–110), including the commodities ranking first, sixth, and seventh in value, accounts for about 28 per cent of the

4. Milwaukee's imports of newsprint for 1958–63 were 57,000 short tons, 70,000 short tons, 69,000 short tons, 65,000 short tons, 66,000 short tons, and 43,000 short tons while the seven cities together imported 499,000 short tons, 528,000 short tons, 562,000 short tons, 492,000 tons, 601,000 short tons, and 612,000 short tons, respectively.

5. Chicago Association of Commerce and Industry, *U.S. Great Lakes Ports Monthly Statistics for Overseas and Canadian Waterborne Traffic*, 1963.

TABLE 5-5

PORT OF MILWAUKEE, OVERSEAS WATERBORNE TRAFFIC, 1963

		Exports		Imports	
No.	Commodity	Dollars	Short tons	Dollars	Short tons
	Total	60,353,626	410,258	35,996,916	282,558
010	Meat and products, fresh	320,939	706		
013	Meat and products, canned	30,597	29		
017	Meat and products, nec*	49,573	102		
018	Meat and prod, incl canned, nec			122,681	178
020	Animal oils and fats, edible	1,044,009	5,220		
035	Dried milk	4,483,462	36,905		
037	Cheese	305,235	1,163	95,461	109
039	Dairy products, nec	346,336	1,139		
047	Fish and products, incl canned, nec			492,221	840
049	Shellfish and products			67,700	72
060	Hides and skins, raw	627,425	3,094	1,479,724	2,598
065	Leather and mfrs	104,807	232	277,260	86
075	Furs and mfrs			674	
095	Animal products, inedible, nec			613,498	1,154
098	Animal products, ined, nec	16,688	66		
100	Corn	9,730,192	219,423		
102	Barley and rye	110,775	2,798	6,323,490	118,097
103	Wheat	873,726	11,920		
107	Wheat flour	3,515,339	41,304		
109	Flour, flour-grain prep, nec	2,664,795	33,668	12,678	52
110	Animal feeds, nec	126,624	3,192		
123	Vegetables and prep, canned	153,214	836		
125	Veg and prep, incl canned, nec			495,810	976
127	Vegetables and prep, nec	2,396,339	5,911		
130	Fruits and prep, fresh			1,493	5
136	Fruit juices			18,466	59
138	Fruits, prep, incl canned, nec			282,609	1,045
140	Nuts and prep			56,908	251
150	Veget oils and fats, edible	3,865	12		
167	Table beverage materials, nec			17,687	44
170	Spices			3,279	9
185	Molasses, sugar prod, edible	170,693	516	26,101	40
190	Liquors and wines	22,112	117	2,503,029	4,751
195	Beverages and sirups, nec			413	2
200	Rubber, crude, and allied gums			837,994	1,736
203	Rubber scrap			1,662	8

TABLE 5-5 (*continued*)

No.	Commodity	Exports		Imports	
		Dollars	Short tons	Dollars	Short tons
205	Rubber tires and inner tubes			29,534	34
207	Rubber manufactures, nec	2,121	0.5	33,062	33
220	Drugs, herbs, roots, crude			20,281	2
231	Soybeans	1,010,847	11,619		
235	Oilseeds, nec	18,012	126		
236	Oilseeds, nec, exc castor beans			3,415	17
250	Dyeing, tanning materials, veg			10,973	57
260	Seeds, except oilseeds	16,903	25	520,217	957
285	Tobacco, manufactured			46,957	28
297	Vegetable prod, inedible, nec	138,982	1,080	26,048	130
300	Cotton unmanufactured			15,317	11
310	Cotton semi-manufactured			9,701	76
320	Cotton manufactures	5,813	48	57,998	16
326	Sisal and jute unmanufactured			74,532	670
335	Vegetable fiber mfrs, nec			2,052,863	6,362
350	Wool manufactures	114,516	1,012	88,164	14
381	Man-made fibers and mfrs	4,512	41	10,098	3
390	Textile products, nec	803,534	768	155,367	244
400	Logs	67,290	358		
408	Wood, nonmanufactured, nec			42,600	35
413	Lumber and shingles	16,043	47	51,082	266
416	Plywood, veneers, cont mat	48,277	218	25,325	238
421	Wood manufactures	10,591	8	150,589	157
441	Wood pulp			173,954	2,011
445	Paper base stocks, nec			3,720	5
450	Standard newsprint paper			6,941,703	55,380
457	Paper and mfrs, nec			133,519	587
475	Paper, related prod, nec	395,118	1,035		
517	Lubricating oils and greases	804	0.5		
523	Building cement			102	
526	Stone and mfrs, nec	600	0.5	152,109	1,588
530	Glass and glass products	1,862	2	149,593	555
540	Clays and earths	27,531	1,047		
543	Brick and tile			51,920	278
547	Clay products, nec			58,754	75
551	Limestone crushed	596	8		
553	Salt			220,492	35,905
554	Sand, gravel, and crushed rock			493	34

TABLE 5-5 (*continued*)

No.	Commodity	Exports		Imports	
		Dollars	*Short tons*	*Dollars*	*Short tons*
555	Nonmetallic minerals, mfrs, nec	285,377	2,271	82,549	606
600	Iron ore and concentrates			262	61
601	Pig iron			339,397	6,231
602	Iron and steel scrap			33,993	753
603	Iron, steel semifinished prod			384,351	4,123
605	Ferrous castings and forgings			1,563	1
606	Tools and basic hardware	82,782	42	121,439	494
607	Kitchen and hospital utensils	35,689	18	19,073	18
608	Iron and steel pipe			194,992	880
609	Rolled, finished stl mill prod	305,090	881	3,116,100	25,043
611	Metal mfrs, parts, nec, exc sci†	1,538,686	3,000		
612	Metal mfrs and parts, nec			435,170	555
614	Chrome			19,034	13
618	Aluminum metal and alloys			172,856	374
620	Copper ore, concent, scrap	14,209	27		
622	Refined copper crude forms	471,798	786		
624	Copper semifabricated forms			148,304	157
632	Copper alloy forms and scrap	142,089	255	127,705	156
642	Lead and alloys			15,967	93
652	Nickel ore, concent, scrp, fms	55,925	321	233,996	40
662	Tin ore, concent, scrap	82,296	178		
665	Tin metal forms			127,159	56
682	Other nonferrous ores			47,694	665
690	Precious metals and mfrs			4,828	2
700	Electrical machinery			374,816	197
701	Electrical machinery, exc sci	1,513,306	720		
710	Engines, turbines, parts, nec	4,183,475	2,347	57,808	59
722	Const, mining mach, parts	6,885,049	5,310		
730	Metalworking machinery, parts			1,072,322	450
731	Metalworking mach, pts, exc sci	2,500,650	978		
740	Textile, shoe mach, parts	109,464	8	61,239	19
742	Industrial mach, parts, nec	7,428,191	3,297		
745	Machinery, parts, nec, exc agri			569,878	282

TABLE 5-5 (*continued*)

No.	Commodity	Exports		Imports	
		Dollars	Short tons	Dollars	Short tons
770	Agricultural mach, parts	1,536,418	1,326	556,299	628
780	Motor vehicles			44,776	46
781	Motor vehicles, exc sci	997,704	750		
782	Motor vehicle parts			235,049	162
783	Watercraft and parts			30,337	14
785	Watercraft and parts, exc sci	19,564	11		
786	Railway equipment	660	2	800	8
787	Motor vehicles parts, exc sci	958,429	800		
790	Aircraft and parts			880	
793	Com and civil aircraft	6,775	1		
796	Vehicles and parts, nec	96,069	28	494,865	266
805	Other coal-tar products			10,819	3
806	Other chemical products	2,886	1		
810	Medicines and preparations	21,679	10	45,971	10
828	Other ind chem, exc sci	18,608	113		
829	Industrial chemicals, nec			81,170	286
837	Syn resins, exc fin form	47,197	148		
844	Chemical spec, nec	239,828	172		
847	Pigments, paints, varn, exc carb blk	9,478	10		
848	Pigments, paints, varnishes			15,597	57
859	Fertilizers and material, nec			5,396	202
860	Miscellaneous chemical prod			99,737	184
900	Commodities, nec			1,111,953	352
901	Commodities, nec, exc sci	983,558	646		
920	U.S. articles returned			459,452	1,137

Source: Chicago Association of Commerce and Industry, Research and Statistics Division, *U.S. Great Lakes Ports Monthly Statistics for Overseas and Canadian Waterborne Traffic*, 1963 Monthly Data.

*nec = not elswhere classified.

†sci = Defense Department controlled shipments.

Figures have been rounded.

total; the machinery and machine parts group (Commodity Nos. 700–770), including the second, third, fifth, ninth, eleventh, and twelfth leading value commodities, accounts for about 40 per cent of the total. Dried milk, the fourth-ranking commodity export, accounts for about 7 per cent of the total. Together, the top twelve commodities equal approximately 80 per cent of the total.

Import tonnage, like export, is dominated by a single commodity —

barley and rye, with 42 per cent of the total. This is typical of Milwaukee's import pattern, for barley is used in the brewing industry. Newsprint ranked second with almost 20 per cent; salt was third with over 12
per cent; rolled and finished steel mill products ranked fourth with almost
9 per cent of the total. The leading commodities in terms of dollars were
newsprint, barley and rye, and rolled and finished steel mill products, respectively, accounting for 45.5 per cent of the total. A wide variety of
other commodities have significant shares of the total import value.

Table 5-6 lists all foreign countries with which Milwaukee traded in
1963. In terms both of tonnage and value, Milwaukee's chief trading
partners were western and southern European countries and Canada,
but there was considerable export trade to such countries as India, the
Republic of Korea, and the then Belgian Congo. Canada led in both tonnage and value, with 24 per cent and 49 per cent, respectively. It was followed by Spain, the Netherlands, the Congo, Italy, the United Kingdom,

TABLE 5-6

PORT OF MILWAUKEE, SUMMARY OF EXPORTS AND IMPORTS
BY ORIGIN AND DESTINATION, 1963

Country	Exports		Imports	
	Dollars	Short tons	Dollars	Short tons
Canada	7,099,956	156,198	15,983,382	234,983
Dominican Republic	398,041	1,559		
El Salvador	51,339	353		
Honduras	45,716	254		
Jamaica	834,086	2,238		
Trinidad	10,030	17		
Haiti	71,043	432		
Greater Antilles	1,260	5		
French West Indies	2,794	2		
Colombia	522,951	1,889		
Venezuela	491,649	1,450		
Brazil	913,246	5,427		
Argentina	286,031	395		
Uruguay	8,060	48		
Sweden	2,228,597	3,976	438,927	2,502
Norway	1,387,336	882	753,844	3,767
Denmark	292,972	567	1,439,366	3,729
United Kingdom	5,258,479	10,716	3,812,876	4,956
Ireland	324,136	5,438	31,111	66
Netherlands	3,809,653	25,233	1,918,981	4,363
Belgium	1,306,911	3,119	1,143,088	6,179
France	2,990,187	2,750	2,033,170	2,549
West Germany	2,953,223	9,050	2,665,787	5,404
East Germany			13,003	46

TABLE 5-6 (*continued*)

Country	Exports		Imports	
	Dollars	*Short tons*	*Dollars*	*Short tons*
Austria	107,380	79	100,981	65
Czechoslovakia	661,722	3,294	936	3
Switzerland	1,170,166	1,414	383,295	180
Hungary			695	2
Finland	67,190	133	33,597	202
Poland	98,203	866	20,550	48
U.S.S.R.	256,219	85		
Spain	4,257,967	64,720	143,357	401
Portugal	296,465	2,182	201,739	750
Malta	630	2		
Italy	4,247,514	13,406	1,745,430	3,481
Yugoslavia	720,685	1,217	24,032	193
Greece	1,748,830	2,497	16,352	23
Turkey	1,686,330	2,757		
Cyprus	15,575	9		
Syria	5,385	3		
Lebanon	360,593	2,416		
Iraq	12,088	14		
Iran	196,794	662		
Israel	541,790	1,132	7,749	14
Jordan	32,880	71		
Kuwait	538,152	1,643		
Saudi Arabia	36,189	125	738	
Afghanistan	33,704	392		
Arabia	41,520	34		
India	2,127,426	6,860	1,670	18
Aden	540	30		
Pakistan	234,068	1,259		
Nepal	6,904	97		
Ceylon	18,598	103		
Burma	77,280	956	643	3
Thailand	3,345	125	591,796	1,832
Cambodia			5,130	11
Viet Nam	280,836	3,090		
Laos	19,362	113		
Federation of Malaya	1,652	43	465,264	886
Singapore	570	31	15,317	11
Indonesia	486,063	3,470	2,345	6
Philippine Republic	354,902	2,415	97,558	633
Macao	115,732	298		
South Korean Republic	1,309,256	13,149	2,456	10
Hong Kong	189,573	567	117,211	181
Taiwan	420,191	2,742	598,806	1,254
Japan	852,245	5,547	978,618	3,075
New Zealand			86,688	5

TABLE 5-6 (*continued*)

Country	Exports		Imports	
	Dollars	*Short tons*	*Dollars*	*Short tons*
Nansei Islands	10,708	5		
Morocco	199,377	446		
Australia	230,421	162	72,694	668
Republic South Africa	6,141	337	441	
Algeria	441,996	2,999	368	1
Seychelles	1,200	66		
Tunisia	133,221	1,239		
Nigeria	40,714	224	1,329	4
Libya	70,233	346		
Ghana	189,200	1,166		
Egypt	828,414	6,472		
Togo	906,369	3,673		
Liberia	220,377	210		
British West Africa	126,971	597		
Ethiopia	70,802	417		
Belgian Congo	1,914,936	17,893	24,630	50
Kenya	32,417	1,774		
Mauritius	2,210	89		
Madeira			685	2
Cameroons	6,984	57		
French Equatorial Africa	725	40	20,281	2
Total	60,353,626	410,258	35,996,916	282,558

Source: Chicago Association of Commerce and Industry, *U.S. Great Lakes Ports Monthly Statistics for Overseas and Canadian Waterborne Traffic*, 1963, Tables 3 and 4. Place names are given as in source.

Figures have been rounded.

West Germany, and the Republic of Korea in tonnage and by the United Kingdom, Italy, the Netherlands, West Germany, France, Spain, Belgium, and India in value, respectively. The high ranking of such countries as the Republic of Korea and the Congo in tonnage totals is explained by the shipping of government relief cargoes such as dried milk and wheat flour through the Port of Milwaukee.

Appendixes A and B present a complete breakdown of Milwaukee's imports and exports by both commodity and country. As might have been anticipated from Tables 5-5 and 5-6, Canada's dominant position in import traffic is based on its shipments of barley and rye, newsprint, and rolled and finished steel mill products; all of Milwaukee's imported barley came from Canada. On the export side, Canada's dominance is explained by the corn traffic which accounts for over 142,000 tons out of Milwaukee's total export tonnage to Canada of about 156,000 tons. Canada ships all of Milwaukee's imported newsprint and 74 per cent of its imported rolled and finished steel mill products. Belgium and West Germany ship most of the remaining steel products, Belgium supplying 15 per cent and West Germany 5 per cent of the total.

It is much harder to summarize the cross-classification of exports (Appendix B). Milwaukee's shipments of machinery and vehicles (group 7) were primarily to free Europe. The United Kingdom received more in value than any other nation, with Italy and France ranking second and third, respectively. However, it is interesting and possibly significant for the future that Milwaukee also shipped sizeable amounts of machinery to a large number of non-European countries and that this machinery went not only to industrialized countries such as Japan and Israel but also to the underdeveloped countries. For example, India, Liberia, Togo, and Jordan each imported machinery amounting to over half the value of their total shipments from Milwaukee. In fact, India was Milwaukee's seventh largest market for machinery exports. This machinery did not amount to half the total tonnage of any of these countries because they also received large quantities of government relief cargo such as dried milk or wheat flour, which were low in value but heavy.

Milwaukee's role as a producer of heavy machinery is well known. As industrialization proceeds in Asia and Latin America, these areas may prove to be steadily expanding markets for Milwaukee's products, and, if producers and purchasers can be persuaded to ship via Milwaukee, the port may have an extremely bright future as a general cargo port.

Corn, the first export in terms of tonnage, went primarily to Canada, which was the recipient of 64 per cent of corn exports, and to Spain, which received about 21 per cent.

The government relief commodities went primarily to non-European countries, although the Netherlands received 8.6 per cent of the dried milk exports and Italy received 11.1 per cent of the wheat flour. The Congo received the greatest amount of the wheat flour with 38.8 per cent, and Korea received 12,915 short tons of flour and flour grain preparations or 47.7 per cent of that commodity. India received the largest amount of dried milk with 13.7 per cent of Milwaukee's shipments, and Indonesia and Japan were the recipients of 9.1 per cent and 7.4 per cent of the 37,000-ton total, respectively.

These government relief commodities, as indicated in Table 5-5, play a major role in Milwaukee's exports, particularly to non-European countries. In the event that the relief program is discontinued, however, Milwaukee may be able to develop a traffic in machinery that could replace it as a source of general cargo.

6

THE PORT'S ECONOMIC HINTERLAND
AND ITS UTILIZATION

THE ECONOMIC HINTERLAND

THE significance of the Port of Milwaukee may also be measured in another way, by estimating the port's share of the traffic between its hinterland and overseas. The hinterland may be conveniently defined here as the area for which the port forms an economic outlet because of lower transportation costs. It is not singular; transportation costs are different for different commodities, and as a consequence the port may have several distinct hinterlands at the same time. The port's hinterland may also vary, depending on the area with which it is trading. Milwaukee's hinterland for European ports extends farther west than for Asian or Australian ports, since the latter may realize lower costs on some commodities by shipping to west coast ports and using land carriers to the Midwest. Geographers have distinguished three components of the typical hinterland: (1) the immediate metropolitan area of the port; (2) the "noncompetitive hinterland," in which the port has a freight-rate advantage; and (3) a peripheral region "wherein rates are equal or the rate differential is low enough so that a port may compete for traffic here, on the basis of factors other than rates."[1]

In the study of the import traffic of Chicago, Draine estimated the hinterlands of ten Great Lakes ports based on Docket No. 28300, "domestic class freight rates." Milwaukee's hinterland, based on class rates, in-

---

1. Draine, *Import Traffic of Chicago*, p. 55. (Also see Harold M. Mayer, "Port Operation: United States," in *Encyclopaedia Britannica*.)

cludes most of the state of Wisconsin, the northeastern corner of Iowa, and the central portion of the Upper Peninsula of Michigan. The border-line between Duluth and Milwaukee is approximated by a straight line from La Crosse to Wausau and extending to Lake Superior; Eau Claire and Superior are the only other Wisconsin cities of at least 25,000 population to fall within the Duluth hinterland. The line between Chicago and Milwaukee is the Illinois-Wisconsin border, and Dubuque lies on it; no other important cities in Iowa lie within the Milwaukee class rate hinterland, nor do any in Michigan.

While Draine's description of the Great Lakes hinterlands is quite ac-curate when considering only class rates, the resulting picture would be rather different if we were to identify hinterlands based on general or special commodity rates. There is considerable evidence to support the contention that a definition of hinterlands by class rates does not provide us with a true-to-life picture of the relative significance of each port. In fact, "an analysis by the Interstate Commerce Commission showed that, of the carload traffic originating on all railroads in the country, approxi-mately 15 per cent moves on class rates and 85 per cent moves on com-modity rates."[2] The traffic manager of the Port of Milwaukee has con-tended that Milwaukee's true hinterland, based on commodity rates of the specific commodities that make up about 70 per cent of the port's traffic, would form a corridor extending west to Nebraska and having a north-south span approximately equal to the distance from Green Bay to Chicago. Since it is not feasible to construct a hinterland map based on all of the various general and special commodity rates, Figure 6-A por-trays the geographic hinterland of the Great Lakes area without any at-tempt to distinguish between the territories tributary to the respective ports.

Figure 6-A is also a good approximation of the hinterlands with re-spect to the total costs of shipping overseas, including both the domestic freight rates and the rates on shipping between the Great Lakes port and the port overseas. This is possible because many of the shipping rates between the Great Lakes and overseas are the same as those between the Atlantic Coast and overseas.[3] Similarly, many overseas shipping rates for Great Lakes and Gulf Coast ports are the same; in fact, railroads serv-ing these two ports are currently engaged in a "rate war" for government

2. Schenker, "Southern State Port Authorities and Florida," *Land Economics*, XXXV, No. 1, 42.
3. Milwaukee, Board of Harbor Commissioners, *Impact of the Milwaukee Port*, p. 11.

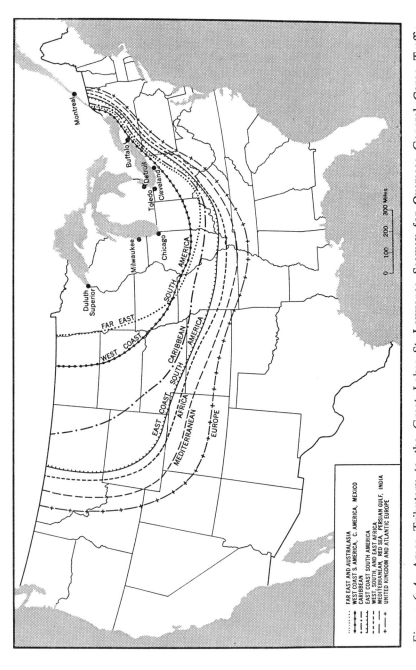

Figure 6-A. Areas Tributary to the Great Lakes–St. Lawrence Seaway for Overseas General Cargo Traffic. *Source:* U.S. Corps of Engineers, *General Cargo Traffic Analysis Great Lakes Harbors Study* (Office of Division Engineer, North Central Division, Sept., 1960). Map drafted by the University of Wisconsin Cartographic Laboratory.

relief cargo, with those railroads serving the Gulf Coast attempting to get rates for flour from areas such as Kansas and Colorado reduced below those to the Great Lakes in order to divert this traffic to Gulf ports.

The importance of equalized overseas rates was evidenced in the Draine study, which noted that, for Chicago, the hinterland based on both land and water rates "agrees to a considerable extent" with the hinterland based on domestic land rates only.[4] The boundary between Chicago and Milwaukee remained the Wisconsin-Illinois state line; for the nine general cargo commodities used to define the class rate hinterlands, Dubuque fell within Chicago's hinterland twice and had identical transport costs via both ports for the other seven commodities.[5]

On the other hand, shipping rates to overseas ports are *not* the same between Milwaukee or Chicago and Duluth; the Lake Michigan ports are cheaper by 9 or 10 cents per hundred pounds of general cargo, according to Draine,[6] and 5 to 10 cents per hundred, according to Professor Krueger.[7] Therefore, the borderline between Milwaukee and Duluth as shown in Figure 6-B is surely unfavorable to Milwaukee, by a distance which varies according to the railroad and ocean shipping rates on particular commodities. One reason for the unfavorable rate to Duluth is that it is the only significant port on Lake Superior. "[A] ship must sail the entire length of Lake Superior to service only Duluth-Superior. Whereas a ship may stop at Green Bay, Muskegon, Milwaukee and Kenosha with little additional sailing time if it is heading for Chicago anyway, Duluth-Superior must generate enough cargo on its own to justify the round trip from the head of Lake Huron to Duluth-Superior." [8] Professor Krueger estimated that the "round trip" requires three days and would cost the steamship line about $9,600.[9]

Therefore, it should not be surprising that Milwaukee does in fact export goods produced in cities which are closer to Duluth in terms of land transport costs. The traffic manager of the Port of Milwaukee has supplied a list of U.S. cities which exported via Milwaukee for the years 1960–64, making it possible to gain an idea of Milwaukee's actual traffic

4. Draine, *Import Traffic of Chicago*, pp. 55–56.

5. *Ibid.*, pp. 62–63; Dubuque is erroneously omitted from the Chicago hinterland on "window glass," as can be seen from *ibid.*, Table 16, p. 88.

6. *Ibid.*, p. 56.

7. Krueger, *Impact of the St. Lawrence Seaway*, p. 29.

8. *Ibid.*, pp. 16–17.

9. *Ibid.*, p. 32. (This figure seems rather high since it is generally estimated that the cost amounts to between $1,500 to $3,000 per day or closer to $7,000 for the trip.)

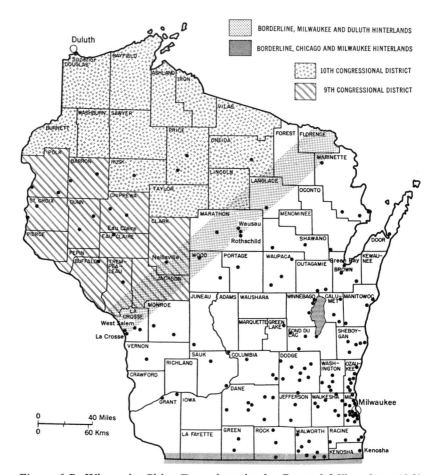

Figure 6-B. Wisconsin Cities Exporting via the Port of Milwaukee, 1963 and/or 1964. Map by the University of Wisconsin Cartographic Laboratory.

hinterland, as compared to its theoretical hinterland based on freight rates. A summary of this list is provided in Table 6-1, and a breakdown by county for the state of Wisconsin for 1963 and 1964 appears in Figure 6-B. Figure 6-C indicates the cities in each state shipping via Milwaukee to foreign ports in 1963 or 1964, or both. It should be stressed that this list is not weighted for value nor volume; it does not show either the value or tonnage originating in any city or state. One shipment of any size is enough to place a city on the list in Table 6-1.

Despite this handicap, Figures 6-B and 6-C are instructive. Of the 150

TABLE 6-1

INLAND CITIES FROM WHICH EXPORT CARGO VIA THE PORT OF
MILWAUKEE ORIGINATED, COMPARISON BY NUMBER, 1960–64

State	Number of cities in each state				
	1964	1963	1962	1961	1960
Wisconsin*	125	117	84	83	76
Illinois	27	27	26	12	22
Iowa	25	24	18	18	15
Minnesota	54	34	28	26	31
South Dakota	5	6	4	2	5
Nebraska	5	8	5	5	5
Colorado	4	2	3	2	6
Michigan	8	9	10	10	10
North Dakota	3	4	1	2	3
Kansas	8	6	10	18	7
Missouri	3	4	5	4	6
Indiana	4	4	4	2	5
Ohio	5	7	3	1	2
Wyoming	1	1	0	0	1
California	0	4	1	0	4
New York	1	4	2	1	1
New Jersey	0	2	0	0	1
Pennsylvania	2	4	0	1	1
Maryland	1	1	0	0	1
Alabama	0	1	0	0	2
Mississippi	0	0	0	0	1
Washington	0	0	0	1	1
Canada	0	1	0	2	4
Utah	0	0	1	0	0
Oregon	1	1	0	0	0
Georgia	0	1	0	1	0
Connecticut	0	1	0	0	0
Texas	0	3	0	1	0
Massachusetts	0	1	0	0	0
Florida	0	0	0	1	0
Montana	3	3	1	1	0
Cities	285	280	206	194	210
States	19	27	17	20	22
Canadian provinces	0	1	0	2	3

Source: Milwaukee, Board of Harbor Commissioners records, compiled by Jorgensen.

*Milwaukee County municipalities are counted as individual units in 1963 and 1964. They are all independent governing units, and thirteen of the sixteen listed have populations in excess of 10,000.

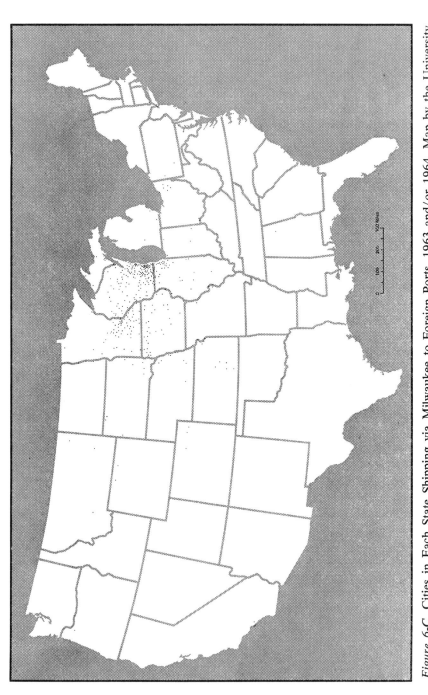

Figure 6-C. Cities in Each State Shipping via Milwaukee to Foreign Ports, 1963 and/or 1964. Map by the University of Wisconsin Cartographic Laboratory.

Wisconsin cities exporting via Milwaukee in 1963 or 1964, 18 lie in Duluth's "domestic" hinterland, as calculated by Draine, and 10 more lie about on the borderline. Ninety-four cities exported in both years; 8 of these (Bloomer, Eau Claire, Rhinelander, Clear Lake, Menomonie, Mondovi, New Richmond, and Jim Falls) lie within the Duluth hinterland, 5 others (La Crosse, Neillsville, Wausau, Rothschild, West Salem) on the borderline. Duluth's domestic class rate hinterland includes 7 Wisconsin cities with 1960 populations of at least 10,000; [10] of these, only Chippewa Falls did not export via the port of Milwaukee in 1960–64.

Consequently, the boundary line in Figure 6-B is unfavorably distorted with respect to Milwaukee's hinterland, on either the "theoretical" basis of domestic freight rates or on the practical criterion of what cities ship via Milwaukee. But even if the boundary is accepted as accurate, Duluth's share of Wisconsin is far more impressive on the map than it is economically. The twenty-five counties lying entirely inside Duluth's hinterland (including Forest and Florence) contain over two-fifths of the land area of Wisconsin (41 per cent); together with the five "border" counties of La Crosse, Jackson, Clark, Marathon, and Langlade, Duluth's hinterland contains just over half of the area (50.3 per cent). But this hinterland includes only 12.5 per cent of the state's population, or 18 per cent if the "border" counties are added. And it produced only 5.5 per cent of the state's value added by manufacturing in 1960, with an additional 3.8 per cent accounted for by the border counties, almost all of it by La Crosse and Marathon. Duluth's hinterland does better in agriculture: in 1960 it produced 21 per cent of the value of Wisconsin's farm products, and another 9 per cent came from the additional five counties.[11] Even at the very worst, Milwaukee's hinterland produced by far the largest share of the goods likely to be exported.

ORIGIN OF EXPORTS

The Commerce Department's study of 1960 exports was also broken down by congressional districts,[12] making it possible to estimate the value of exports manufactured in each port's share of Wisconsin. Figure 6-B also shows the boundaries of Wisconsin's Ninth and Tenth Congressional Districts as they were in 1960, and it appears that these districts are a reasonable approximation of Duluth's hinterland. The districts do not

10. U.S. Bureau of the Census, *United States Census of Population, 1960, Final Report PC (1) — 51C; Wisconsin, General Social and Economic Characteristics*, p. 51-163.

11. U.S. Bureau of the Census, *County and City Data Book, 1962*, pp. 412–31. far the largest share of goods likely to be exported.

12. U.S. Department of Commerce, "Export Origin Study," 1962.

include La Crosse and Wausau (Marathon County), but, since these are at best on the borderline, the omission is probably justifiable.

Wisconsin's exports of manufactures in 1960 were estimated at $411.4 million, of which $270.0 million was actually reported in the study. Of this $270.0 million, only $2.8 million was produced in the Ninth and Tenth Congressional Districts. This is just barely over one per cent of the state's total. These districts did better in agricultural exports (which overlaps the manufactured exports, since both include manufactured agricultural products): their "equivalent share" of agricultural exports was 21 per cent of the state's share.[13] However, since the manufactured agricultural commodities are far more likely to be shipped as general cargo than are the raw commodities such as corn, Duluth's equivalent share, even if it were all shipped via that port, would produce a relatively small amount of revenue for the port.

It is, therefore, only a slight exaggeration to say that Milwaukee's hinterland includes all of Wisconsin. This simplification permits analysis of the port's share of its hinterland's total exports for each of the two-digit industries of the Standard Industrial Classification (S.I.C.), since this breakdown is not available by congressional district but only for each state and some metropolitan areas. This breakdown is presented in Table 6-2 which uses 1963 updated data.[14]

Because Census Bureau data on exports and imports are classified on a different system than the Standard Industrial Classification, it has been necessary to attempt to reconcile them. It is possible that some commodities have been erroneously classified. This has certainly happened in the case of instruments and related products (Standard Industrial Classification, S.I.C., No. 38); firms producing these goods, according to the Commerce Department study, have provided information that they do in fact export some goods via the Port of Milwaukee, but it has not been possible to determine which foreign trade classifications include them. Therefore, we may be sure that the percentage of instrument exports is higher than zero and, conversely, that the percentages in one or more other classifications (presumably fabricated metal products or machinery) is too high.

As indicated in the table, the food and kindred products industry has

13. The "equivalent share" is a statistical device. If an area produces one per cent of the national output, e.g., of corn, then its "equivalent share" of the nation's corn exports is also one per cent.

14. U.S. Bureau of the Census, *Survey of the Origin of Exports of Manufactured Products, 1963*; and Chicago Association of Commerce and Industry, *U.S. Great Lakes Ports, Monthly Statistics for Overseas and Canadian Waterborne Traffic*, 1963.

TABLE 6-2

WISCONSIN EXPORT PRODUCTION AND PORT OF MILWAUKEE
EXPORTS, 1963

S.I.C. No.	Major industry group	Wis. export production (millions of dollars)	Milwaukee exports (millions of dollars)	Milwaukee port's share of Wis. export production (%)
20	Food & kindred products*	88.4	27.5	31.1
21	Tobacco products	0	0	0
22	Textile mill products	1.4	0.9	64
23	Apparel & related products	0.9	0	
24	Lumber & wood products	5.8	0.1	2
25	Furniture & fixtures	0.5	0	0
26	Paper & allied products	5.6	0.4	7
27	Printing & publishing	3.6	0	0
28	Chemicals & allied products	5.2	0.3	6
29	Petroleum & coal products	0	†	†
30	Rubber & plastics products	2.6	†	†
31	Leather & leather products	2.8	0.6	21
32	Stone, clay & glass products	8.4	0.3	4
33	Primary metal industries	8.2	0.6	7
34	Fabricated metal products	18.5	2.0	11
35	Machinery, exc. electrical	241.8	22.6	9
36	Electrical machinery	42.2	1.5	4
37	Transportation equipment	61.5	2.1	3
38	Instruments & related products	23.8	0	0
19 & 39	Miscellaneous mfg.	23.6	1.0	4
	Total	544.8	59.9	11

Source: U.S. Bureau of the Census, *Survey of the Origin of Exports of Manufactured Products, 1963*; Chicago Association of Commerce and Industry, *U.S. Great Lakes Ports Monthly Statistics for Overseas and Canadian Waterborne Traffic*, 1963.

*Includes unprocessed agricultural commodities.

†Less than $50,000 and less than 0.5%.

been expanded to include unprocessed agricultural commodities. Wisconsin's estimated exports of food products in 1963 amounted to $43.7 million, while its equivalent share of total agricultural exports was $78.4 million. The equivalent share has been divided into unprocessed and manufactured exports on the basis of a study by the Bureau of Labor Statistics, which estimated that "in the farm sector 13 per cent of total farm employment is required for producing exports. Of this 13 per cent, almost 8 per cent is for direct export of farm commodities, and slightly less than 6 per cent is for farm commodities consumed in manufacturing exports." [15] Assuming that the same ratio holds for the value of output as for employment and does not vary from state to state, then $44.7 million of Wisconsin's agricultural exports may be said to have been shipped in unprocessed form, while $33.7 million were processed and were included in the $43.7 million of food and kindred products exported by the state. As should be clear from the tenuous nature of the assumptions, these figures are to be treated as, at best, rough approximations, but they are sufficient for the illustrative purposes of Table 6-2.

No probable modification of the figures for individual industry groups is likely to change the conclusion to be drawn from Table 6-2: the Port of Milwaukee ships only a small share of the exports originating in its hinterland. Of the four industries which comprise about four-fifths of the state's exports, Milwaukee ships a large share only of agricultural commodities, and even here it ships only about one-third of the state's total output. Despite the important role played by machinery in the port's shipments,[16] those shipments are a small fraction of what might be shipped.

However, small as it is, 11 per cent is certainly an overstatement of the port's share of the exports originating in its hinterland, since Milwaukee does in fact draw export cargo from outside Wisconsin and even from outside its theoretical freight hinterland. In the case of Michigan, Milwaukee draws largely from the Upper Peninsula, but relatively little of the port's traffic originates in that part of Michigan lying east of the lake. In fact, the larger part of the comparatively nonindustrial Upper Peninsula lies within the boundaries of Duluth's theoretical hinterland. It may, therefore, be reasonable to assume that Michigan exports do not constitute a large share of Milwaukee's cargo and that the most important part, economically speaking, of that state lies outside Milwaukee's hinterland, both theoretically and actually.

Iowa, the other state falling partly into Milwaukee's theoretical hinterland, presents an entirely different picture. Of the twenty-nine different cities appearing in the traffic manager's list, only three (Waukon, Arlington, and Fredericksburg) appear to lie clearly in the Milwaukee hinterland, while two others (Dubuque and Oelwein) lie about on the Chicago-Milwaukee borderline. What is more surprising is that eight of the

15. U.S. Bureau of Labor Statistics, *Domestic Employment Attributable to U.S. Exports, 1960*, p. 4.

16. See above, p. 63. Commodity Group 7 probably includes all of the machinery and transportation equipment industries.

other twenty-four cities lie clearly within the Chicago domestic hinterland, which, as stated previously, very nearly coincides with its foreign hinterland. Thus Milwaukee is reaching into an area where it probably does not have a rate advantage or even parity. While it is true that six of these eight cities are served by one or both of the railroads serving Milwaukee (the Chicago & North Western, and the Chicago, Milwaukee, St. Paul & Pacific), these railroads also connect directly to Chicago. In addition, these railroads connect Milwaukee with twelve of the sixteen cities in Duluth's hinterland, but these same cities plus Ft. Dodge are also connected to Chicago by rail.

The important point derived from an analysis of Iowa's exports through Milwaukee is that they appear to play a significant role in the port's export traffic as a whole and that, therefore, Milwaukee's share of Wisconsin exports is most certainly less than the 11 per cent (closer to 8 or 9 per cent) shown in Table 6-2. This conclusion is still further reinforced by considering the state of Minnesota, which is second only to Wisconsin in number of cities shipping via Milwaukee. Despite the fact that the entire state lies within Duluth's theoretical hinterland, cities in all parts of the state, including Duluth itself and cities well to the north and northwest of Duluth, export via Milwaukee.

The picture of the sources of Milwaukee's export traffic may be rounded out by noting that sixteen cities in the Chicago SMSA exported through Milwaukee, as did twenty cities from the rest of Illinois. These shipments reflect the fact that many rail rates from Illinois cities are the same to both Milwaukee and Chicago. For instance, tractors from either Springfield or Peoria pay the same charges in going to either port. The equalization of commodity rates offers justification for including most or all of Illinois in Milwaukee's hinterland, as is done by the Board of Harbor Commissioners in its promotional literature.[17] Finally, although a number of states listed in Table 6-1, such as New York, Pennsylvania, Maryland, Oregon, and California, could not by any stretch of the imagination be described as part of the Milwaukee hinterland, some idea of its outer limits may be gathered from the following list of cities which exported via Milwaukee in both 1963 and 1964: Alton, Illinois; Indianapolis, Indiana; St. Louis, Kansas City, and St. Joseph, Missouri; Topeka and Wichita, Kansas; Omaha, Hastings, and Grand Island, Nebraska; Denver, Colorado; Belle Fourche and Sioux Falls, South Dakota; Fargo and

17. Milwaukee, Board of Harbor Commissioners, *Port of Milwaukee* 1962, p. 27; hereafter cited as *1962 Port Brochure.*

Grand Forks, North Dakota; Three Forks, Montana. It is interesting that the last seven of these cities lie in Duluth's domestic class rate hinterland and the first eight in Chicago's.

EXPORTERS SURVEY

In an effort to determine why Wisconsin firms do not ship a greater share of their exports through the Port of Milwaukee, a questionnaire (see Appendix C) was sent to those firms which were listed as participants in the Commerce Department study. In it, exporters were asked to give the value and tonnage of their annual exports, to estimate the percentage of their exports shipped via Milwaukee and via competitive Atlantic, Gulf, and Great Lakes ports, and to list the reasons why ports competitive to Milwaukee were used.

The Commerce Department study included 250 Wisconsin firms, of which 130 gave permission to be identified in the study as exporters. The 1963 updated reported exports were valued at $343.2 million or 68.6 per cent of the state's estimated total manufactured exports ($500.2 million). Table 6-3 presents a classification by industry of both the reported and the estimated exports, as well as information on each industry's share of the state and national totals. According to the study, the firms included had at least one hundred employees and 1963 exports worth $25,000. "Based on a Census company survey covering 1958, these establishments account for substantially all shipments known to the manufacturer to be destined for export." [18]

The questionnaire was sent to all 130 listed firms. Eight of these replied that they are currently doing no exporting; of the remaining 122 firms, 63 returned the questionnaire with some or all of the desired information. While this is slightly more than half the number of firms, those which did reply reported exports valued at $206.4 million, which is over 60 per cent of the total reported in the Commerce Department study.[19] It is evident that the sample includes most of the state's reported exports, and we may draw the inference that, by and large, the firms which did not reply are not exporting a significant amount.[20] The con-

18. U.S. Department of Commerce, "Export Origin Study," 1962.

19. The $206.4 million in fact includes only fifty-one firms, since eleven which replied did not supply a figure for the value of their exports.

20. Some support for this inference may be drawn from the statements of five companies that their exports were "negligible" or "very few" at present, in addition to the eight which are not currently exporting at all. Fourteen firms said that the statistics were unavailable (only one of these stated that exports were "sizeable"), and forty did not reply.

clusions of the survey, therefore, would probably not be modified greatly if data were available from the other firms. The nature of the sample, however, does not permit any quantification of the probable extent of divergence between the survey results and the "true" figures.

TABLE 6-3

WISCONSIN REPORTED EXPORTS AND ESTIMATED TOTAL EXPORTS OF MANUFACTURING ESTABLISHMENTS,* 1963

Industry group	Reported export value (millions of dollars)	Estimated total exports of manufactured prod., 1963			
		Value (millions of dollars)	% of U.S. total	% State distribution	Rank in state
Food & kindred prod.	15.5	43.7	2.6	8.7	3
Tobacco manufactures	0	0	0	0	0
Textile mill prod.	0	1.4	0.5	0.3	16
Apparel & related prod.	0	0.9	0.8	0.2	17
Lumber & wood prod.	†	5.8	3.0	1.2	10
Furniture & fixtures	0	0.5	1.9	0.1	18
Paper & allied prod.	1.7	5.6	1.0	1.1	11
Printing & pub.	‡	3.6	2.1	0.7	13
Chemicals & allied prod.	2.7	5.2	0.3	1.0	12
Petroleum & coal prod.	0	0	0	0	0
Rubber & plastics prod.	1.4	2.6	1.1	0.5	15
Stone, clay, glass prod.	6.5	8.4	4.2	1.7	8
Primary metal ind.	6.2	8.2	1.0	1.6	9
Fabricated metal prod.	13.7	18.5	3.4	3.7	7
Leather & leather prod.	0.8	2.8	4.6	0.6	14
Machinery, exc. elect.	184.1	241.8	7.0	48.3	1
Elect. machinery	34.8	42.2	3.5	8.4	4
Transportation equipment	52.5	61.5	2.4	12.3	2
Instruments & related prod.	4.8	23.8	3.4	3.8	5
Misc. mfr.	§	23.6	3.5	4.7	6
Total	343.2‖	500.2	3.1	100.0	

Source: U.S. Bureau of the Census, *Survey of the Origin of Exports of Manufactured Products, 1963.*

Figures have been rounded.

*Establishments with one hundred or more employees which exported $25,000 or more in 1963.

†Less than $1.0 million.

‡$1.0 million to $4.9 million.

§$10.0 million to $24.9 million.

‖Total includes †, ‡, §.

Table 6-4 shows the percentage of export tonnage and value shipped by Milwaukee and by competitive ports. It demonstrates once again the dominance of Atlantic Coast ports, and to a lesser extent of Gulf coast ports. Milwaukee attracts only about 8.5 per cent of the tonnage exported by these firms and only about 6 per cent of the value.[21] The reasons why exports via other Great Lakes ports are almost non-existent have been suggested earlier: overseas shipping rates from Milwaukee are generally the same as those from other Lake Michigan ports and cheaper than those from Duluth, so that for most firms, other things being equal,

TABLE 6-4

PORTS UTILIZED BY WISCONSIN EXPORTERS

Ports	% of tonnage shipped via	% of value shipped via
Milwaukee	8.51	5.98
Atlantic	57.34	68.88
Gulf	26.01	17.59
Other Great Lakes	.21	.39
Other	7.75	6.54
Unreported	.16	.62

Source: Exporters Survey Questionnaire.
Figures have been rounded.

shipping from Chicago or Duluth increases total transportation costs by at least the difference between domestic freight rates to these ports and to Milwaukee.

Further analysis of the data in Table 6-4 suggests some considerations for promotional activities by the Port of Milwaukee. Over 87 per cent of the total export tonnage in the survey was produced by only four firms, with thirty-nine others sharing the remainder. (Twenty firms did not supply tonnage figures.) Shipments of these four via Milwaukee amounted to only 7.97 per cent of their total tonnage, while smaller exporters shipped 12.26 per cent. If the big exporters can be induced to ship a larger fraction through Milwaukee, they might be a potent stimulus to the port's overseas traffic. To offer an example of the possible effect, if the largest four exporters doubled their Milwaukee shipments, which would amount to only 16 per cent of all their shipments, the port's general cargo exports would rise by about 15 to 20 per cent.

Although the biggest exporters ship less through Milwaukee, relatively

21. The result with respect to value supports the earlier conclusion that Table 6-2 overstates Milwaukee's share of Wisconsin exports.

speaking, it should be stressed that they are not behaving in a particularly different way from the other firms. The following frequency distribution emphasizes this point:

% tonnage shipped via Milwaukee	Number of firms
0	16
0.1–5.0	18
5.1–10.0	9
10.1–20.0	5
20.1–30.0	3
30.1–50.0	9
Over 50.1	3

The median figure reported was 5 per cent. The sixteen firms which ship nothing at all via Milwaukee accounted for only 1.5 per cent of the total tonnage; the value of their exports was $31 million.

According to the Commerce Department study, the Milwaukee SMSA's reported exports amounted to $148.3 million, or 43 per cent of the state as a whole. Table 6-5 presents the breakdown by industry for the metropolitan area and the other data on exports that was given in Table 6-3 for the state. Nineteen exporters from Milwaukee County replied to the questionnaire, which was sent to fifty-two companies; these nineteen reported exports amounting to $107.7 million, 72.6 per cent of the Commerce Department figure for 1963. The distribution of their export shipments is shown in Table 6-6. It does not vary substantially from the pattern for all of Wisconsin in Table 6-4; the port does a little better in terms of tonnage and not so well in terms of value in its own metropolitan area. Only one Milwaukee firm did not use the port at all, seven shipped up to 5 per cent via Milwaukee, and six more used the port up to 10 per cent of the time. Of the other firms, two reported percentages between 20 and 30, one between 30 and 50, and two use the port for over half of their exports. The median figure was 10 per cent.

The questionnaire asked the firms to explain why they did not use Milwaukee more frequently. The replies to this question are tabulated in Table 6-7. Though the firms were asked to rank the reasons in their order of importance, a number of respondents preferred simply to indicate which reasons were important to them, without a ranking. These replies are tabulated in a separate column of Table 6-7. Two reasons were cited most consistently, with "control of shipment by buyer, who specifies port" being both slightly more important and slightly more frequent

TABLE 6-5

MILWAUKEE SMSA, VALUE OF MANUFACTURED PRODUCTS EXPORTS
OF FIRMS REPORTING EXPORTS IN 1963*

S.I.C. No.	Industry group	Value (millions of dollars)	% of U.S. total	Distribution in area (%)	Rank in area
20	Food & kindred prod.	3.5	0.5	2.3	7
27	Printing & publishing	†	‡		
28	Chemicals & allied prod.	1.8	0.1	1.2	8
31	Leather & leather prod.	†	‡		
32	Stone, clay & glass prod.	†	‡		
33	Primary metal industries	5.9	0.8	4.0	5
34	Fabricated metal prod.	6.7	1.7	4.5	4
35	Machinery, exc. elect.	95.3	3.6	64.5	1
36	Electrical machinery	23.7	2.4	16.0	2
37	Transportation equipment	7.1	0.3	4.8	3
38	Instruments & related prod.	3.8	0.9	2.6	6
	Total	148.3§	1.3	100.0	

Source: U.S. Bureau of the Census, *Survey of the Origin of Exports of Manufactured Products, 1963.*

Figures have been rounded.

*Establishments with one hundred or more employees which reported $25,000 or more in 1963.

†Less than $1.0 million.

‡Percent not calculated.

§Total includes ranges for Nos. 27, 31, 32.

TABLE 6-6

PORTS UTILIZED BY MILWAUKEE COUNTY EXPORTERS

Ports	% tonnage shipped via	% value shipped via
Milwaukee	9.13	4.56
Atlantic	51.73	64.86
Gulf	30.06	23.54
Other Great Lakes	.18	.63
Other	8.91	6.31
Unreported	—	.10

Source: Exporters Survey Questionnaire.
Figures have been rounded.

TABLE 6-7

REASONS GIVEN BY WISCONSIN EXPORTERS FOR NOT SHIPPING VIA MILWAUKEE

Reason	Most important reason	Second	Third	Fourth	Fifth	Sixth	Seventh	Listed without ranking
Control of shipment by buyer, who specifies port	16	6	4	2	2	1	0	11
Greater frequency of sailings from Gulf & Atlantic ports	10	11	4	2	0	0	0	12
Sailings from Gulf & Atlantic ports to destinations not available from Milwaukee	6	4	7	4	1	1	0	7
Seasonal nature of St. Lawrence Seaway	2	3	3	5	3	0	0	8
Gulf or Atlantic forwarder	0	5	3	3	4	1	0	3
Rate differential	2	0	3	3	3	0	1	2
Longer transit time from Milwaukee	1	0	3	0	0	0	0	3
Shipments are consolidated with those of other companies in New York	0	1	1	0	0	0	0	3
Most of firm's exports are produced by plants not in Wisconsin	0	0	0	0	0	0	0	5
Banking facilities available elsewhere	0	0	0	0	0	0	0	3
Firm has export office in N.Y.	0	0	0	0	0	0	0	2
Lack of U.S.-flag vessels from Milwaukee	0	0	0	1	0	0	0	0

Source: Exporters Survey Questionnaire

than the larger number of sailings available from other coasts. This result, however, deserves further analysis. While the fact that buyers may determine the routing of their purchases explains why Wisconsin exporters do not make greater use of Milwaukee, it is not a reason in any economic sense: if the foreign buyers were asked why *they* do not make greater use of Milwaukee, their answers would fall into the other categories of more frequent sailings from other ports, rate differentials, the seasonal nature of the Seaway, and so forth.

But it is also likely that foreign buyers may not ship via Milwaukee simply because they are unfamiliar with the port and its facilities. It is both costly and time-consuming for them to obtain information about Milwaukee and the Seaway (or any other new form of transport), and they may prefer to use their already established shipping routes. This is purely a short-run consideration; eventually, foreigners who could profitably utilize Milwaukee will find out about it. All this means is that the changes in overseas shipping routes, due to the opening of the Seaway, have not fully worked themselves out yet.

In the meantime, there is no reason why Milwaukee cannot speed up the process of change, and the port has, in fact, begun to aim part of its promotional activities at the foreign buyers. In 1962 Milwaukee sent its first overseas trade mission to Europe, visiting seventeen major shipping centers in nine countries. The Board of Harbor Commissioners considered the reaction in Europe to the mission to be "exceptionally favorable." [22] In addition, a special four-page feature section on the port appeared on June 27, 1963, in the *Journal of Commerce and Shipping Telegraph*, a widely read trade newspaper of the shipping industry, published in Liverpool, England. Recent discussions with the Board of Harbor Commissioners indicate that the port intends to devote more effort in the future to reaching overseas customers of the area's industry. This barrier to the growth of Milwaukee's shipping traffic will probably be reduced in the next few years.

The second most important reason — that Atlantic and Gulf ports offer more frequent sailings than does Milwaukee — is of particular importance to exporters who have promised delivery of their merchandise by a specified date. Even when there is no deadline to meet, the credit and storage costs of goods waiting for a ship can be substantial. These costs are an important consideration to any exporter and may easily outweigh the savings in transport costs. While sailings from Milwaukee have grown

22. Milwaukee, Board of Harbor Commissioners, Chairman's *1962 Annual Report*, p. 11.

steadily since World War II and reached 439 in 1964 (see Table 5-1), the Port of New York had approximately 13,000 departures in 1963, and Philadelphia had 6,308 in the same year.

Milwaukee's disadvantage in relation to New York, however, becomes an advantage in relation to Duluth. Table 6-8 brings out this point, explaining to a great extent why Milwaukee is consistently able to reach far into Duluth's theoretical freight hinterland for overseas cargo.

TABLE 6-8
NUMBER OF SAILINGS FROM GREAT LAKES PORTS TO
OVERSEAS DESTINATIONS, 1958–64

Ports	*1958*	*1959*	*1960*	*1961*	*1962*	*1963*	*1964*
Milwaukee	223	261	333	368	391	359	439
Chicago	365	511	482	519	562	552	674
Duluth	0	235	243	204	280	220	299
Detroit	503	610	714	761	801	789	864
Cleveland	475	574	497	584	587	570	548
Green Bay	—*	—	—	—	102	99	99
Kenosha	—	—	—	—	94	117	92

Source: Unpublished correspondence between author and the port directors.
*Dash = data not available.

Duluth suffers from a unique disadvantage: among Great Lakes ports, it is the only one not lying on the route to Chicago. This has already been noted in connection with Duluth's higher shipping rates (see p. 57), but it is perhaps even more important in terms of number of sailings. The additional cost of stopping at Milwaukee is small, in terms of both time and money, to a ship already sailing to or from Chicago, and, consequently, relatively small cargoes will be required to induce them to stop. Thus, while Milwaukee must compete with Chicago for much of its cargo, it also benefits from its proximity to the larger city.[23] In every year from 1958 to 1964 Milwaukee sailings averaged between 60 and 70 per cent of those from Chicago.

The most obvious way for Milwaukee to increase the number of its sailings would be to persuade Chicago's remaining 30 to 40 per cent to stop at Milwaukee also. This is only a short run measure, however; ultimately Milwaukee and all other Great Lakes ports must more or less simultaneously persuade more shippers and more ships to use them.

23. When the Fjell Line began sailings to the Great Lakes in 1933, its service went to Chicago, with stops at Milwaukee and some other ports en route. See above, p. 37.

The third most important reason — the lack of ships to specific ports — is in reality a special case of the second. Information obtained from replies to the eleventh question as to the destination of each company's exports provides a basis for further analysis of both reasons. In response to this question, thirty-six companies provided data on value and thirty on tonnage. Though these companies represent only half of all partici-

TABLE 6-9

DESTINATION OF WISCONSIN-MANUFACTURED EXPORTS

Destination	% of total value	% of total tonnage
Europe	40.47	10.66
Mediterranean	11.59	10.56
East coast of South America	8.86	17.83
West coast of South America	3.95	16.14
Canada	4.91	1.37
Central America, Cuba, Mexico	4.48	24.46
Islands of the Atlantic	1.62	1.39
Far East	5.10	1.17
Indonesia	.16	3.88
Red Sea, Persian Gulf	3.39	.30
India, Pakistan, Burma	5.43	5.65
Africa (East, West, & South)	6.48	2.21
Australia, New Zealand, and Pacific Islands	2.80	4.26
Other	.76	.12
Total	100.0	100.0

Source: Exporters Survey Questionnaire.

pants in the survey, they accounted for over 66 per cent of the reported value and over 77 per cent of the reported tonnage. Their responses are summarized in Table 6-9.

Comparison of this table with Appendix B, showing the 1963 export shipments of Milwaukee by commodity and country of destination, is illuminating. It was pointed out earlier (see page 53) that a large percentage of Milwaukee's machinery shipments went to free Europe. When combined with the non-European countries bordering the Mediterranean, this area received 84.4 per cent of Milwaukee's machinery shipments in 1963. But only about 40 per cent of the value of all reported manufactured exports went to Europe, and only about 12 per cent to the Mediterranean countries. By contrast, Central and South America received over 17 per cent of reported exports, but only 4 per cent of Milwaukee's shipments; similar situations occurred for Asia and Africa. The data are not precisely comparable, since a few of the participants in the survey do not manufacture machinery, but removing them from the data would not change the results to any significant degree.[24]

Five of the six companies which listed "sailings from Gulf and Atlantic ports to destinations not available from Milwaukee" as the chief drawback to making greater use of the port also provided information on the destination of their shipments. In the light of the preceding paragraph, it is not surprising that as a group these companies shipped more heavily to Asia, Africa, and Australia than did the others. Four of them each sent more than half of their exports there, as against 23 per cent by all companies in terms of value, or 17 per cent in terms of tonnage. Milwaukee does, in fact, now have ships to ports on all three continents, though the first two sailings to Australia occurred only in 1962. It appears probable that Milwaukee can overcome this difficulty to the same extent and in the same ways that it manages to attract more frequent sailings.

Use of Gulf or Atlantic forwarders is a difficulty of another kind. General cargo often requires special services in preparing it for shipment, and the greater availability of companies with this specialized know-how is one reason for the concentration of exports at the Atlantic and Gulf ports, in particular New York. That port's position as the financial and commercial capital of the nation enables it to offer superior services to shippers which can offset its rate disadvantage. In economic theory, these services are called an example of "economies of scale." They are not available in all ports in proportion to the traffic of each, but are concentrated in the largest ports. Consolidation of shipments and banking facilities, which were given as answers by some companies, are other examples of services of this kind. Taken as a group, the relative absence of these services is a handicap to every Great Lakes port.

As is not surprising, rate differentials are not a very important drawback for these Wisconsin firms. Interestingly enough, the two firms which gave this as the most important reason manufacture the same product. This could be considered as the exception that proves the rule, since any rate differentials against Milwaukee are likely to be confined to a few special cases. For a number of firms, the rate differential was the only one of the five listed reasons that they did not consider applicable to themselves.

The seasonal nature of the St. Lawrence Seaway was an important

---

24. Those companies not manufacturing machinery accounted for between 5 and 6 per cent of both the value and tonnage reported.

factor, perhaps as important as the absence of freight forwarders and other services. There is nothing that Milwaukee can do about the fact that the Seaway is closed for three or four months of the year. Senator William Proxmire of Wisconsin has sponsored a bill calling for a study of ways to keep the Seaway open for a longer period each year. Such a study, of course, is only a first step, and there is certainly no guarantee that the study will recommend keeping the Seaway open or that Congress will accept such a recommendation. For the foreseeable future, the eight-month shipping season must be accepted as unavoidable.[25]

Among the other reasons given, only the longer transit time from Milwaukee needs further analysis. The platitude that "time is money" is especially relevant to firms which face credit costs during the period of transport, and it is undeniably true that rail transportation to coastal ports is faster than using the Seaway, especially when the ship stops at several Great Lakes ports along the way. Professor Krueger estimated that the differential to Liverpool would average about two days, with a wide variation around that average.[26] A good idea of the variation may be obtained from a study of transit times between Milwaukee and overseas ports, prepared by the traffic manager for the Board of Harbor Commissioners and reproduced here as Appendix D. For example, twenty-three voyages to London are recorded, with an average time of about twenty-five days, but the range is between seventeen and thirty-four. Similarly, for Liverpool the average was between twenty-four and twenty-five days, with a range of twenty to forty, and these are merely the first ports of call. Some of the other ranges in Appendix D are comparably wide; the most extreme is Yokohama, Japan, with fourteen voyages, ranging from forty-four to ninety-one days. With a range so great for both Milwaukee and competitive ports, one should not place too much emphasis on the greater average transit time from Milwaukee. Against the seven companies which considered this a drawback may be weighed the testimony of another firm which found that a shipment to Scandinavia via Milwaukee and the Seaway went faster than by any other possible route.[27]

On the other hand, if, in fact, we do wish to retain average transit

25. It is possible that either Wisconsin shippers or their foreign customers might change their inventory practices to permit shipment of all exports during the present season. Such a change would be quite expensive, however, and is highly unlikely to occur.

26. Krueger, *Impact of the St. Lawrence Seaway*, p. 13.

27. Municipal Port Director to Board of Harbor Commissioners, Dec. 13, 1962, in records of Board of Harbor Commissioners, Milwaukee.

time as a useful measure, we are able to get a much more meaningful picture by adjusting the average so as to discount the extremes. For example, by dropping the longest and shortest voyages to Yokohama from the computation, the average transit time is reduced by over two and one-half days, and, by similarly adjusting the figure for Liverpool, the average time in transit is reduced by over one full day. Similar adjusted average transit times are shown in Appendix D.

In some cases the modal, or most recurring, figure for days in transit may prove to be a more meaningful representative than the average. As is seen in Appendix D, there were twenty-six sailings to Le Havre, France, studied in the 1964 analysis. Even though the various sailings had a time variation of over a week, sixteen of the twenty-six trips were made in precisely twenty-two days. In cases similar to this it is evident that such a recurring figure may certainly be more meaningful to a potential exporter than an average that might be distorted by some unusual instance. The graphs at the end of Appendix D demonstrate that there undoubtedly was such a modal time-in-transit figure for sailings to virtually all parts of the world.

Throughout this chapter it was assumed that Milwaukee's most important nearby competitors are Chicago and Duluth. In conclusion, this assumption may itself by analyzed briefly. While there are fourteen ports in Wisconsin with terminal facilities for large vessels,[28] only five handled any general overseas cargo at all in 1963, and one of these (Manitowoc) handled less than 200 tons.[29] Besides Superior, which is classified with Duluth in foreign trade statistics, only Green Bay (96,000 tons) and Kenosha (52,000 tons) handled any sizeable amount of traffic.

The possible extent of competition from these ports may be gauged from a report of the Wisconsin Business Research Council, in which Wisconsin manufacturers of exports were asked which of the state's ports they would use if all had adequate facilities.[30] Only nine manufacturers indicated a preference for Kenosha, seven of them in Kenosha County

28. The ports are Superior, Washburn, and Ashland on Lake Superior; Marinette, Green Bay, Sturgeon Bay, Kewaunee, Two Rivers, Manitowoc, Sheboygan, Port Washington, Milwaukee, Racine, and Kenosha on Lake Michigan. See Schenker, *General Cargo Capacity at Wisconsin Lake Ports.*

29. U.S. Army Corps of Engineers, *Waterborne Commerce of the United States,* Annual Report, 1963, Part 3, p. 31.

30. Wisconsin Business Research Council, *The Economic Significance of the St. Lawrence Seaway to Wisconsin.* Some of the material was published in *Wisconsin Manufacturers and Foreign Trade* by the Wisconsin Department of Resource Development.

and two in Ozaukee County. It can, therefore, be stated with some confidence that Kenosha is likely to compete with Milwaukee only in its home county, though it should be remembered that some Kenosha County manufacturers are very large firms.

Green Bay, on the other hand, was listed by 63 manufacturers, second only to Milwaukee with 265. In a separate question, the participants in the survey were asked to choose only between Green Bay, Milwaukee, and Chicago. The results were about the same: "a dividing line between Milwaukee and Green Bay might run in an east-west direction and through the southern portion of Lake Winnebago." [31] In effect, Green Bay's hinterland might consist of the Fox and upper Wisconsin River valleys, together with Manitowoc and perhaps Eau Claire. Green Bay's general cargo exports totaled 58,000 tons in 1963, and two-thirds of this total was government relief cargo (dried milk and wheat flour). Consequently, it can hardly be said to have a large share of its hinterland's traffic.[32] The port has a drawback in that it lies on Green Bay rather than Lake Michigan, and large ships must go somewhat out of the way to get to it, around the Door County Peninsula. It also suffers from the absence of export services to a much greater extent than Milwaukee.

In general, therefore, it seems legitimate to treat all of Wisconsin as lying in the hinterland of Milwaukee, at least for the time being.

31. Wisconsin Department of Resource Development, *Wisconsin Manufacturers and Foreign Trade*, pp. 16–17; Wisconsin Business Research Council, *The Economic Significance of the St. Lawrence Seaway to Wisconsin*, Appendix B.

32. In the exporters survey questionnaire, only five manufacturers listed Green Bay as an "other Great Lakes port." All five firms, with total shipments of only 28 tons, are located in the Fox River Valley area.

7

FEDERAL GOVERNMENT INFLUENCE
ON PORT ACTIVITIES

THE federal government has historically participated in port development. Milwaukee's first permanent white settlers had no sooner arrived
than they sought support from Washington for river and harbor improvements. In 1835, when the first settlement of Juneautown was being established and the population was about two hundred, a petition was sent
to the War Department asking for a survey of the river.[1] The survey was
made in the following year, but then the great depression that began in
1837 intervened, and no improvements were made for several years, except for the building of a lighthouse in 1838 for which Congress appropriated $5,000.[2]

The situation which confronted the early residents urgently demanded
some sort of improvement. The confluence of the Menomonee and the
Milwaukee offered a potentially fine harbor, but below that junction the
river wound a tortuous path to Lake Michigan. At one point (the site
of the present harbor entrance), only a sand bar separated it from the
lake, but then the river turned inland again to meet the Kinnickinnic before eventually reaching the lake, leaving a peninsula about 3,000 feet
long and 300 to 700 feet wide connected to the mainland north of it by
that sandbar.[3] It was not possible for the lake vessels to navigate the shal-

1. Bruce, *History of Milwaukee*, I, 271. Population estimate from Austin, *The
Milwaukee Story*, p. 22.

2. Austin, *The Milwaukee Story*, p. 60.

3. A good sketch of the area, showing the nature of the problem, appears in Hamming, *The Port of Milwaukee*, Figure 5, p. 25. A diagram of the present harbor is
given in Chapter 8 as Figure 8-A; the location of the original river mouth was about

low river to the village, a mile upstream. Instead, passengers and cargo were transferred to a smaller craft which brought them to the settlement. The trip was graphically described by a Swedish immigrant in 1841: "The water splashed over the deck of the unpleasant little freight boat, which had no railings. There was no way of sitting down or holding on to anything. The passengers stood tightly packed together, balancing themselves, as the small boat kept rolling from one side to the other. This passage seemed to me to be the most adventurous part of the entire journey. It was a miracle that neither passengers nor luggage tumbled overboard. Finally, wet and weary, we came to the mouth of the Milwaukee River, and in an hour we were ashore." [4]

The danger was a real one: the predecessor to this ship had run aground in 1840 during a high wind,[5] and its predecessor — "a timber deck and nothing more" — had gone aground in 1837. At least five persons drowned in the lake during transfers in 1839 and 1840.[6]

HARBOR IMPROVEMENTS

The War Department survey had recommended that a "straight cut" be made through the sand bar at the present entrance, which was also preferred by the residents. Congress finally appropriated $30,000 in 1843 "for the construction of a harbor at the most suitable situation at or near Milwaukee, in the Territory of Wisconsin," [7] and later additions raised the total to $50,000. But the work that was actually done in 1845 consisted instead of channel improvements at the natural mouth of the river. It was charged that those merchants with warehouses at the river mouth had bribed the engineers, but the charge was never proven.[8]

Since these improvements were not very useful for most of the merchants and other residents, several groups of private citizens built piers out into the lake at more convenient locations, about 3,000 to 6,500 feet north of the river mouth (that is, between the present harbor entrance and the Municipal Passenger and Auto Pier). For several years this was

where South Pier No. 2 is now located. Jones Island had a much more irregular shore line at that time.

4. G. Unonius, *A Pioneer in Northwest America*, trans. Jonas O. Backlund (Minneapolis: Swedish Pioneer Historical Society, 1950), I, 111–12, quoted in Hamming, *The Port of Milwaukee*, p. 24.

5. Austin, *The Milwaukee Story*, p. 53.

6. Bruce, *History of Milwaukee*, I, 283–85.

7. *Ibid.*, p. 275 .

8. *Ibid.*, pp. 275–76; Austin, *The Milwaukee Story*, p. 95. For further discussions of this period see Gregory, *History of Milwaukee, Wisconsin*, and Whitbeck, *The Geography and Economic Development of Southeastern Wisconsin*.

Milwaukee's waterfront district. The federal government, however, abandoned its plans and improvements at the mouth by 1854, and the city thereupon appropriated $50,000 and built the straight cut itself in 1857. The sand bar and swampland between the two river mouths were filled in to make Jones Island. Shipping activity then ceased at the lakefront piers and was concentrated on the river banks inland.[9]

Subsequent relations with the federal government have been more satisfactory. The first breakwater was constructed between 1881 and 1902; it now constitutes the northernmost 7,650 feet of the harbor's north breakwater. A number of improvements in the inner harbor were authorized between 1902 and 1910, but were not carried out. The authorization was terminated in 1922, when Congress approved the existing project.

The River and Harbor Act of 1922 authorized the U.S. Army Corps of Engineers to extend the breakwater another 1,760 feet to the south and to build a new breakwater, 9,650 feet long, starting 500 feet south of the first one. This formed a protective basin, now known as the outer harbor. In 1935 the Engineers were authorized to dredge about half of the outer harbor to a depth of 21 feet, in cooperation with the city. Over the years, other parts of the project have included deepening the original straight cut to 21 feet (the cut is now 358 feet wide at its lakeward end, 552 feet wide at the shoreward end, and some 1,600 feet long; it is lined by a pier on each side for its entire length, also constructed by the Engineers). In addition, the 21-foot depth was extended in two directions: (1) from the mouth of the straight cut almost to the gap between the breakwaters, creating an entrance channel to the port; (2) upriver on all three rivers, to Kinnickinnic Avenue on the Kinnickinnic, Twenty-fifth Street on the Menomonee, and Humboldt Avenue on the Milwaukee.[10]

Nearly all of this project had been completed by the time the St. Lawrence Seaway was opened, though some deepening remained to be done in the outer harbor north of the entrance channel, and in the Milwaukee River, between Buffalo Street (just above the junction with the Menomonee) and Humboldt Avenue.[11] The Seaway has a minimum depth of 27

9. Hamming, *The Port of Milwaukee*, p. 26.

10. Based on U.S. Army Engineer District, *Great Lakes Harbors Study, Interim Report on Milwaukee Harbor, Wisconsin*, pp. 8–10; hereafter cited as *Milwaukee Interim Report*.

11. It may be noted in passing, as a further significant example of the federal government's relation to the port, that the Seaway itself was created by the government, jointly with Canada.

feet, which meant that Milwaukee's harbor was no longer deep enough for the larger ships now able to ply the Great Lakes. The situation was by no means unique to Milwaukee; not one of the fifty-six federally improved commercial harbors on the Great Lakes had a project depth of 27 feet.[12]

In these circumstances, Congress in 1956 authorized the Engineers to determine "the advisability of further improvements of the harbors on the Great Lakes . . . with due regard to the scheduled time of completion of the St. Lawrence Seaway and the connecting channels between the Great Lakes."[13] Accordingly, the Engineers held a public hearing concerning Milwaukee on November 29 of that year. The city sought "27-foot navigation" in the entrance channel, in the previously dredged outer harbor area south of it, in the straight cut, and upriver on both the Milwaukee and the Kinnickinnic to the first bridge on each.[14] It also asked for a 22-foot depth on all three rivers, for as far inland on each as had already been dredged to 21 feet, and on the South Menomonee and Burnham canals in the Menomonee Valley. In substance, the Chicago district engineer recommended approving the former request and rejecting the latter. A 28-foot depth is to be provided in the entrance channel, the straight cut, and the outer harbor, and one of 27 feet on each river. In addition, an approach channel will be dredged to 30 feet from the present entrance channel to a point beyond the opening between the breakwaters.[15]

Congress approved the project in the Rivers and Harbors Act of 1962, authorizing expenditures of $4,029,000.[16] Dredging operations began in 1965, and the U.S. Army Corps of Engineers has pushed the project

12. Schenker, "Federal Expenditures and the St. Lawrence Seaway," *Public Utilities Fortnightly*, LXIII, no. 13, 3. The maximum depth was 26 feet at each of three ports: Two Harbors, Minnesota; Presque Isle, Michigan; and Calumet Harbor, Illinois. The first two ship large amounts of iron ore, while Calumet Harbor, near U.S. Steel's South Works, both receives iron ore and ships bituminous coal.

13. Resolution of the Senate Committee on Public Works, May 8, 1956; and Resolution of the House Committee on Public Works, June 27, 1956, both quoted in U.S. Army Engineer District, *Milwaukee Interim Report*, p. 1.

14. "In referring to 27-foot channels throughout this document, we refer to depths 27 feet below federal low water datum, which would produce available operating draft of 28 feet to 30 feet within the average range of water level fluctuation in Lake Michigan." Statement of the Board of Harbor Commissioners, Public Hearing, Milwaukee, November 29, 1956, p. 3.

15. U.S. Army Engineer District, *Milwaukee Interim Report*, pp. 30–46.

16. Milwaukee, Board of Harbor Commissioners, Chairman's *1962 Annual Report*, pp. 9–10.

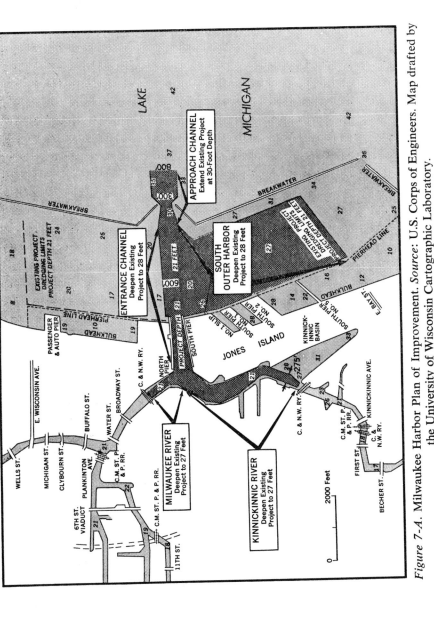

Figure 7-A. Milwaukee Harbor Plan of Improvement. *Source:* U.S. Corps of Engineers. Map drafted by the University of Wisconsin Cartographic Laboratory.

continuously in order to complete it in 1966 instead of the three- or four-year period that was earlier contemplated. Figure 7-A is a map of the Milwaukee Harbor area showing the present dimensions as well as the new capacity which should be completed by the 1966 navigation season. The present project, when fully completed, will enable large, fully loaded ocean cargo vessels and lake carriers to reach piers in the two rivers as well as in the south outer harbor.

SHIPPER OF GENERAL CARGO

The federal government's sizeable impact on the port's construction need not be further stressed. It has long been widely believed in this country that 'internal improvements" are a legitimate function of the government, and the importance of these improvements, both to individual areas and the nation as a whole is generally recognized.[17]

What is far less generally recognized is that the federal government has, in recent years, acquired an important new relationship with the nation's ports: it has become a major shipper of general cargo. Its shipments fall into two categories: agricultural commodities for needy persons in other countries (usually termed "relief cargo") and goods used by our armed forces stationed around the world, including both military hardware and supplies for the day-to-day living needs of servicemen and their families.

RELIEF CARGO

Since World War II, the volume of this traffic has grown steadily, and it has been an important "base cargo" for seaboard ports, particularly for those on the Gulf coast. Though there was some movement of government-controlled cargo via the Great Lakes before 1959, it was only with the opening of the St. Lawrence Seaway that Milwaukee and other lake ports became major participants in the traffic. (The pattern is exemplified in Table 7-1). Milwaukee, in particular, has consistently been a leading port in shipments of relief cargo, although defense cargo plays a very minor role at this port.

Relief cargo consists primarily of agricultural surplus commodities. The principal goods in the traffic are wheat flour, powdered milk, and cereal products such as corn meal (classified in foreign trade data under

17. In recent years increasing concern has been expressed by transportation experts regarding the methods and procedures by which federal navigation projects are evaluated and recommended for development by the Corps of Engineers. For discussion of this problem see Schenker, "Public Investment in Navigation Projects: A Case Study," *Land Economics*, XXXVI, 212–16.

TABLE 7-1

TYPES OF GOVERNMENT RELIEF CARGO SHIPPED OVERSEAS VIA GREAT LAKES PORTS, 1955–63
(Short tons)

No.	Commodity	1955	1956	1957	1958	1959	1960	1961	1962	1963
035	Dried milk	33	2,480	985	4,092	20,334	57,631	113,621	91,859*	199,282
107	Wheat flour semolina	6,107	2,564	2,550	7,518	34,383	166,935	198,246	212,261†	138,212
109	Other flour, flour & grain preparations nec	1,361	1,416	1,087	3,364	11,670	39,623	72,209	111,017	111,717‡
	Total	7,501	6,460	4,622	14,974	66,387	264,189	384,076	415,137	449,211

Source: Great Lakes Commission, *Great Lakes Overseas Commerce*, Annual Reports, 1955–56; Great Lakes Commission, *Great Lakes Foreign Commerce*, Annual Reports, 1957–60; U.S. Bureau of the Census, *United States Foreign Waterborne Commerce, Great Lakes Area*, Annual Reports, 1961–63.

*Includes 5 tons shipped to Canada via the Atlantic.
†Includes 17,020 tons shipped to Canada via the Atlantic.
‡Includes 6,218 tons shipped to Canada via the Atlantic.

TABLE 7-2

DESTINATION OF GOVERNMENT RELIEF CARGO SHIPPED OVERSEAS VIA GREAT LAKES PORTS, 1955–63

(Short tons)

Area	1955	1956	1957	1958	1959	1960	1961	1962	1963
Caribbean	1,883	1,873	1,859	5,267	20,176	3,649	181	9,534	26,941
United Kingdom & Eire	2,786	641	269	961	2,010	2,492	3,599	2,520	1,875
Baltic & Scandinavia	618	2,822	2,051	3,039	1,558	14,294	10,424	16,364	7,312
Bayonne-Hamburg range	781	64	26	2,993	10,681	4,624	1,456	10,897	20,546
Portugal & Spanish Atlantic	0	92	66	178	58	373	1,896	6,128	0
Mediterranean & Black Sea	1,433	0	4	3,315	14,355	177,358	215,613	174,082	126,643
Africa (South, East, & West)	0	0	0	181	2,087	0	11,381	0	43,816
India, Persian Gulf, & Red Sea	0	0	0	0	14,870	37,015	66,073	59,850	58,084
Southeast & East Asia	0	0	0	0	0	16,622	68,130	81,847	118,646
Other & Unreported	0	968	346	40	592	7,741	5,236	53,915*	45,348†
Total	7,501	6,460	4,621	15,974	66,387	264,168	383,989	415,137	449,211

Source: Great Lakes Commission, *Great Lakes Overseas Commerce*, Annual Reports, 1955–56; Great Lakes Commission,*Great Lakes Foreign Commerce*, Annual Reports, 1957–60; U.S. Bureau of the Census, *United States Foreign Waterborne Commerce, Great Lakes Area*, Annual Reports, 1961–63.

*Includes 17,025 tons shipped to Canada via the Atlantic.

†Includes 6,218 tons shipped to Canada via the Atlantic.

Commodity No. 109, "other flour, flour and grain preparations not elsewhere classified"). Virtually no study of this traffic has been made heretofore. In particular, government relief shipments have not been separated in the data from commercial shipments of the same commodities; both are included without differentiation in the publications of the U.S. Army Corps of Engineers and the Census Bureau. It has not been possible to determine what share of the traffic reported in these commodities is relief cargo. The figures used in this analysis include both government relief and commercial shipments. For our purposes, this procedure is reasonably satisfactory.

The shipments via the Great Lakes of each of the three leading relief commodities since 1955 are represented in Table 7-1. The effect of the Seaway on this traffic needs little comment. It should be noted that while 1959 figures showed exports more than four times those of 1958 the increase in tonnage is dwarfed by comparison with the increase between 1959 and 1960, when shipments again quadrupled.

Until 1963, flour had always accounted for at least half of the overseas relief shipments via the Great Lakes-Seaway route. This, of course, was not surprising since wheat is the major crop of the plains to the west of the lakes. In that year, however, the "rate war" between the Great Lakes and the Gulf ports (which will be discussed later in the chapter) played a major role in reducing the Great Lakes share of wheat flour exports. This reduction, coupled with a 107,000-ton increase in dried milk shipments, relegated wheat flour to second place among the relief cargo exports of the Great Lakes.

The growth of relief exports was accompanied by a striking shift in the regional pattern of their destinations. Prior to the opening of the Seaway, Great Lakes trade was primarily with northern European ports and the Caribbean, although Table 7-2 also shows that in 1958 the Mediterranean area (including ports in Europe, the Near East, and North Africa) received more relief cargo than any of the northern European port groups. The opening of the Seaway in 1959 brought a quadrupling of trade with the Caribbean, which temporarily remained the largest single recipient, but more significant is the fact that the shipments to Persian Gulf and Red Sea ports (including India) occurred in such quantities that this region stood second, though Great Lakes trade with these ports was nonexistent before 1959. Also, the Mediterranean area received slightly more relief cargo than all of northern Europe combined, while in 1958 it had received slightly less than half as much.

The tremendous increase in 1960 brought even more pronounced shifts. Shipments to the Mediterranean ports alone accounted for over

80 per cent of that increase; shipments to the two Asian regions [18] more than accounted for the remainder. In the face of a fourfold increase in all relief cargo shipments, exports to the Caribbean declined by more than 80 per cent, and shipments to the ports between Bayonne and Hamburg by more than 50 per cent. About the same pattern appears in the 1961 figures. Southeast and East Asia recorded the largest increase in receipts, and sub-Saharan Africa traffic rose from zero to over 11,000 tons. The Bayonne-Hamburg range lost a further two-thirds of its receipts, and trade with the Caribbean virtually disappeared.

In 1962 and 1963 relief shipments to the Mediterranean dropped from the 1961 peak while those to the Bayonne-Hamburg range reached their highest level to that date (still less than one-fifth of those to the Mediterranean). The Caribbean regained its losses of the previous two years and reached its highest level in 1963 while shipments to Southeast and East Asia continued to grow significantly. A major factor contributing to the total increase in 1962 was an export trade of 17,000 tons of wheat flour to Canada via the Seaway and Atlantic. Unlike lake traffic, this cargo must be carried in ocean-going vessels and may be classified as overseas trade. The largest increase in 1963 was in shipments to the west coast of Africa. This gain, together with increased shipments to East Asia and the Caribbean, more than accounted for the total gain experienced in 1963.

It may be doubted whether shipments to the United Kingdom, northern continental Europe, and Canada were in fact relief cargo, particularly in recent years. Certainly it is highly likely that most of the commercial shipments went to these prosperous countries. Any attempt to make allowances for commercial shipments, however, would be sheer guesswork, and rather than make some arbitrary judgment of what to include in the statistics, we have preferred to present figures for all overseas recipients and to let the reader draw his own conclusions. Lake trade with Canada is excluded, but overseas shipments from U.S. Great Lakes ports which were transhipped at Canadian ports are included in the tables.

In the first five years of Seaway operation, Milwaukee consistently shipped a large share of relief cargo; the port ranked first or second among all Great Lakes ports every year in every commodity. The ton-

18. "Southeast and East Asia" includes three Census Bureau trade areas: (1) Malaya, Singapore, and Indonesia; (2) Far East-Southern Area, including Taiwan and Philippines; (3) Far East-Northern Area, including Japan. The three are combined in Great Lakes Commission, *Great Lakes Foreign Commerce*, Annual Report, 1960.

TABLE 7-3

GREAT LAKES PORTS OF SHIPMENT FOR WHEAT FLOUR, 1958–63
(Short tons)

Port	1958	1959	1960	1961	1962	1963
Milwaukee	1,955	17,242	38,590	52,506	44,337	41,304
Chicago	4,088	8,162	63,293	38,516	35,229	25,744
Duluth-Superior	0	561	4,320	29,419	19,025	11,753
Buffalo	448	4,676	12,113	22,889	20,458	14,905
Green Bay	0	0	13,959	20,665	28,483	7,503
Kenosha	0	0	15,887	20,122	18,329	9,023
Toledo	930	1,645	13,323	11,830	24,800	24,530
Cleveland	56	341	2,293	1,560	3,745	1,013
Oswego	0	0	3,134	0	0	0
Rochester	0	1,670	0	0	0	0
Other	40	87	23	139	823	2,433
Total	7,518	34,383	166,935	197,646	195,229	138,208

Source: U.S. Army Corps of Engineers, *Waterborne Commerce of the United States*, Annual Reports, 1958–63.

TABLE 7-4

GREAT LAKES PORTS OF SHIPMENT FOR DRIED MILK, 1958–63
(Short tons)

Port	1958	1959	1960	1961	1962	1963
Milwaukee	1,936	8,460	18,761	45,403	34,960	36,952
Green Bay	509	2,573	29,089	42,888	16,768	30,495
Duluth-Superior	0	322	250	18,744	21,271	77,214
Chicago	0	2,276	3,216	2,389	8,339	14,423
Ogdensburg	0	0	0	2,153	886	3,818
Kenosha	0	0	3,110	1,677	1,766	2,200
Toledo	600	0	0	196	2,923	3,866
Buffalo	0	5,426	2,164	113	0	917
Cleveland	1,048	1,276	939	58	245	6,016
Other	0	0	102	0	4,693	23,337
Total	4,092	20,334	57,631	113,621	91,851	199,238

Source: U.S. Army Corps of Engineers, *Waterborne Commerce of the United States*, Annual Reports, 1958–63.

Figures have been rounded.

TABLE 7-5

GREAT LAKES PORTS OF SHIPMENT FOR "OTHER FLOUR &
PREPARATIONS," 1958–63

(Short tons)

Port	1958	1959	1960	1961	1962	1963
Chicago	2,913	8,805	15,042	35,369	57,011	59,046
Milwaukee	281	2,714	18,922	25,407	27,512	27,181
Oswego	0	0	3,896	7,881*	7,267	0
Toledo	0	0	218	1,741	855	1,424
Kenosha	0	0	0	1,731	2,037	4,206
Green Bay	169	95	1,515	0	0	1,619
Other	0	56	30	80	16,332	12,091
Total	3,363	11,670	39,623	72,209	111,014	105,567

Source: U.S. Army Corps of Engineers, *Waterborne Commerce of the United States*, Annual Reports, 1958–63.

Figures have been rounded.

*Listed as "imports" in *Waterborne Commerce of the United States*, Part 3, p. 193, but as "exports" in *U.S. Great Lakes Ports Monthly Statistics*, November, 1961, p. 2.

nages for 1958 to 1963 are shown in Tables 7-3, 7-4, and 7-5. Milwaukee's dominant position is clear. Only Chicago in 1960 has topped it in total relief cargo tonnage for any year since the opening of the Seaway. Except in the case of wheat flour, the western Great Lakes ports have had virtually all of that cargo moving via the Great Lakes. Wisconsin's boast that it is America's Dairyland is borne out by the statistics on dried milk; 73 per cent of Great Lakes shipments went via four Wisconsin ports in 1963 (including Duluth-Superior). Cereal products shipments have been virtually a monopoly of Chicago and Milwaukee,[19] and the same ports ranked first and second in wheat flour exports for each of the four years, though shipments of the latter commodity have been much more dispersed among several ports of origin, with the Lake Erie ports of Buffalo and Toledo getting significant shares of the traffic, in addition to the western ports.

The significance of government relief cargo to the Great Lakes can

19. It is pointed out in the note to Table 7-5 that Oswego's cereal products traffic (and its other overseas trade) is listed as "imports" in the Corps of Engineers' statistics and as "exports" in the data published by the Chicago Association of Commerce and Industry. Both get their figures from the Census Bureau. The error, almost certainly, is in the engineers' data, for the total export tonnage, published independently by the Census Bureau, is equal to the sum of the individual ports tonnages as reported by the engineers only if Oswego's traffic is counted as exports.

be seen in Table 7-6, comparing all general cargo exports for the major ports (as shown in Table 2-4) with their relief cargo (taken from Tables 7-3, 7-4, and 7-5). Milwaukee and Buffalo are clearly the ports most heavily dependent on government-controlled shipments, but Buffalo's relief tonnage was only about one-seventh as great as Milwaukee's in 1963. Duluth's share of relief cargo, primarily dried milk, in-

TABLE 7-6

GOVERNMENT RELIEF CARGO AS A PERCENTAGE OF GENERAL CARGO EXPORTS, MAJOR GREAT LAKES PORTS, 1958–63

Port	1958	1959	1960	1961	1962	1963
Buffalo	0%	48% 62*	58%	77%	40%	79%
Chicago	7	5 14*	24	22	21	15
Cleveland	2	3 5*	4	3	7	9
Detroit	0	0 1*	0	0	5	8
Duluth	0	5 10*	11	56	29	29
Milwaukee	9	23 48*	71	80	64	64
Toledo	18	6 10*	42	18	56	44

Source: U.S. Army Corps of Engineers, *Waterborne Commerce of the United States*, Annual Reports, 1958–63.

*Assumes that half of "General Miscellaneous Commodities, n.e.c." is relief cargo. For explanation of alternative percentages, see note 20.

creased substantially from 1960 to 1963. Only Cleveland and Detroit, both major manufacturing centers and both somewhat removed from the heart of the Farm Belt do not depend on government relief cargo for a sizeable share of their general cargo export trade. Green Bay and Kenosha, not shown in Table 7-6, are also heavily dependent upon relief cargo: 60 per cent of Green Bay's and 37 per cent of Kenosha's overseas exports were government relief commodities in 1963.[20]

20. The alternative percentages for 1959 in Table 7-6 (marked with an asterisk) are based on Great Lakes Commission, *Great Lakes Foreign Commerce*, Annual Report, 1959, p. 17, note a: "The category 'General miscellaneous commodities, n.e.c.,' which totals 192,322 tons, is not included due to the vagueness of the classification. A major portion of this traffic is shipments by U.S. relief agencies. The principal ports handling the above-mentioned classification of commodities

Milwaukee's status as a leading relief cargo port has given it an opportunity to increase its commercial general cargo traffic at the same time. Its importance in this respect has been well described by H. C. Brockel, municipal port director at Milwaukee: "The availability of agricultural products as base cargo permits many steamship lines to come into the Seaway trade with some confidence and to supplement this base traffic with a variety of commercial cargo. It is of great economic importance to the area in this respect — in other words the availability of government cargo attracts the shipping lines, which in turn makes new services available to commercial shippers, which in turn stimulates and facilitates our general import and export trade, and diversifies the economy of the Middle West by offering direct and low-cost shipping services to foreign markets." [21] Confirmation of Brockel's statement can be seen in Appendix B. The Port of Milwaukee shipped directly to fifty Asian, African, and Middle Eastern countries in 1963, and, in all but six cases, at least part of the traffic was relief cargo. The point has been made in Chapter 6 that Milwaukee ships a relatively small share of the state's total machinery exports to Asia and Africa; it seems clear that relief cargo is largely responsible for this traffic being even as big as it is. Without relief cargo, Milwaukee might well have no trade at all with either continent.

But heavy dependence on government-controlled shipping has drawbacks as well as advantages. Especially since 1961, the traffic has been irregular and sporadic. The 1962 experience was summarized by Brockel: "We have generally had a 'cliff-hanging' feeling throughout this season because of apparent sudden changes in policy and method which have alternately produced large volumes of traffic, or almost dried it up." [22]

There are a number of possible factors which may cause large shifts in the relief-cargo routings. In June, 1962, for example, Milwaukee's traffic almost disappeared, and the port found that relief groups were requiring that flour be shipped through Gulf Coast ports. A year earlier, the International Cooperation Administration (ICA) required shipment of relief cargoes in U.S.-flag vessels, which would have virtually eliminated Seaway traffic and lake port shipments. The ICA subsequently reversed its ruling after protests from the lake ports.

were: Chicago, 77,753; Milwaukee, 61,902; Green Bay, 34,507; Toledo, 5,977; Buffalo, 5,085; Cleveland, 3,287; Detroit, 1,743; and Duluth-Superior, 1,612." In other years tonnages in the classification were quite small.

21. Personal conversation with author.
22. *Ibid.*

However, such requirements have been exceptional. The general policy of the Department of Agriculture and other relief agencies has been to use the lowest-cost routes for all shipments, as determined on the basis of competitive bids from individual milling companies and milk processors. Where bids through different ports are identical, the policy has been to allocate shipments to each. Such a policy might be expected to result in relatively stable quantities being shipped regularly through the individual ports, but it has not worked out that way in practice. The chief competitors for relief cargo traffic are the Great Lakes and Gulf Coast ports, and it was pointed out in Chapter 6 that many overseas shipping rates are the same from these two coasts. In this situation, domestic transport costs and Seaway tolls become the determining factor, but at present railroad rates on flour from many milling centers are the same to both coasts. As a result, a "rate war" (referred to in Chapter 6) developed.

The rate war began in August, 1961, when the Gulf area railroads reduced the rate on flour for export from Kansas and Nebraska by five cents per hundred pounds. The Western Trunk-Line railroads (serving Milwaukee and the western Great Lakes ports) were apparently caught napping and failed to follow suit, and most of the relief cargo shipping that fall was diverted to the Gulf.[23] Despite the fact that the western railroads matched the rate reduction from Missouri River origins prior to the 1962 Seaway shipping season, the Great Lakes ports were able to regain only a fragment of the wheat flour traffic that they had shipped in the previous year. Encouraged by this sizeable gain, the railroads serving the ports on the Gulf of Mexico published new rates on wheat flour in December, 1962, which would cut an additional ten cents off the Midwest-Gulf rates for the following season. Obviously, this action would have deprived the Great Lakes ports of a major portion of their base cargo and would have diverted both the wheat flour traffic and sizeable quantities of commercial cargo that accompany these relief shipments from the Great Lakes to Gulf ports.

Milwaukee and other Great Lakes ports protested these proposed rates to the ICC on the grounds that they were "noncompensatory" and would establish a monopoly for the Gulf ports while depriving the Great Lakes ports of the commodity upon which much of their commercial traffic relies. In 1964, after some delay, the ICC denied these further rail-rate reductions, and Milwaukee and other Great Lakes ports

---

23. The amount of relief flour shipped from Great Lakes ports was 86 per cent of the national total in April, 1961; 77 per cent in May; 14 per cent in September. It rebounded slightly to 30.5 percent in April, 1962.

were able to hold their relative position on wheat flour traffic. However, as a result of the rail reductions of 1961, the Gulf ports still enjoyed a relative advantage in western Kansas and Nebraska. The two cent per hundred pound Seaway toll spells the difference in this region. However, on April 24, 1965, the ICC approved a two cent per hundred weight rate increase for export and import coastwise freight. This increase equalized costs on wheat flour to the Middle and Far East and gave the Great Lakes a two cent per hundred weight advantage to the Mediterranean from certain producing points. The rate war has thus reached a stand-off, but we can expect further efforts by both camps to gain an advantage in the future. Once again it should be emphasized that this base cargo is vital to the Great Lakes-Seaway shipping industry because it sustains service and makes it available for other users.

It can be seen in Tables 7-4 and 7-5 that other Great Lakes ports are beginning to lessen the Milwaukee-Chicago dominance of relief traffic. Duluth has made substantial gains in the export of dried milk in recent years. The 56,000-ton gain made in 1963 can be attributed to a single large shipment, for the Japanese school-lunch program, which went entirely via Duluth.

In the face of continuing uncertainty over the routing of government relief cargo, the port has taken action on several fronts. The municipal port director, his staff, and board members have sought clarification of policy and assurances of equal treatment from the Department of Agriculture and other relief agencies. A Great Lakes conference of U.S. senators has been established recently to promote the use of the Seaway. When Milwaukee's flour allotments fell in early 1963 substantially below those of previous years, the port traffic manager made a series of promotional visits to the major milling centers in Nebraska and Kansas and to the Department of Agriculture office in Minneapolis. He was unable to pinpoint any definite reason for recent fluctuations in traffic patterns, but three distinct possibilities were brought to light.

First, the Department of Agriculture hypothesized that, if the milling companies suspect that the Department of Agriculture will favor Great Lakes ports, they might submit higher bids for these ports, feeling that they will be able to get their price because of the assumed Department of Agriculture predisposition. This, of course, gives the Gulf coast ports a relative rate advantage, and, in the final result, the Great Lake ports are the losers since the Department of Agriculture will allocate a greater share of the shipments to the Gulf ports due to the relatively lower bids. Second, it was revealed that on certain lots of relief flour cargo the buying country controls the movement and may prefer to use the Gulf ports where they can make their own arrangements for stevedoring and vessels at rates advantageous to themselves. Third, regarding dried milk shipments, it was learned that the Commodity Credit Corporation, an agency of the Department of Agriculture, selects ports on the basis of lowest inland rail-freight costs from the processor's plant to the port of export. This is an obvious inconsistency within the Department of Agriculture since routes are usually determined on the basis of total transport costs from the point of origin to the final destination. The Commodity Credit Corporation's criteria ignore the higher shipping costs from Lake Superior ports (see p. 57), giving to the Port of Duluth a preference, difficult to justify, over Milwaukee and other Lake Michigan ports. Continued efforts are also being made to attract commercial general cargo and diversify the port's trade, but Milwaukee's present heavy dependence on government relief cargo places the port in a vulnerable position, as recent experience has shown.[24]

Defense Cargo

Evaluations of the importance of defense cargo at different ports are hampered by the fact that this type of cargo is excluded from the statistics published by both the Census Bureau and the U.S. Army Corps of Engineers. However, the lack of data is not as great a drawback to this study as might first appear, since Milwaukee has only a very small volume of defense cargo. There have been no large overseas shipments of defense cargoes, and total overseas military shipments have been nominal; by comparison, overseas commercial and relief cargo in 1964 amounted to 463,061 tons. The lack of military tonnage reflects the Milwaukee area's industrial production; its manufacturers are not major suppliers of military hardware. Other Great Lakes ports, notably Detroit, Toledo, and Kenosha, have a much greater interest in defense cargo. Kenosha, which has special facilities for handling military vehicles, is particularly heavily dependent on military shipping. In 1959, for example, over 70 per cent of its overseas traffic appears to have been defense cargo.[25]

The history of defense cargo shipping via the Great Lakes since the opening of the Seaway presents an interesting example of some prob-

24. The foregoing discussion of the port's difficulties since 1961 is largely based on recent reports and correspondence of the Board of Harbor Commissioners, City of Milwaukee.

25. Based on a comparison of the report of the Kenosha Board of Harbor Commissioners with data published by the Corps of Engineers. See Schenker, *General Cargo Capacity at Wisconsin Lakes Ports*, p. 22.

lems faced by the lake ports in attracting government cargo. In 1959, the Defense Department shipped 90,000 tons via the Great Lakes ports, announcing that it had saved the taxpayers an average of $7.00 per ton, or $630,000. Despite this, Great Lakes defense cargo shipments declined in 1960 and declined again in 1961. A group of lake port managers met in July, 1961, and secured the support of the twelve U.S. senators of the region for a joint letter to the Secretary of Defense about the situation. The Secretary ordered the appointment of a task force, which made an investigation and reported its findings in January, 1962.[26]

The task force found only one significant drawback to making greater use of Great Lakes ports: the lack of U.S.-flag shipping. The Defense Department is legally obligated to use American ships when they can provide service at "reasonable rates." The task force reported that only two American lines provided service from the Great Lakes, and both went to the Mediterranean.[27]

If U.S.-flag shipping were available, considerable transportation savings could have been realized by routing defense cargo through the Great Lakes. The task force estimated that $203,000 could have been saved on the shipping of tanks alone, and added that "further savings from the shipment of other commodities could also have been realized." It recommended that the Military Sea Transportation Service supply controlled ships in the Great Lakes if U.S.-flag ships could not be induced to provide service.

The report specifically mentioned that comparative transit times (via the Great Lakes and the seaboard) presented no obstacle to making increased use of the Seaway. It also listed ten Great Lakes ports with adequate terminal facilities for handling military general cargo and vehicles, including Chicago, Kenosha, Milwaukee, and Duluth.

One conclusion of the task force is significant: although present procedures were deemed generally sufficient to ensure use of the most economical ports and routes, "unrealistic cost factors have prevented the recognition of actual lowest over-all landed cost in some cases."[28] It recommended that deficiencies and inconsistencies in the published cost factors be corrected and that a periodic review be instituted. The group

---

26. U.S. Department of Defense, *Surface Movement of Export Cargo.*

27. The predominance of foreign-flag shipping in the Great Lakes can be seen from a breakdown of the overseas sailings in 1962 from Milwaukee. Only 17 of 391 sailings were by American-flag vessels. By contrast, 116 German-flag sailings were recorded; 54 Norwegian; 37 British; 36 Dutch; 36 Swedish; 21 French. Two Japanese lines, serving only the Far East, had 15 sailings from Milwaukee.

28. U.S. Department of Defense, *Surface Movement of Export Cargo,* p. 4.

also found that one major shipper, the Army-Air Force Exchange Service, was not being informed of potential opportunities to use the Great Lakes.

The Great Lakes ports were quite satisfied with the report, but were somewhat less pleased with its implementation during 1962. The situation in that year was described by Brockel: "The movement of defense cargo has been spotty in terms of the Seaway trade. Some ports are enjoying a greater volume, but at Milwaukee we recently saw the spectacle of 1,500 tank trucks being moved overland at staggering cost to a depot in Pennsylvania for final processing, and overseas shipment through the Atlantic seaboard. These units could readily have moved through the Port of Milwaukee to the desired theatres without difficulty and at substantial savings." [29]

The situation of the Great Lakes ports with respect to defense cargo is a good example of the competitive pressures and delays inherent in the process of adjustment to technological improvement and new transportation routes. It is tempting to speculate that similar frictions may be responsible for the uneven flow of relief cargo, but this is less likely.[30]

In September, 1965, a special subcommittee of the U.S. Senate Committee on Commerce published a report which highlighted two of the primary reasons why the Great Lakes area continues to handle less government cargo than would be economically prudent.[31] First, under Section 22 of the Interstate Commerce Act, railroads can offer special rates for government shipments. This enables the railroads to discriminate against lake ports by offering lower rates from the Midwest to Atlantic ports than from the Midwest to Great Lake ports. The railroads, quite naturally, will take advantage of this opportunity to discriminate as long as it exists. They will do so because Great Lakes-overseas shipping operations are a direct competitor to railroad lines that carry traffic from the Great Lakes area to Atlantic Coast ports. If these government commodities were shipped directly from the area in which they are pro-

29. *Ibid.*, p. 6.

30. Early in 1962, the Port of Milwaukee persuaded the Department of Agriculture to list the four American seacoasts, including the Great Lakes, on its relief cargo bidding forms. Prior to that date, the forms merely asked the bidder to specify a port, and Milwaukee felt that, as the newest shipping route, the Great Lakes would benefit from being listed, while the other three coasts were much better known to shippers. The incident forcefully demonstrates the length of time needed to adjust to new transport conditions.

31. U.S. Senate, *Great Lakes–St. Lawrence Seaway Transportation*, report of a Special Subcommittee of the Committee on Commerce.

duced, i.e., from the Great Lakes ports, these railroad lines would be left without this substantial traffic.

Second, the Cargo Preference Laws, which group the Great Lakes and North Atlantic ports into one administrative jurisdiction, contribute to the scarcity of American-flag ships on the Great Lakes. The Cargo Preference Laws state that a Department of Defense shipment cannot leave a port in a foreign ship if an American ship is available at any port in that administrative jurisdiction. By coupling the Great Lakes ports and Atlantic ports into one jurisdiction, these laws encourage American shipowners to avoid using the Great Lakes. After all, why should they sustain the additional time and expense that it would require to sail to the Great Lakes if they can pick up the same cargo at an Atlantic coast port? However, though these Cargo Preference Laws may hold down costs for certain American shipowners, they increase aggregate costs, since it would be far less expensive to sail these ships to the Great Lakes than it is to transport virtually all Midwest-produced defense exports overland to the Atlantic coast. They also tend to retard the development of the Great Lakes shipping industry.

It may be worth noting that, among its recommendations, this special Senate subcommittee recommended both a change in Section 22 of the Interstate Commerce Act and a revamping of the Cargo Preference Laws. Whether these recommendations will be followed remains to be seen, but their adoption would seem to be both logical and economically prudent, and the Great Lakes ports would certainly stand to benefit.

8

LOCAL GOVERNMENT INFLUENCE
ON PORT ACTIVITIES

THE preceding chapter may have created the impression that Milwaukee's harbor development has been chiefly paid for by the federal government, but such is not the case. At the 1956 public hearing, the Board of Harbor Commissioners pointed out that the city had spent twice as much as the federal government had on the harbor, dating back over a century to the digging of the original "straight cut" and even before.[1] Municipal expenditures through the end of 1955 had totaled $16,187,412, compared with federal outlays (through 1953) of $7,973,122. Since then the city-financed permanent improvements have cost $10,751,780, in an ambitious program designed to enable the port to take full advantage of the Seaway;[2] additional federal expenditures amounted to about $2,600,000, nearly all of it maintenance work. About $400,000 worth of work on the pre-Seaway federal project (described on p. 81) is being completed at the present time; the Seaway-inspired deepening and improvements, authorized by Congress in 1962, are expected to cost at least another $4,029,000.[3]

1. Statement of the Board of Harbor Commissioners, Public Hearing, Milwaukee, November 29, 1956, pp. 5–6.
2. Records of the Board of Harbor Commissioners, Milwaukee; see also the annual *Budget, City of Milwaukee, Wisconsin,* Permanent Improvement Fund Expenditures.
3. U.S. Army Engineer District, *Milwaukee Interim Report,* pp. 9–10, p. 35. This estimated cost, however, may prove to be somewhat high since the dredging is now being done by the Corps of Engineers' large hopper dredge, Markham. Besides accelerating the completion of the project by two years, it is estimated that the use of this ocean-going dredge will reduce the cost by about $1.8 million.

The financial aspects of the city's relations with its port will be discussed in greater detail later in this chapter. The above figures are cited only to emphasize the magnitude of municipal expenditures and to show that local government activity is a long-standing tradition.

PORT IMPROVEMENTS

The first recorded dredging expenditures were in 1854, but the earliest municipal activity in connection with the harbor occurred twelve years prior to that date, during the early agitation for a federally financed straight cut. The trustees of the town of Milwaukee appointed two residents, Increase A. Lapham and F. Randall, to make a survey both of local commerce and of the traffic on all of Lake Michigan, in order to demonstrate the need for federal harbor improvements. These men, termed "Milwaukee's first harbor commission" by William M. Bruce, made their report on February 17, 1842.[4] It attempted to list everyone killed and all vessels lost or damaged in lake accidents between 1834 and 1841 and to estimate the value of these vessels and their cargo. The report enumerated 118 deaths, naming many of the victims, 89 lost ships, and $1,052,450 in lost property, "being over $131,000 yearly, and enough each year to construct two harbors." It claimed that many or all of these accidents could have been averted by providing harbors; most of them apparently occurred during docking or cargo transfers at the ports, often in storms.

Despite this report, the federal government did not dig the straight cut (see pp. 80, 81); the city itself finally spent $50,000 to construct it in 1857. It was the first sizeable outlay by the city on the harbor, although dredging and docking operations had begun in 1854 at a cost of $3,050.[5] After 1860 dredging expenditures became an annual item in the budget; however, they rarely exceeded $40,000 in any year until 1900. Much more important to the future of the city and the port was the establishment of a Canal Commission in 1868; the activities of this commission began the transformation of the Menomonee River Valley from a useless marshy swamp to the industrial complex that it is today.

Milwaukee was one of the first Great Lakes ports to establish a public port authority. The original impetus came from the fact that Great Lakes freighters were continually getting larger around the turn of the cen-

4. Bruce, *History of Milwaukee*, I, 277; the text of the report is given in full on pp. 277–87.

5. A complete list of annual expenditures on dredging and docking appears below in Tables 8-6 and 8-7.

tury, and the inner harbor along the rivers was increasingly inadequate for their needs. In 1900, Mayor David S. Rose recommended that the city acquire properties on the lake shore and build municipal terminals. A number of surveys were made, eventually culminating in an advisory Harbor Commission, established by the Common Council in 1911 and reconstituted in 1912. This commission served until 1920, with Bruce as chairman throughout that period; it recommended the acquisition of Jones Island as the basis of municipal development. Condemnation proceedings began in 1914, and the city acquired title to the island three years later, at a cost of about $500,000. The Harbor Commission engaged a New York port consultant, H. McClellan Harding, in 1919 to draw up a long-range plan for development; his report was adopted in that year and still serves as the basis of outer harbor improvements. A year later the advisory Harbor Commission was abolished and replaced by the present Board of Harbor Commissioners, with power to construct and operate port facilities, contingent on the approval of the Common Council.[6]

The development of the municipal port may be traced most conveniently by reference to Figure 8-A, a diagram of the Milwaukee harbor area showing the location of both public and private port facilities as of March 1, 1962. The numbering system used in Figure 8-A will be followed in the rest of this chapter, the number of each facility usually being cited in parentheses following the first mention of the facility by name.

A listing of facilities constructed since 1920 does not sufficiently emphasize the changes in the harbor since then. Even the physical geography has been changed. For example, the Municipal Mooring Basin (74 in Figure 8-A) was then a swampy area with shallow water of no economic use. The entire south breakwater and part of the north one had not yet been built by the U.S. Army Corps of Engineers. The Jones Island area, south of the present river mouth, was smaller, with an irregular shore line.

The first publicly owned port facility was the Municipal Car Ferry Terminal (86), which went into operation on July 9, 1929. It was leased to the Chesapeake & Ohio Railway Company on a long-term basis. It was followed in the same year by the Municipal Open Dock Terminal (84), designed primarily to handle heavy-bulk commodities, such as steel, iron, and scrap metal. Most of the decade of the 1920's had been

6. Bruce, *History of Milwaukee*, Vol. I, chap. xx; Milwaukee, Board of Harbor Commissioners, *Port of Milwaukee*, 1957, pp. 25–26.

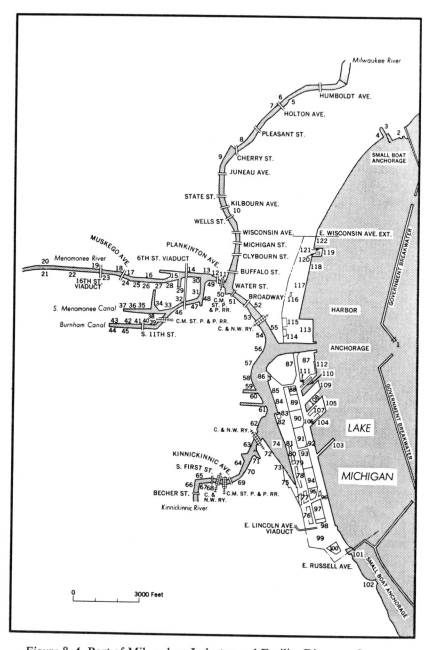

Figure 8-A. Port of Milwaukee, Industry and Facility Diagram. *Source*: Board of Harbor Commissioners, City of Milwaukee. Map drafted by the University of Wisconsin Cartographic Laboratory.

1 Breakwater Light Station
2 Milwaukee County Marina
3 Milwaukee Yacht Club
4 U.S. Coast Guard Station
5 A. F. Gallun & Sons, Corp.
6 Schlitz Brewing Co. Coal Dock
7 Albert Trostel & Sons, Co.
8 Schlitz Bottle House
9 Wisconsin Electric Power Co.
10 Wisconsin Electric Power Co.
11 C. M. St. P & P RR. House No. 3
12 C. M. St. P & P RR. House No. 4 & 5
13 C. M. St. P & P RR. House No. 10
14 Great Lakes Dredge & Dock Co.
15*
16 Northwestern-Hanna Fuel Co., N. 12th St.
17 Schneider Fuel & Supply Co., N. 13th St.
18 Northwestern-Hanna Fuel Co., N. 13th St.
19 Northwestern-Hanna Fuel Co., N. 16th St.
20 Milwaukee Gas Light Co.
21 Wisconsin Reading Coal & Dock Co.
22 Wisconsin Ice & Coal Co., N. 16th St.
23 Municipal Service Building & Dock
24 Wisconsin Ice & Coal Co., N. 13th St.
25 Milwaukee Fuel & Dock Co.
26 Sand Products Co.
27 Inland Lime & Stone Co.
28 Universal Atlas Cement Co.
29 United Coal & Dock Co.
30 Municipal Bridge Shop
31 Morton Salt Co.
32 United Coal & Dock Co.
33 Marquette Cement Co.
34 Youghiogheny & Ohio Coal Co.
35 Lincoln Iron & Steel Co.
36 Lincoln Iron & Steel Co.
37 Schneider Fuel & Supply Co.
38 Cargill Inc. Elevators
39 Schneider Fuel & Supply Co.
40 Huron Portland Cement Co.
41 Manitowoc Portland Cement Co.
42 Miller Bros. Iron & Metal Co.
43 Miller Compressing Co.
44*
45 Penn-Dixie Cement Corp.
46 P. & V. Atlas Industrial Center Inc.
47 C. M. St. P & P RR. House No. 14
48 C. M. St. P & P RR. House No. 8 & 9
49 C. M. St. P & P RR. Open Dock
50*
51 Great Lakes Towing Co.
52 Marine Terminal Building
53 C. & N.W. Ry. Rialto Elevator
54 P. & V. Atlas Water St. Terminal
55 Hansen Storage Co.
56 Evinrude Motors Testing Dock
57 United Coal & Dock Co.
58 Afram Bros. Scrap Yard
59 Afram Bros. Scrap Yard
60 Sinclair Refining Co.
61*
62 U.S. Coast Guard Depot
63 Milwaukee Solvay Coke Co.
64 C. & O. Ry. Co. (inactive)
65*

66 Leszczynski Fuel Co.
67 Edward E. Gillen Co.
68 Sommers Boat Yard
69 State Sand & Gravel Co.
70 P. & V. Atlas Hilbert St. Terminal
71 Grand Trunk Ry. Car Ferry Slips
72 C. & N.W. Ry. Elevators–Continental Grain Co.
73 C. & N.W. Ry. Open Dock
74 Municipal Mooring Basin
75 Miller Compressing Co.
76 Schwerman Trucking Co.
77 Ruan Transport Corp.
78 International Salt Co.
79 Edward E. Gillen Co.
80 Advance Boiler & Tank Co.
81 Pittsburgh Steamship Co.
82 Lelond La Fond Fisheries
83 Island Yachts Inc.
84 Municipal Open Dock Terminal
85 Heavy Lift Cranes
86 Municipal Car Ferry Slip–C. & O. Ry.
87 Milwaukee Sewage Disposal Plant
88 The Jacobus Co.
89 American Oil Co.
90 Mobil Oil Co.
91 Shell Oil Co. Inc.
92 West Shore Pipe Line Co.
93 Cities Service Oil Co.
94 Texaco Inc.
95 Aurora Gasoline Co.
96 Harbor Restaurant
97 Phillips Petroleum Co.
98 Indianhead Truck Lines Inc.
99*
100 U.S. Naval & Marine Corps Reserve Center
101 U.S. Navy Submarine Dock
102 South Shore Yacht Club
103 Municipal South Pier No. 5 (Tanker Pier)
104 Municipal South Slip No. 3
105 Municipal South Pier No. 2
106 Mun. General Cargo Terminal No. 3 (P. & V. Atlas Terminal Corp.)
107 Mun. General Cargo Terminal No. 2 (Hansen Seaway Service Ltd.)
108 Municipal South Slip No. 2
109 Municipal South Pier No. 1
110 Municipal South Slip No. 1
111 Mun. General Cargo Terminal No. 1 (P. & V. Atlas Maritime Corp.)
112 East Berth (Mun. General Cargo Terminal No. 1)
113 20 Acre Land Reclamation–Fill in Progress
114 Nackie Paper Co.
115 C. & J. Transport Inc.
116 Administration Building (former airport)
117 U.S. Military Reservation–Nike Battery
118 Municipal Small Boat Launching Ramp
119 Municipal Passenger & Auto Pier
120 Municipal Passenger Terminal Building (Wisconsin-Michigan Steamship Co.)
121 Harbor Restaurant Site
122 Municipal Small Boat Excursion Pier

*Area not in use at present time.

spent in further detailed port planning, acquiring riparian rights, and other preliminaries.

There could hardly have been a less auspicious time to launch new port facilities. Milwaukee's waterborne commerce dropped by 40 per cent between 1929 and 1932, and the public facilities, which handled nearly 423,000 short tons in their first full shipping season (1930), did not equal that mark again until 1936. Nevertheless, the Board of Harbor Commissioners continued to develop the harbor, with an extensive construction program between 1931 and 1933. The first lakeside facilities since 1854 were opened in 1933: Municipal South Pier No. 1 (109), like the open dock designed for bulk commodities, and Transit Shed No. 1 (111), now General Cargo Terminal No. 1, opened in the same year that the Fjell Line began direct overseas-Great Lakes service. At the same time the Municipal Mooring Basin was dredged and sixty-five acres of new land were created on the lake front, partly meeting the long-recognized need to expand Jones Island and straighten its shorelines.

The tonnages handled by each of these facilities are shown in Table 8-1; the public port's share of all traffic in Table 8-2. The Car Ferry Terminal accounted for over half the tonnage of the municipal facilities each year until 1940, even after the opening of South Pier No. 1 and the Transit Shed, and despite the fact that the Chesapeake & Ohio kept its old car ferry facilities (64) in operation until 1960, when it finally consolidated all ferry operations at the municipal terminal.[7] No further facilities were constructed until 1950, but the public port achieved two major milestones in the later 1930's: the board showed a surplus for the first time in 1935, with operating income $335 above expenses; and in 1938, the city purchased the Illinois Steel Company tract, south of Jones Island, after nineteen years of negotiations. The purchase added 132 acres and riparian rights to more than a mile of the lake shore to the public holdings and greatly facilitated rail connections and access to Jones Island.

The development of port traffic in petroleum products, which had begun in 1936, led to the construction of Municipal South Pier No. 5 (103) in 1950, the first postwar addition to the harbor. The pier is for the exclusive use of tanker ships, with pipelines connecting it to the marine petroleum terminals on the South Harbor Tract.[8] In the same year the

7. The Grand Trunk Western still maintains its own car ferry terminal and slips on the Kinnickinnic River (71).

8. The opening of the West Shore Pipe Line, drastically reducing waterborne traffic in petroleum products beginning in 1962, has been discussed on pages 35 and 36.

TABLE 8-1

TOTAL WATERBORNE TONNAGE, IN VOLUME, HANDLED AT MUNICIPAL HARBOR FACILITIES, 1929–63

(Short tons)

Year	Mun. Mooring Basin Mun. Open Dock Terminal Mun. South Pier No. 1 Mun. South Pier No. 5 Cargo tonnage (combined)	Mun. Car Ferry Terminal No. cars handled	Frt. tons† (loaded cars)	Mun. General Cargo Terminals Cargo tonnage No. 1‡	No. 2‡	No. 3‡	Mun. Passenger-Auto Pier* (tonnage of new cars only)	Total tonnage
1929§	18,751	12,454	198,550					217,301
1930	41,433	26,721	381,525					422,958
1931	43,334	19,545	278,250					321,584
1932	29,720	16,670	247,550					277,270
1933	52,570	18,899	282,975	15,716				351,261
1934	22,037	19,477	296,100	17,504				335,641
1935	43,258	17,909	288,900	16,899				349,057
1936	101,169	20,286	348,125	19,026				468,320
1937	130,594	19,171	317,500	12,068				460,162
1938	75,588	16,645	272,150	9,550				357,288
1939	192,700	19,346	314,500	12,515				519,715
1940	379,167	22,203	362,275	2,300				743,742
1941	436,433	26,106	473,600	1,800				911,833
1942	449,631	25,653	564,129	0				1,013,760
1943	588,715	26,445	670,574	0				1,259,289
1944	667,296	24,664	606,889	0				1,274,185
1945	680,137	24,259	640,406	0				1,320,543
1946	646,492	23,258	573,655	668				1,220,815
1947	790,997	25,261	612,532	4,078				1,407,607
1948	823,544	27,572	647,213	8,335				1,479,092

TABLE 8-1 (continued)

Mun. Mooring Basin
Mun. Open Dock Terminal
Mun. South Pier No. 1
Mun. South Pier No. 5

Year	Cargo tonnage (combined)	Mun. Car Ferry Terminal No. cars handled	Mun. Car Ferry Terminal Frt. tons† (loaded cars)	Mun. General Cargo Terminals Cargo tonnage No. 1‡	No. 2‡	No. 3‡	Mun. Passenger-Auto Pier* (tonnage of new cars only)	Total tonnage
1949	1,134,149	21,695	574,701	6,744				1,715,594
1950	1,261,886	26,559	606,495	17,271				1,885,652
1951	1,575,624	24,095	599,115	8,365				2,183,104
1952	1,683,917	16,504	386,303	17,712				2,087,932
1953	1,860,016	24,171	573,580	28,086				2,461,682
1954	2,015,074	21,937	533,730	30,129				2,578,933
1955	2,205,512	26,389	578,345	55,744				2,839,601
1956	2,256,942	20,210	615,192	59,208				2,931,342
1957	2,234,983	19,258	578,318	42,302				2,855,603
1958	2,231,930	19,828	598,607	58,585				2,889,122
1959	2,477,656	22,447	672,063	138,719				3,288,438
1960	2,451,714	30,830‖	917,500	91,163			181,083	3,641,460
1961	2,380,180	46,882	1,482,409	110,893	22,798	13,987	131,834	4,142,101
1962	959,091	45,483	1,525,548	65,039	49,583	58,728	106,920	2,764,909
1963	753,756	46,011	1,616,396	60,660	75,408	42,564	72,685	2,621,469

Source: Records, office of the Municipal Port Director, Milwaukee.

*Passenger-Auto Pier placed in service April, 1960.

†Car ferry tonnage based on actual average load per car each year.

‡Terminal 1 placed in service 1933; Terminal 2 placed in service August, 1961; Terminal 3, October, 1961.

§First (partial) season of operation of public docks.

‖Chesapeake & Ohio Car Ferry operations consolidated at Municipal Car Ferry Terminal, October, 1960.

TABLE 8-2

DIVISION OF WATERBORNE COMMERCE BETWEEN PUBLIC
AND PRIVATE PORT FACILITIES

PORT OF MILWAUKEE, 1929–63

(Short tons)

Year	Total port traffic	Public port facilities	Private terminals	Public port % of tonnage	Private terminals % of tonnage
1929*	8,564,863	217,301	8,347,562	2.54	97.46
1930	7,703,182	422,958	7,280,224	5.49	94.51
1931	6,576,277	321,584	6,254,693	4.89	95.11
1932	5,247,267	277,270	4,969,997	5.28	94.72
1933	6,351,588	351,261	6,000,327	5.53	94.47
1934	6,083,400	335,641	5,747,759	5.52	94.48
1935	5,838,583	349,057	5,489,526	5.98	94.02
1936	6,951,964	468,320	6,483,644	6.74	93.26
1937	6,617,802	460,162	6,157,640	6.95	93.05
1938	5,849,466	357,288	5,492,178	6.11	93.89
1939	6,329,802	519,715	5,810,087	8.21	91.79
1940	6,880,088	743,742	6,136,346	10.81	89.19
1941	7,633,365	911,841	6,721,524	11.95	88.05
1942	7,599,321	1,013,760	6,585,561	13.34	86.66
1943	7,677,919	1,259,289	6,418,630	16.40	83.60
1944	8,052,249	1,274,185	6,778,064	15.82	84.18
1945	8,023,961	1,320,543	6,703,418	16.46	83.54
1946	7,900,892	1,220,815	6,680,077	15.45	84.55
1947	8,520,940	1,407,607	7,113,333	16.52	84.48
1948	8,601,122	1,479,092	7,122,030	17.20	82.80
1949	7,099,476	1,715,594	5,383,882	24.17	75.83
1950	8,926,964	1,885,652	7,041,312	21.12	78.88
1951	8,314,358	2,183,104	6,131,254	26.26	73.74
1952	7,479,224	2,087,932	5,391,292	27.92	72.08
1953	8,165,023	2,461,682	5,703,341	30.15	69.85
1954	7,781,559	2,578,933	5,202,626	33.14	66.86
1955	8,711,557	2,839,601	5,871,956	32.60	67.40
1956	8,600,655	2,931,342	5,669,313	34.08	65.92
1957	8,410,509	2,855,603	5,554,906	33.95	66.05
1958	7,658,689	2,889,122	4,769,567	37.72	62.28
1959	8,799,519	3,288,438	5,511,081	37.37	62.63
1960	8,519,044	3,641,460	4,877,584	42.74	57.26
1961	8,369,684	4,142,101	4,227,583	49.49	50.51
1962	6,724,912	2,764,909	3,960,003	41.11	58.89
1963	6,626,442	2,621,469	4,004,973	39.56	60.44

Source: U.S. Army Corps of Engineers, *Annual Reports of the Chief of Engineers*, 1959–63; Milwaukee Board of Harbor Commissioners, operating records, 1965.

*First (partial) season of operation of public docks.

port also installed the largest dock crane on the Great Lakes (85), designed to handle loads of as much as ninety short tons. The crane is especially useful to the heavy machinery industries of the Milwaukee area, but it has also served to draw heavy-lift cargo for other areas through the port. For example, some imported exhibits for the 1950 Chicago Trade Fair were too heavy for the cranes at that port; they were unloaded at Milwaukee and shipped to Chicago by rail.[9] In 1965, South Pier No. 5 began a new type of operation when its facilities were expanded to include one of the most modern terminals in the country for handling the growing international traffic in fats and oils used in the manufacture of soap, foods, and many other products. This facility, which will enable Midwest fat and oil producers to take advantage of lower shipping rates through the Seaway, is operated by the General American Transportation Corporation which has invested close to $500,000 in the terminal and equipment. The city of Milwaukee also has in excess of $250,000 invested in the operation, but it is believed that the added revenue resulting directly from this terminal plus the additional inducement for ships to stop at the port will more than repay the city for this outlay.

Exports of tallow, grease, and lard will form the largest share of this terminal's traffic. Steam from boilers melts the semisolid substances into a fluid while still in railroad cars, and then this liquid is pumped through pipes into a waiting ship. The entire process takes between twenty-four and thirty-six hours, and eighty-seven cars can be heated simultaneously. The liquid-bulk terminal is also able to pump similar substances from ship to shore, but in this case, the ship heats its own cargo. The new terminal is expected to handle approximately 35,000–40,000 tons of cargo this year, but a minimum of 100,000 tons per year is predicted for the future.

The passage of the Wiley-Dondero Act in May, 1954, authorizing the construction of the St. Lawrence Seaway, was the signal for a number of other new municipal facilities. Over $10,000,000 was spent in the years 1956–61 in an unprecedented expansion program. The largest single item was Municipal South Pier No. 2 (105), costing over $4,000,000. The pier is located at the site of the original river mouth. On it stand Municipal General Cargo Terminals Nos. 2 and 3 (106–107), completed in 1961 at a cost of over $2,000,000. These terminals are among the most modern in the country; they have approximately

9. *Chicago Journal of Commerce*, July 27, 1950, cited in Hamming, *The Port of Milwaukee*, p. 58.

doubled the overseas general cargo capacity of the port, from about 360,000 short tons annually to 688,000.[10]

Another major new facility is the Municipal Passenger and Auto Pier (119), the first lake-shore pier north of the river mouth; it was opened in 1960. The pier is used by the "Milwaukee Clipper" and the "Highway 16," both operated, between Milwaukee and Muskegon, by the Wisconsin and Michigan Steamship Company. Besides serving the last important passenger route on the Great Lakes, the "Clipper" has been used during the winter season as a companion to the "Highway 16" in the movement of new automobiles across the lake, enabling Detroit auto manufacturers to reach the northwestern states without having to ship through Chicago.[11] The pier has cost almost $1,900,000.

The development program has also included sizeable investments in additional cranes, including three with fifty tons capacity each, and in a seven-mile expansion of the railroad yards and connecting tracks on the waterfront. The municipal railroad system now contains about eighteen miles of track.[12] The complete record of the program appears in Table 8-3, listing all expenditures from the Permanent Improvement Fund in the 1957–64 period. Though the program began in 1956, the only major expenditure in that year was $148,669 for the initial work on South Pier No. 2. The development was essentially completed by the end of 1961.

In the table, "General Cargo Terminal at South Pier No. 2" includes the cost of both the terminals and the pier itself. This pier and the Municipal Passenger and Auto Pier account for nearly three-quarters of the development expenditures. The "steel bulkhead construction" items in 1957 and 1958 represent most of the cost of creating twenty acres of land just north of the harbor entrance. The area has been filled with waste materials and is intended for commercial use in the future. Including the new twenty-acre tract, about half of all municipal harbor property (two hundred out of four hundred acres) has been created from the lake. This aspect of public port activity will be discussed in more detail later in this chapter.

The new cranes and their accessories have cost over $730,000. The

10. Schenker, *General Cargo Capacity at Wisconsin Lake Ports*, p. 73.

11. Very recently, the cross-lake auto traffic has been substantially diverted to all-rail routes through Chicago as a result of the development of tri-level railroad cars which can carry the autos at reduced rates. On May 23, 1963, the ICC upheld the legality of the lower all-rail rates: Motor Vehicles—Wayne & Wixom, Michigan, to Milwaukee, Wisconsin, ICC No. 33945.

12. Milwaukee, Board of Harbor Commissioners, *1962 Port Brochure*, p. 25.

TABLE 8-3

MILWAUKEE PORT DEVELOPMENT PROGRAM, 1957–64

Improvement	1957	1958	1959	1960	1961	1962	1963	1964	Total
Construction and repair of dock walls	$ 92	$ 80,514	$ 19,717	0	0	$ 959	$ 11,766	$ 920	$ 113,968
Passenger and auto pier	610,226	384,390	496,202	$ 382,970	16,418	2,730	0	0	1,892,936
Miller Compressing Co. lease improvement fund	9,539	15,375	4,440	52,071	17,975	16,294	15,704	4,853	136,251
Locomotive and gantry cranes	0	0	3,644	242,396	293,331	189,824	590	1,045	730,830
General Cargo Terminal at South Pier No. 2	220,312	1,932,114	379,096	1,308,515	1,576,923	101,395	4,009	9,452	5,531,816
C & O Railroad Co. lease improvement fund	0	0	1,015	168,032	68,270	5,032	1,266	0	243,615
South Harbor Tract water & sewer lines	2,408	5,136	0	17,224	22,905	1,954	45,214	69,957	164,798
Harbor launch	53,060	0	0	3	46,849	2,141	0	0	102,053
Fender system for South Pier No. 5	49,778	0	0	0	0	0	0	0	49,778
Steel bulkhead constr. & related expenses	601,382	81,320	11	0	0	0	622	301	683,636
Additional berth & improvements at General Cargo Terminal No. 1	0	0	0	63,546	22,246	0	0	955	86,747

TABLE 8-3 (continued)

Improvement	1957	1958	1959	1960	1961	1962	1963	1964	Total
South Harbor Tract filling, grading, paving & related improvements	0	0	0	0	3,272	32,403	66,798	60,103	162,576
Dredging mooring basin and inner harbor	0	0	0	0	30,752	478	99,119	19	130,368
Service road to area west of mooring basin	0	0	62	84	13,285	36	0	0	13,467
Channel Wale for East Berth and South Slip No. 1	0	0	0	0	0	33,827	33,852	18,108	85,787
Place decking at Municipal Open Dock	0	0	0	0	0	2,637	0	0	2,637
Dock office addition	0	0	0	0	0	830	8,179	74,969	83,978
Railroad yard and track extension	0	0	1,589	106,328	0	2,518	0	0	110,435
Car ferry terminal renewal	0	0	0	0	0	0	0	27,026	27,026
Liquid bulk terminal	0	0	0	0	0	0	0	220,487	220,487
Off harbor industrial development	0	0	0	0	0	0	0	886	886
Other	1,362	444	0	0	0	0	0	0	1,806
Total	$1,548,159	$2,499,293	$905,776	$2,341,169	$2,112,226	$393,058	$287,119	$489,081	$10,575,881

Source: Accounts of Board of Harbor Commissioners, Milwaukee.

seven miles of new railroad trackage, have been almost as expensive, costing over $450,000. This expense shows up in several different categories in the Permanent Improvement Fund accounts, such as "Miller Compressing Company lease improvement fund" and "Chesapeake & Ohio Railway Company lease improvement fund." The railroad system is carried as a single fixed asset on the balance sheets of the Board of Harbor Commissioners, however; comparison of the 1965 figure ($1,031,589.21, as shown in Table 8-5) with the entry in 1958 ($470,156.00) reveals the cost of the new tracks *in toto*, since this phase of the expansion program was not begun until 1959.

Another useful (and inexpensive) improvement is the East Berth (112) at General Cargo Terminal No. 1 (111). The berth was established on a 20-foot strip of property east of the Milwaukee Sewage Disposal Plant (87); the strip had remained under the board's jurisdiction. It was paved and lighted, mooring bollards and dock fenders were installed, and dredging to a depth of 25 feet was carried out for 600 feet alongside it. In its first season (1961), the new berth served to allow 26-foot deep-draft ocean-going ships to load or unload small volumes of general cargo, thus freeing the berths at the terminal (110) for the use of ships needing to dock for a relatively long period of time. The cost of the completed East Berth project was shown in a list of "improvements in process" attached to the 1962 balance sheet; it was $48,266.13. In the 1962–64 period, in addition to the liquid-bulk terminal mentioned above, the major expenditures were for the construction of a new dock office addition and for general land improvements on the South Harbor Tract.

Of the two large harbor launch entries (Table 8-3), the 1957 figure represents the "Harbor Escort," used for harbor inspection and similar purposes; the 1961 entry was the cost of the "Harbor Seagull," a unique vessel which removes surface debris from the harbor. The "Seagull" was designed by the board staff; it went into operation in April, 1962, and in that year removed about 160 tons of timber, dead alewives, and other debris.[13]

13. "The city government has received a remittance from the Wisconsin Conservation Department, covering payment for items for 1962 water safety patrol operations of 'M.V. Harbor Escort,' 'M.V. Harbor Seagull' and the Launch, 'Harbor Scout.'

"A claim was filed with the State in the sum of $10,313.71 for water safety patrol activities conducted by the Board of Harbor Commissioners in 1962. Remittance has been received from the State in the full amount of the claim.

"The remittance from the State is a substantial offset to the cost of govern-

A summary of Permanent Improvement Fund expenditures since 1949, when the postwar development program began, appears in Table 8-4. The federal and state expenditures in the first three years were part of the cost of the Maitland Airstrip for private planes, which was subsequently closed because of lack of traffic and earnings. The city spent over

TABLE 8-4

HARBOR COMMISSION PERMANENT IMPROVEMENT FUND
EXPENDITURES, 1949–64

Year	City	State	Federal	Total
1949	$ 139,095	0	$ 10,323	$ 149,418
1950	577,419	$20,000	21,171	618,590
1951	317,498	25,000	85,470	427,968
1952	86,298	0	0	86,298
1953	89,478	0	0	89,478
1954	103,578	0	0	103,578
1955	154,572	0	0	154,572
1956	175,899	0	0	175,899
1957	1,548,159	0	0	1,548,159
1958	2,499,293	0	0	2,499,293
1959	905,776	0	0	905,776
1960	2,341,169	0	0	2,341,169
1961	2,112,226	0	0	2,112,226
1962	393,058	0	0	393,058
1963	287,119	0	0	287,119
1964	489,081	0	0	489,081
Total	$12,219,718	$45,000	$116,964	$12,381,682

Source: Records of the Board of Harbor Commissioners, Milwaukee.

$132,000 on the airstrip in the years 1949–51, $92,000 of it in 1950. South Pier No. 5 also helps to account for the relatively large outlays in 1950 and 1951; $291,000 was spent on it in the former year and $103,000 in the latter. The year 1950 includes a further large item of $131,000 for dock and work equipment, chiefly the 90-ton heavy-lift crane. Over $176,000 in 1954 and 1955 went to a 20,000-square-foot addition to Transit Shed No. 1 (General Cargo Terminal No. 1). The

mental operations in the water safety field as conducted under the direction of the Board. The 1962 remittance, in excess of $10,000, compares with the State's 1961 grant of approximately $6,600 for this purpose. The 1962 remittance reflects the first full year of operation of 'M.V. Harbor Seagull,' and indicates that the city is recovering a substantial part of the cost of 'M.V. Harbor Seagull.'" H. C. Brockel to Milwaukee, Board of Harbor Commissioners, September 11, 1963.

balance of the expenditures during the period were for a number of relatively small construction and rehabilitation projects, such as dock walls. The general nature of these projects can be seen from the smaller items in Tables 8-3 and 8-5.

INVESTMENT ANALYSIS

The Seaway-inspired improvements have raised the public port investment in fixed assets to almost $20,000,000. A complete list of these assets is given in Table 8-5. This table does not include the figure for "improvements in process." This item in the balance sheet amounted to $309,571.37 at the end of 1964.

The figures shown are historical costs, not market values or replacement costs. In looking at Table 8-5, therefore, the historical sequence of development should be kept in mind. The Car Ferry Terminal, the earliest facility, was one of the smallest items under "Piers, Wharves, Slips, Basins and Bulkheads," because nearly all of the outlay on it was the initial cost of construction in the 1920's; the only major expenditure since was some $38,000 for rehabilitation in 1954. On the other hand, there have been continuing improvements in the Kinnickinnic dock (84, the Municipal Open Dock), which was built at the same time; over $250,000 was spent in recent years. The rise in the general price level since 1941 means that disproportionate weight is given to the most recent improvements. It also means that the board and the city are the recipients of substantial capital gains, in accounting terms, on the early projects.

The largest of the capital gains has almost certainly been in the value of the land, especially that created or purchased by the board before World War II. The city has an investment of almost $3.5 million in harbor land, as shown in Table 8-5. Nearly 90 per cent was spent on the South Harbor Tract, although only 75 per cent of the public harbor land lies in that tract. The discrepancy is partly due to the fact that much of the original 80-acre North Harbor Tract was filled in during the 1920's, at an average cost of $5,000 per acre. Filled-in land on Jones Island (the South Harbor Tract) cost $12,000 per acre, while the Illinois Steel Company Tract south of Jones Island cost $22,000 per acre in 1938.[14]

The firm of Lloyd-Thomas, real estate appraisers, has recently completed a professional appraisal of the public port facilities under the

14. Milwaukee, Board of Harbor Commissioners, *Impact of the Milwaukee Port*, p. 7. The land investment costs in Table 8-5 do not reflect the full expenditures, since some of the land was later sold or transferred to other city departments.

TABLE 8-5

FIXED ASSETS OF THE BOARD OF HARBOR COMMISSIONERS,
CITY OF MILWAUKEE, AS OF JANUARY 1, 1965

Property	Historical Cost	Total
Land:		
North Harbor Tract	$ 230,372.71	
South Harbor Tract	3,079,172.79	
General South (Abbott Tract)	144,932.70	$ 3,454,478.20
Piers, wharves, slips, basins, and bulkheads:		
North Harbor Tract	2,166,620.76	
South Harbor Tract	7,317,274.31	9,483,895.07
Buildings:		
North Harbor Tract	618,314.36	
South Harbor Tract	2,669,506.05	3,287,820.41
Electric light and power lines:		
North Harbor Tract	683.57	
South Harbor Tract	47,111.22	47,794.79
Fencing:		
North Harbor Tract	6,905.16	
South Harbor Tract	10,437.17	17,342.33
Dredging		398,823.60
Inner harbor dock walls —		
street and alley ends		318,046.73
Small boat pier		3,069.44
Railroads:		
South Harbor Tract		1,031,589.21
Sewers:		
South Harbor Tract		147,914.64
Water lines:		
South Harbor Tract		229,720.12
Roads:		
South Harbor Tract		76,235.62
Maitland Airstrip		434,788.56
Track scale:		
South Harbor Tract		7,252.36
Truck scale:		
South Harbor Tract		14,204.01
Channel improvements		27,669.05
Gasoline fueling system		2,534.82
Other directional signs		2,919.99
Equipment:		
Cranes	666,380.49	
Launch "Harbor Escort"	57,796.63	
Motor vessel "Harbor Seagull"	48,993.88	
Crane accessories	42,563.14	
Tractors	779.10	
Scow	4,944.75	

TABLE 8-5 (*continued*)

Property	Historical Cost	Total
Motor launch accessories	$ 3,920.82	
Fork lift	17,238.76	
Office furniture & fixtures	41,742.95	
Tools & small equipment	14,429.36	898,789.88
Total assets		$19,884,888.83

Source: Records of the Board of Harbor Commissioners, Milwaukee.

authorization of the Board of Harbor Commissioners. The appraisal of land values ranged from $33,225 to $60,000 per acre on the North Harbor Tract and from $15,000 to $87,120 per acre on the South Harbor Tract, depending on location and docking facilities. It was further estimated that the most typical harbor land ranged in value from $50,000 to $60,000 per acre and that a normal rental would be 6 per cent of the value on most of the land and 7.3 per cent of high-value dock property. This additional 1.3 per cent was to allow for eventual replacement of the dock wall which had an estimated life of seventy-five years.[15]

As a result of this appraisal, municipal harbor leases are now based on land values of $50,000 per acre for dockside land and $40,000 per acre for "back land," and a rental of 5.5 per cent plus wharfage and shipping charges is assessed.

The city does not by any means receive rent reflecting this value on all of the publicly owned harbor land; at least one-third of it is tied up in nonrevenue public uses, such as auto parking for the War Memorial, the proposed southern extension of Lincoln Memorial Drive, and a twenty-acre buffer zone on the South Harbor Tract between the harbor area and the homes and parks south of it. In addition, a large section of the North Harbor Tract (the site of the Maitland Airstrip) is occupied by a Nike base and military reservation, leased rent-free to the Defense Department. Theoretically speaking, the land used for these purposes is producing satisfactions for the community (and in the case of the Nike base, for the country), worth at least $40,000 to $50,000 per acre, and there are at present no plans of any kind to turn the land over to commercial harbor use. The land does not, however, produce any revenue for the city government.

The Lloyd-Thomas appraisal also established the current replacement

15. Milwaukee, Board of Harbor Commissioners, *Review of Municipal Harbor Leases.*

value (as of December 31, 1962) of the port's physical assets at
$32,507,359. When this figure is compared with the accumulated his-
torical costs of the Milwaukee Public Port's accumulated appraised
assets of $18,490,058,[16] it is evident that the city's investment has nearly
doubled over the years.

The dredging cost shown in Table 8-5 includes only amounts spent
by the board for new dredging work. It leaves out both the dredging
undertaken by the city before 1920 and maintenance dredging of already
existing projects since the board was established. By far the greater part
of public outlays on dredging falls into one or the other of these classifications. Table 8-6 lists the annual expenditures on dredging and docking
from 1854 to 1918. It includes the $50,000 spent on the original straight
cut in 1857 and extraordinary expenses in five later years, as explained
in the notes to the table. The figures shown here are also historical costs;
since the period included major inflations during the Civil War and
World War I, one of the worst depressions in the nation's history beginning in 1873, and twenty-three years of steadily falling prices from
1873 to 1896, the total shown should not be taken as any sort of economic measure of dredging costs or value.

The same applies to Table 8-7, maintenance dredging from 1919 to
1964. The amounts in this table resulted entirely from work in the three
rivers. More was done in the Menomonee than in the other two combined;
$600,093.18 was spent to dredge 1,459,456 cubic yards from it. Dredg-
ing in the Kinnickinnic cost $324,156.29 to remove 613,918 cubic
yards; the remainder, $158,556.85 and 461,370 cubic yards, was taken
from the Milwaukee. These figures reflect the relative economic importance of the rivers. No work has been done by the city in the Milwaukee
River since 1943, a fact which explains the small outlay there relative to
the amount of material removed. That river is becoming less important
to the harbor as time goes on. As long ago as 1922, Bruce asserted that
"the Milwaukee River has seen its best days as a navigable stream and
that its service will lessen rather than increase in the future." [17] Traffic
on the river dropped from over 1,000,000 tons in 1917, to 200,000 tons
in 1940, to 45,000 tons in 1950.[18] In 1960 the district engineer reported
that "commerce on the upper reaches of the Milwaukee River in recent
years has usually been limited to two or three medium-sized cargoes of

16. Total historical costs of physical assets = $19,583,983
     Assets not appraised = $ 1,093,926
     —————————
     $18,490,058
17. Bruce, *History of Milwaukee*, I, 301.
18. Hamming, *The Port of Milwaukee*, p. 141.

TABLE 8-6
EXPENDITURES FOR DOCKING AND DREDGING, 1853–1918

Year	Expenditure	Year	Expenditure
1853	—*	1886	$ 23,977.26
1854	$ 3,050.00	1887	14,576.28
1855	1,521.63	1888	31,010.75
1856	736.81	1889	23,694.94
1857	72,763.57†	1890	27,081.88
1858	—	1891	23,829.33
1859	—	1892	25,400.83
1860	7,186.86	1893	37,194.63
1861	981.60	1894	35,590.88
1862	1,722.91	1895	21,560.82
1863	5,416.44	1896	30,721.77
1864	12,316.91	1897	31,989.53
1865	9,960.43	1898	19,598.67
1866	9,073.95	1899	16,145.17
1867	21,165.67	1900	14,473.58
1868	8,227.97	1901	19,971.86
1869	44,489.83‡	1902	21,538.21
1870	85,855.83‡	1903	18,626.23
1871	56,026.50‡	1904	19,058.02
1872	68,974.36‡	1905	17,921.69
1873	21,501.09	1906	31,237.27
1874	40,935.34	1907	181,137.39§
1875	20,522.07	1908	9,493.83
1876	17,063.10	1909	48,946.44
1877	14,846.35	1910	37,921.43
1878	21,923.06	1911	25,699.34
1879	25,665.96	1912	58,361.45
1880	31,243.32	1913	70,530.61
1881	14,216.15	1914	53,697.10
1882	22,171.62	1915	41,926.09
1883	18,645.18	1916	31,906.00
1884	15,111.89	1917	21,166.64
1885	24,217.08	1918	27,058.71
Total			$1,810,578.11

Source: Official Records of the city of Milwaukee.

*There is no record of dredging and docking expenses in 1853 and 1858; possibly no river work was done in those years. There are no records of 1859 extant.

†Includes Milwaukee's first investment of $50,000 in the "straight cut."

‡The expense in these four years was augmented by payments in liquidation of the Hasbrouck claim growing out of the construction of the "straight cut."

§Includes the sum of $142,724.30 which was awarded to owners for land taken for a turning basin in the Kinnickinnic River and for widening the river.

TABLE 8-7

MAINTENANCE DREDGING, CITY OF MILWAUKEE, 1919–64

Year	Cubic Yards	Cost	Year	Cubic Yards	Cost
1919	160,378	$24,362.26	1942	30,165	$17,767.19
1920	133,885	30,659.66	1943	58,949	33,306.19
1921	140,560	34,999.44	1944	0	0
1922	146,393	42,087.99	1945	29,450	19,437.00
1923	115,784	42,145.37	1946	0	0
1924	119,964	52,484.25	1947	0	0
1925	110,966	48,270.21	1948	0	0
1926	124,858	53,064.65	1949	44,966	32,375.52
1927	261,182	94,025.52	1950	0	0
1928	131,646	56,476.13	1951	0	0
1929	0	0	1952	0	0
1930	40,908	19,840.38	1953	0	0
1931	154,321	50,000.00	1954	54,687	48,507.37
1932	0	0	1955	0	0
1933	67,627	19,561.18	1956	0	0
1934	111,500	38,746.25	1957	0	0
1935	105,437	38,220.81	1958	38,752	57,740.48
1936	0	0	1959	0	0
1937	165,491	66,342.40	1960	0	0
1938	51,165	20,593.91	1961	9,450	27,688.50
1939	0	0	1962	0	0
1940	0	0	1963	29,933	82,315.75
1941	96,327	31,787.91	1964	0	0
			Total	2,534,744	$1,082,806.32

Source: Records of the Board of Harbor Commissioners, Milwaukee.

coal, and there has been a continuing decline in the use of the upper Milwaukee River terminals. No renewal of commerce there is considered probable." [19]

Since 1947 the federal government has undertaken maintenance dredging on the rivers also, under the River and Harbor Act of March 2, 1945. The government has spent $886,178.74 to remove 906,553 cubic yards from the rivers, including $118,537.03 to remove 108,131 cubic yards from the Milwaukee in 1955, 1957, 1960, and 1962, and $16,204.69 to remove 21,617 cubic yards from the river entrance channel in 1957 and 1962. Most of the rest has been spent on the Menomonee (something over half of the total), but a precise breakdown is not available because some figures are given jointly for the Menomonee and the

19. U.S. Army Engineer District, *Milwaukee Interim Report*, p. 34.

Kinnickinnic.[20] The municipal dredging expenditures since then have been either for sections of the rivers not included in the Act or for emergency work when federal funds were not available, as happened in 1954.[21]

All of the dredging costs have been paid for through annual budget appropriations. Budget funds have also been used to acquire about a third of the $20,000,000 in fixed assets held by the Board of Harbor Commissioners. The balance — $13,725,000 — has come from bond issues. The first harbor bond issue was authorized by the Common Council in 1914 — $250,000 to buy Jones Island — but no bonds were actually issued until 1916.[22] A series of eleven Permanent Harbor Improvement issues were marketed between 1916 and 1931, having a total par value of $5,030,000. Between 1932 and 1948 the city did not issue any bonds whatsoever; under Mayor Daniel W. Hoan, Milwaukee had set up an amortization fund in 1923, intending to retire all indebtedness within fifty years. By 1944 the amount in the amortization fund equaled the city's bonded debt.[23] The "debt-free" policy was reversed in 1949, but bonds for harbor development were not issued until 1957; such major investments as the $2,744,000 purchase of the Illinois Steel Company Tract in 1938 and the $400,000 for the tanker pier in 1950 and 1951 were financed on a pay-as-you-go basis.

The cost of the Seaway development program, however, was clearly beyond the capacity of budget financing. Beginning in 1957 the city marketed $8,695,000 worth of bonds to help pay for the new general cargo terminals and other improvements. The last series of these bonds was issued in 1964.

Table 8-8 provides detailed information on all of the harbor bond issues. The interest rates and years until maturity, where available, have been used to compute the interest cost of the bonds. The total interest paid for harbor improvements, if the 1957–64 issues are retired at their dates of maturity, will amount to $4,650,599.16. Well over half of it — $2,523,675 — was paid for the prewar bonds, despite the fact that their total par value was much smaller than the par value for the more

20. Statement of the Board of Harbor Commissioners, Public Hearing, Milwaukee, November 29, 1956, pp. 3–4, Exhibit 2; letters from Harbor Engineer, Board of Harbor Commissioners, September, 1963. At least 463,903 cubic yards were dredged from the Menomonee, costing $461,386.36; at least 201,926 cubic yards from the Kinnickinnic, costing $205,766.56.

21. *Ibid.*, p. 4.

22. Bruce, *History of Milwaukee*, I, 297.

23. Austin, *The Milwaukee Story*, p. 188.

TABLE 8-8

BOND ISSUES FOR HARBOR IMPROVEMENTS, 1916–64

Year (1)	Amount (2)	Interest rate (%) (3)	Years until maturity (4)	% retired each year (5)	Total interest charge paid to date (6)	Total interest charge until maturity (7)
1916	$200,000	4.0	20	5.0*	$84,000.00*	$84,000.00*
1917	150,000	4.0	20	5.0	63,000.00	63,000.00
1917	50,000	4.5	20	5.0	23,625.00	23,625.00
1918	150,000	5.0	20	5.0	78,750.00	78,750.00
1919	200,000	4.5	20	5.0	94,500.00	94,500.00
1920	500,000	6.0	20	5.0	315,000.00	315,000.00
1922	500,000	5.0	20	5.0	262,500.00	262,500.00
1926	1,500,000	4.5	20	5.0	708,750.00	708,750.00
1929	1,000,000	5.0	20	5.0	525,000.00	525,000.00
1930	280,000	4.5	20	5.0	132,300.00	132,300.00
1931	500,000	4.5	20	5.0	236,250.00	236,250.00
1957†	2,750,000	2.81994	20	5.0	485,911.24	814,703.50
1958†	2,750,000	2.54656	20	5.0	365,055.00	739,307.00
1959‡	150,000	2.97830	20	5.0	21,643.00	44,851.01
1960	2,500,000	2.691998	13	7.69	233,692.05	471,680.23
1961	245,000	2.6810	15	6.67	15,923.63	52,819.92
1962	0	0	0	0	0	0
1963	0	0	0	0	0	0
1964§	300,000	2.375	1.5	0	0	3,562.50
Total	$13,725,000				$3,645,899.92	$4,650,599.16

Source: Records of the Board of Harbor Commissioners, Milwaukee.

*For the years 1916 to 1931 inclusive, records of the city comptroller are not itemized as to interest paid and principal paid. Total interest charges are approximate.

†Amounts shown for 1957 and 1958 are exact.

‡Beginning with 1959 the city began issuing corporate purpose bonds. Interest charges are distributed to the various purposes on a percentage basis. Total interest charges are approximate.

§The amount borrowed in 1964 is a short-term obligation to run for 18 months. The note is callable in 6 months and the interest shown is for 6 months.

recent issues. The higher interest costs, of course, are largely due to the uniformly higher rates paid to float the 1916–31 issues; interest rates on state and local government bonds have fallen since World War II because interest on these bonds is constitutionally exempt from the federal income tax, making the bonds especially attractive to investors in the higher tax brackets. The interest costs for the Seaway-inspired improvements will have amounted to $2,123,361.66 by 1979, the retirement date for the last twenty-year issue.

Of the $16,187,412 municipal outlay for the port mentioned at the 1956 public hearing, $3,412,427 represented the accumulated annual expenses incurred in operating the public port through the end of 1955. In the nine years since then, operating expenses have come to another $3,851,712. However, this is by no means the full story; Table 8-9 shows that income has exceeded expenses in every year since 1935, and over the whole period of public port operation an operating surplus of over $4,400,000 has been accumulated; after making adjustments for such items as major repairs and the cost of the governmental services performed by the port, the actual net surplus is over $3,500,000.

TABLE 8-9

HARBOR OPERATING INCOME, DEPARTMENTAL EXPENSE, AND
NET SURPLUS OR DEFICIT FROM THE PERIOD PRIOR
TO 1921 TO DECEMBER 31, 1964

Year	Operating income	Departmental expense	Net surplus	Net deficit
Prior to 1921	0	$43,798.67		$43,798.67
1921	0	20,262.80		20,262.80
1922	0	28,326.78		28,326.78
1923	$600.00	24,494.34		23,894.34
1924	710.00	27,532.96		26,822.96
1925	2,101.00	28,108.56		26,007.56
1926	2.00	40,548.62		40,546.62
1927	2,233.67	55,205.44		52,971.77
1928	2,271.50	61,513.43		59,241.93
1929	14,905.19	69,409.81		54,504.62
1930	60,964.44	100,539.32		39,574.88
1931	52,804.09	71,863.70		19,059.61
1932	53,983.59	62,602.42		8,618.83
1933	60,245.93	75,691.20		15,445.27
1934	57,118.11	58,165.71		1,047.60
1935	72,256.32	71,921.25	$335.07	
1936	88,645.66	69,070.45	19,575.21	
1937	115,128.10	83,949.29	31,178.81	
1938	77,264.18	56,536.69	20,727.49	
1939	116,301.15	75,469.14	40,832.01	
1940	128,449.36	72,627.20	55,822.16	
1941	126,077.69	77,126.82	48,950.87	
1942	106,466.56	56,258.23	50,208.33	
1943	128,674.25	63,654.39	65,019.86	
1944	152,546.62	77,397.36	75,149.26	
1945	155,271.60	80,014.21	75,257.39	
1946	175,587.25	102,050.01	73,537.24	
1947	218,309.30	137,198.81	81,110.49	

TABLE 8-9 (*continued*)

Year	Operating income	Departmental expense	Net surplus	Net deficit
1948	221,227.78	135,757.35	85,470.43	
1949	275,855.08	166,302.52	109,552.56	
1950	287,569.35	162,871.29	124,698.06	
1951	287,211.24	182,957.29	104,253.95	
1952	317,975.05	209,921.07	108,053.98	
1953	374,566.64	236,899.30	137,667.34	
1954	394,611.98	246,912.42	147,699.56	
1955	498,680.48	279,467.95	219,212.53	
1956	546,657.05	317,152.03	229,505.02	
1957	563,574.94	324,739.90	238,835.04	
1958	514,437.76	311,063.73	203,374.03	
1959	746,680.67	381,187.23	365,493.44	
1960	808,698.84	397,851.28	410,847.56	
1961	947,534.14	437,382.32	510,151.82	
1962	941,539.87	537,613.19	403,926.68	
1963	938,758.00	546,670.82	392,087.18	
1964	1,031,959.74	598,051.58	433,908.16	
Total	$11,666,456.17	$7,264,138.88	$4,862,441.53	$460,124.24
Total Net Gain for Period			$4,402,317.29*	

Source: Milwaukee, Board of Harbor Commissioners, *Review of Municipal Harbor Leases.*

*Does not include adjustments to expense and income through surplus account in the amount of $843,573.57. Actual net surplus total for the period equals $3,558,779.73.

A crude comparison of the accumulated net surplus with the bond interest costs indicates that the municipal harbor has so far managed to repay over three-fourths of the interest charges and is still about $1,290,000 in the red for the period during which it has been operated by the Board of Harbor Commissioners. However, such a comparison is seriously inadequate. Most obviously, the surplus covers the period only until 1964, while significant interest costs will continue until 1979. If interest payments on still-outstanding bond issues are calculated only through 1964, it appears that the city has paid $1,112,225 to date for the bond-financed Seaway improvements. Total interest payments to date amount to $3,645,900, indicating that the city has recovered almost 100 per cent of the interest costs to date, in the form of operating surplus ($3,558,780), and is, therefore only about $87,000 in the red.

It is also important to note that the annual surplus in each year since 1957 has been more than sufficient to cover interest costs on the Seaway bonds then outstanding; the net surplus in each year since 1959 has been about $400,000, compared to annual interest on all five bond issues since 1961 of $225,915. This evidence indicates that the board will probably continue to earn surpluses approximately equal to 80 per cent of the annual interest on outstanding bonds.

Such a surplus is not too common among public port enterprises,

TABLE 8-10

TAXES AND ASSESSMENTS ON SOUTH HARBOR TRACT, 1936–64

Year	Real estate & property taxes paid by harbor tenants*	Total assessed value of industrial installations
1936	$667.80	(figures not
1937	3,690.92	available)
1938	6,269.85	"
1939	5,968.31	"
1940	12,441.96	"
1941	23,362.24	"
1942	19,586.49	"
1943	21,086.81	"
1944	16,690.40	"
1945	19,504.47	"
1946	20,622.41	"
1947	36,468.32	"
1948	41,389.71	"
1949	59,522.83	"
1950	68,594.16	"
1951	84,935.41	"
1952	103,000.00	"
1953	155,885.00	"
1954	165,589.00	"
1955	169,219.00	"
1956	179,703.00	"
1957	193,898.00	$3,508,836.00
1958	225,600.08	3,799,900.00
1959	231,283.89	3,973,950.00
1960	248,489.92	4,088,350.00
1961	262,684.46	4,125,070.00
1962	277,208.48	4,161,040.00
1963	286,340.09	4,175,880.00
1964	280,898.65	3,922,070.00
Total	$3,220,601.66	

Source: Milwaukee, Board of Harbor Commissioners, *Review of Municipal Harbor Leases.*
*Includes city-county-state taxes.

which tend to combine commercial and governmental functions in the same organization. It has been a goal of the Board of Harbor Commissioners, since its inception, to put the port on a self-sustaining basis; the fact that this status was achieved within six years of the completion of the first public facility, in the teeth of the great depression, is rather remarkable. By 1945, the accumulated deficit of the first fifteen years was wiped out; the annual surplus has grown steadily, reaching $400,000 and above in the last five years.

The Board of Harbor Commissioners and the harbor staff take some pride in the port's financial situation. The report to the mayor in 1962 discussed the "Direct Earning Power of the Public Port" before anything else, pointing out the mixed nature of its operations and the amount of land devoted to nonrevenue-producing uses. It estimated the surplus as $500,000 to $600,000 per year on an undepreciated investment of $20,400,000, a return which "may not appear to be as lucrative as a prime industrial or utility security . . . but it *is* a net earning, after recovery of all departmental expenses, including those for purely governmental purposes. . . . In the final analysis, the public port was never intended or demanded to earn profits in the commercial meaning of the word, but rather to serve as an economic stimulant and to assure a healthy transportation climate. These objectives it has performed in full measure. Its limited but undeniable financial success is an added dividend, rather than a major objective." [24]

In considering the financial returns of the public port, a further point should be made. The city (and the county and state as well) receives a return on its investment in the form of property taxes paid by the industrial tenants of the municipally owned harbor land. As of 1965, there were thirty such tenants, occupying 106 acres of public land. Table 8-10 shows the real estate and property taxes paid by these firms between 1936 and 1964. The first commercial lease on the North Harbor Tract was not signed until 1960, so that the table is substantially accurate even though it includes only the South Harbor Tract. It appears from the table that the city and other governments are receiving over $2,700 per acre in taxes, or about 7 per cent on the current per-acre valuation. The money is certainly a further return on the city's investment. It should be included in any discussion of the port's financial status. The total tax take shown in Table 8-10 is about $3,220,600 through 1964. Since the taxes may be considered a return on port investment, they are an addi-

24. Milwaukee, Board of Harbor Commissioners, *Impact of the Milwaukee Port*, pp. 4–5.

tional legitimate offset against the interest costs of harbor bonds. Therefore, there is a total surplus as of 1964 taxes and 1964 harbor income in
excess of $3,000,000. Taxes have been running over $200,000 annually
since 1958, suggesting that future property taxes alone will be almost
enough to pay the interest costs on the bonds still outstanding. This
would mean that the annual harbor surplus is actually a surplus, over
and above the total operating and bond expenses.

9

ECONOMIC IMPACT OF THE PORT
ON THE URBAN COMMUNITY

TAKEN together, the municipal port's surplus and the property taxes on its land give the city a sizeable counterbalance on its harbor investment, having grown substantially in recent years to exceed $700,000 in 1964. This sum, however, represents only a very small part of the total economic benefits derived from the port, even of those benefits directly attributable to municipally owned facilities. As the Board of Harbor Commissioners stated, the above dollar return is somewhat in the nature of an added dividend (see pp. 123 and 124).

Precise quantitative measurement of the harbor's economic impact is impossible, but a number of different aspects can be examined. Among them are savings in transport costs, from the fact that water carriers usually are the cheapest means of carriage, and the availability of water transportation as a major inducement to industries to locate near a port. Both forms of economic benefit have been mentioned previously (see pp. 34 and 35) in discussing Milwaukee's car ferries, where their impact is most obvious,[1] but these benefits also exist for lake vessel traffic and foreign shipping through the Seaway. They are derived from both public and

1. The point made previously is worth repeating in a broader context: the savings in transport costs may occur even on commodities which are not shipped by water; railroads, trucks, and other modes of carriage may hold their freight rates at low levels because of *potential* competition from water carriers. Hamming cites an incident in the 1930's to illustrate this point. When the Municipal Open Dock began operations, the railroads sought a reduced rate on steel between Chicago and Milwaukee to forestall diversion of their traffic. The ICC not only refused the reduction but raised the rate to conform with other steel rates in the Midwest, where-

privately owned facilities; the community at large gains from lower transport costs regardless of whether the merchandise is handled through the Municipal Open Dock or a private grain terminal.[2]

The desire for reliable quantitative estimates of at least some forms of port benefits has stimulated research into the direct income-generating powers of port facilities. The economic importance of stevedoring, tugboat service, ship repairs, crew expenditures in port, etc., is seldom recognized except by those personally engaged in supplying the services, and even these persons usually fail to see the full scope of all the services that they provide as a group or to realize how large is the total income derived from them. The range of goods and services provided by a port is shown in Table 9-1, which lists fifty separate items.

CARGO-GENERATED INCOME

A pioneering study by the Delaware River Port Authority in 1953 estimated the direct port expenditures for goods and services produced by each ton of cargo handled by the port.[3] The study is especially useful in that it estimated expenditures for each of the major types of cargo handled by the port. Since many bulk commodities are handled by automated processes, while general cargo is loaded and unloaded by hand, a ton of the latter generates much more income. The Philadelphia study, for example, found that general cargo produced expenditures of $11.33 per ton, while the four leading bulk commodities (coal, tanker cargo such as petroleum products, ore, and grain) generated much smaller sums, ranging from $1.81 per ton for coal to $4.24 per ton for grain.[4] These estimates were based on a questionnaire sent to steamship lines and agencies and to industrial firms operating their own vessels. For some categories, such as port terminal income, estimates were also made by experienced persons who actually provide the services. A copy of the survey questionnaire appears in Appendix E.

The figures obtained by this study, revised occasionally since 1953

upon bulk freighters took much of the traffic away from the rails. After a year the ICC recognized what the railroads had known at the start and permitted a lower rate to the railroads, who then recaptured most of the traffic. See Hamming, *The Port of Milwaukee*, p. 63. The Chicago-Milwaukee rail tariff on steel is still one of the lowest in the country for a comparable distance.

2. It should be pointed out, however, that public facilities at Milwaukee usually handle different types of cargo than do the private docks; they are complementary rather than competitive.

3. Delaware River Port Authority, *The Value of a Ton of Cargo to the Area's Economy*.

4. *Ibid.*, p. 2.

TABLE 9-1

FACTORS OF COMMUNITY INCOME DIRECTLY GENERATED BY SERVICES TO VESSELS AND BY PORT OPERATIONS

Vessel disbursements while in port

Marine services
1. Tug hire
2. Line running
3. Dockage

Federal services
4. Immigration service
5. Entrance and clearance fees
6. Customs overtime

Labor
7. Stevedoring
8. Clerking, checking, watchmen
9. Cleaning, fitting, equipment rental

Repair service
10. Repairs
11. Structural alterations
12. Special cargo fitting

Supplies and chandlery
13. Foodstuffs
14. Hardware
15. Lubricants
16. Laundry and cleaning
17. Cordage
18. Medical
19. Miscellaneous

Fuel
20. Bunker fuel
21. Water

22. Miscellaneous services

Port and terminal income
23. Cargo stevedoring
24. Heavy-lift crane service
25. Car loading and unloading
26. Handling
27. Storage
28. Demurrage
29. Top wharfage

TABLE 9-1 (*continued*)

Inland transport
    30. Local cartage
    31. Local switching
    32. Line-haul truck
    33. Line-haul rail

Vessel crew expenditures
    34. Personal items, drugs & sundries
    35. Haberdashery and clothing
    36. Transportation
    37. Tavern, restaurant, entertainment
    38. Gift shopping
    39. Other

Port services
    40. Steamship agency services
    41. Customs brokerage
    42. Freight forwarding
    43. Warehousing
    44. Marine insurance
    45. Banking
    46. Commodity brokerage
    47. Marine surveys
    48. International trade consultation
    49. Advertising and promotion
    50. Communications (telephone and telegraph)

Source: Milwaukee, Board of Harbor Commissioners, *Impact of the Milwaukee Port*, pp. 7 and 8.

and extended to a wider range of bulk commodities, as these became important in Philadelphia's traffic, have served as basic data in other studies.[5] The most recent estimates were made in 1960; they are uniformly 50 per cent higher than the 1953 figures for those commodities appearing in both lists.

By using the Philadelphia data, it is possible to estimate the income generated at other ports, though allowances should be made for known differences in costs and services between ports. In Tables 9-2 and 9-3, the income generated at the Port of Milwaukee in 1963 is estimated generally on the basis of the 1960 figures for those commodities included in the Philadelphia study. However, for several bulk commodities, the figures have been modified to take account of the findings from an in-

5. See, for example, American Association of Port Authorities, *Annual Report of Committee II, Standardization and Special Research.*

dependent study of the Philadelphia port made in 1958 by Alderson Associates, engineering and economic consultants.[6] This extremely detailed investigation of the port's impact on industry and commerce found that labor costs for handling petroleum products and ore had fallen drastically since 1953, largely because loading techniques were increasingly mechanized. For petroleum products, revenue from vessel dis-

TABLE 9-2

INCOME GENERATED BY OVERSEAS COMMERCE, MILWAUKEE, 1963

Commodity	Tonnage (short tons)	Income per ton	Total income from commodity
General cargo	269,010	$17.00	$4,573,170.00
Grains	338,021	5.45	1,842,214.45
Soybeans	11,619	5.45	63,323.55
Coal	0	2.21	0
Salt	38,868	2.21	85,898.28
Ores	7,910	1.60	12,656.00
Scrap metal	1,158	5.00	5,790.00
Other	778	5.00	3,890.00
Returns	1,071	—	—
Defense Dept. cargo	162	19.00	3,078.00
Total	668,597		$6,590,020.28

Source: U.S. Army Corps of Engineers, *Waterborne Commerce of the United States*, Annual Report, 1963.

bursements (including loading costs) and auxiliary services fell from 96 cents per ton to 17 cents; for ore, from $1.73 to $1.03.[7] The Alderson figures have been used for these commodities in the tables, in combination with the Philadelphia port estimates of 1960 for other income categories.[8]

The Alderson study also found an increase in revenue derived from

6. Alderson Associates, Inc., *The Economic Impact of the Delaware River Ports*; hereafter cited as *Alderson Study*.

7. *Ibid.*, pp. 3–23.

8. For example, in 1953 rail and motor freight revenue and vessel crew expenditures in port were 38 cents per ton of ore; vessel disbursements and auxiliary services cost $1.73, as stated in the text, making total revenue $2.11 per ton. In Tables 9-2 and 9-3 the 1960 estimate of a 50 per cent increase in revenue has been applied to freight and crew expenditures, which are assumed to be 57 cents; the Alderson estimate of $1.03 for vessel disbursements and auxiliary services has been added to this figure, making total revenue $1.60 per ton of ore, as shown in the tables.

general cargo, again largely as a result of changes in loading costs. It did not discuss other bulk commodities specifically, but concluded its analysis of income generation with the comment: "It would appear that, overall, the level of expenditures discovered in each study are confirmed by each other, and that differences over the time period are entirely explainable on the basis of known changes in cost factors." [9] We have

TABLE 9-3

INCOME GENERATED BY INTERLAKE VESSEL SHIPPING, MILWAUKEE, 1963

Commodity	Tonnage (short tons)	Income per ton	Total income from commodity
General cargo	97,128	$17.00	$1,651,176.00
Grains	9,398	5.45	51,219.10
Coal	1,628,296	2.21	3,598,534.16
Salt	145,131	2.21	320,739.51
Ores	20,646	1.60	33,033.60
Scrap metal	7,080	5.00	35,400.00
Petroleum products	851,914	2.67	2,264,610.38
Building materials	772,003	1.50	1,158,004.50
Motor vehicles	66,950	7.81	522,879.50
Other	9	5.00	45.00
Total	3,598,555		$9,635,641.75

Source: U.S. Army Corps of Engineers, *Waterborne Commerce of the United States*, Annual Report, 1963.

interpreted this statement to mean that the Alderson study found no significant changes from the 1953 figures for coal and grain, and we have therefore used the 1953 estimate for vessel disbursements and auxiliary services (the only factors investigated by Alderson), combined with a 50 per cent increase in other categories, as estimated in 1960.

Scrap, building materials, Defense Department cargo, and "other cargo" were evaluated only in 1960, and these estimates have been used without modification. The 1960 figure for general cargo also was used, since Alderson found a sizeable increase in loading costs. Applying these estimates to Milwaukee can be justified on the basis of an investigation by the Board of Harbor Commissioners, which found that "the figure of $17 per ton earned on general cargo compares authentically with local experience. . . . Earnings of export scrap metals compare

9. *Alderson Study*, pp. 3–24.

almost exactly." [10] The investigation was made by the municipal port director. While they were not specifically mentioned, neither "other cargo" nor defense cargo play any important role in Milwaukee's shipping; the estimate for building materials is used on the basis of the general agreement between Milwaukee and Philadelphia revenues noted by the port director, in addition to the specific comparisons already mentioned.

Several bulk commodities important in Milwaukee traffic were not discussed by either study of Philadelphia. These are soybeans, salt, bulk cement, and motor vehicles. In Table 9-2 soybeans are treated as grain. Salt is both shipped and handled in a manner similar to coal (piled on docks when loaded or unloaded and generally stored "in the open" where it is delivered). Building materials in the Philadelphia study consisted only of "sand, gravel, etc." Milwaukee vessel traffic in building materials consists largely of crushed limestone and building cement; it also included gypsum and plaster rock as well as sand and gravel. All of these commodities are shipped in self-unloading vessels which directly serve the private companies having storage facilities in the harbor. (Referring back to Figure 8-A, these companies include 26, 27, 28, 33, 40, and 41, all on the Menomonee River or its tributary canals; and 69 on the Kinnickinnic). Therefore, these commodities have been treated as generating identical revenue in Table 9-3.

Motor vehicles, unfortunately, cannot be treated in a similar fashion. Much of this commerce is handled by the Wisconsin and Michigan Steamship Company, operating the "Milwaukee Clipper" and the "Highway 16" between Milwaukee and Muskegon (see pp. 32 and 109). The traffic has been largely seasonal, during the winter when the all-water route from Detroit to Duluth is closed. The cars are simply driven onto the ships at Muskegon and driven off at Milwaukee.[11]

In the rate litigation before the ICC, the Wisconsin and Michigan Steamship Company offered in evidence the number of automobiles shipped and total revenue received from them, for each year from 1957 to 1961 (see p. 109).[12] Using these figures, the revenue to the company for 1961 was $23.42 per car; the average revenue over the five-year

10. Milwaukee, Board of Harbor Commissioners, *Impact of the Milwaukee Port*, p. 9.

11. The eastbound tonnage shown in Table 4-3, p. 32, comes from the American Motors plant at Kenosha.

12. The Wisconsin and Michigan Steamship Company figures were reproduced in the decision of the hearing examiner, Motor Vehicles—Wayne & Wixom, Michigan to Milwaukee, Wisconsin, ICC No. 33945, pp. 8–9.

period was $22.91. In Table 9-3 the 1961 figure has been used, and one-half the revenue per car is assumed to be income generated in Milwaukee. The "average" automobile is assumed to weigh 1.5 tons, so that revenue generated *per ton* is $7.81.[13]

The car ferries present a still different kind of problem. Table 9-4 shows the estimates of direct revenue generated by a ton of car ferry traffic. For line-haul traffic through Milwaukee, the only revenue generated is assumed to be the charge for switching the cars through the Milwaukee switching district; the cost of the ferry service is included in the rates between eastern cities and Milwaukee. The switching cost is

TABLE 9-4

INCOME GENERATED BY CAR FERRY TRAFFIC, MILWAUKEE, 1963

Type of traffic	Tonnage* (short tons)	Revenue per ton	Total revenue
Local	1,249,744	$3.91	$4,886,499.04
Interstate line-haul	471,601	.90	424,440.90
Intrastate line-haul	636,662	.85	541,162.70
Total	2,358,007		$5,852,102.64

Source: U.S. Army Corps of Engineers, *Waterborne Commerce of the United States*, Annual Report, 1963.

*Tonnage figures for individual classifications are based on percentage estimates furnished by the C. & O. Railroad.

probably completely port-derived income for Milwaukee, since without the ferries the line-haul traffic would be shipped either through Milwaukee to Chicago without stopping, or between Chicago and western cities without going through Milwaukee at all. Switching rates on line-haul traffic in the Milwaukee district are 4.25 cents per hundred pounds or 85 cents per ton for intrastate traffic and 4.50 cents per hundred or 90 cents per ton for interstate traffic; the Milwaukee district includes the car ferry terminals. For traffic with a local origin or destination, switching rates are 5.75 cents per hundred for the Milwaukee Road ($1.15 per ton) and 4.75 cents per hundred for the Chicago & North Western (95 cents per ton).[14] In addition, local traffic must be unloaded or loaded.

13. This average is based on ICC No. 33945, p. 10, where the average weight of a 15-car load on the tri-level railroad car is given as 21.9 tons, or 1.46 tons per auto.

14. Personal interviews with officials of the Chicago & Northwestern Railroad, and the Milwaukee Road. See also Interstate Commerce Commission, *Freight Tariff 2543-U*, p. 17.

The figure used in Table 9-4 for this service is $2.86 per ton; it has been given by Taff as "a representative charge for the simple service of un-loading in one territory." [15] By combining this loading charge with an average switching charge of $1.05 per ton, revenue per ton of local traffic is derived.

Income directly generated by Milwaukee waterborne commerce amounted to about $22.1 million in 1963 (see Table 9-5). According to the Census Bureau, total income in Milwaukee County in 1960 was $2,371 million; total income for the Milwaukee SMSA, including Mil-waukee and Waukesha counties, was $2,716 million.[16] Thus it appears that shipping activities directly generate about 0.93 per cent of Mil-waukee County's income, or 0.81 per cent of income in the SMSA.

TABLE 9-5

TOTAL PORT-GENERATED INCOME, MILWAUKEE, 1963

Type of traffic	Tonnage (short tons) (1)	Direct income (2)	Total income (k = 2.33) (3)	Total income (k = 2.905)* (4)
Foreign	668,597	$6,590,020.28	$15,354,746	$19,144,008
Domestic vessel	3,598,555	9,635,641.75	22,451,044	27,991,540
Car ferry	2,358,007	5,852,102.64	13,635,399	17,000,385
Total	6,625,159	$22,077,764.67	$51,441,189	$64,135,933

Source: Tables 9-2, 9-3, and 9-4.

*Hoch, "A Comparison of Alternate Inter-Industry Forecasts for the Chicago Region," *Papers and Proceedings of the Regional Science Association*, V, 230. The multiplier for water transport is the second lowest among the forty-six industries considered. The multiplier for leather is 2.820.

SECONDARY INCOME

These figures do not take account of secondary income generated by the expenditure of the original $22.1 million. The economic concept of the "multiplier," developed by Richard F. Kahn and given a central place in economic theory by Keynes,[17] can be used to estimate the amount of secondary income generated by these expenditures. The recipients of direct income from shipping services will spend some fraction of that income on purchasing goods and services from other individuals and

15. Taff, *Traffic Management, Principles and Practices*, p. 373.

16. U.S. Bureau of the Census, *County and City Data Book, 1962*, p. 423.

17. Kahn, "The Relation of Home Investment to Unemployment," *Economic Journal*, XLI, 173–98; Keynes, *The General Theory of Employment, Interest, and Money*.

firms in the Milwaukee area; these individuals and firms in turn spend a fraction of their receipts on similar purchases, and so forth.

Use of the multiplier is valid only when the primary income can be treated as exogenous, as coming from "outside." Income from port services can be so treated. To demonstrate this, it is helpful to visualize Milwaukee as a separate economic entity, distinct from the rest of the United States. Its situation would be comparable to that of "free cities" such as Hong Kong, Singapore, or Danzig between the world wars. Shippers who live "outside" Milwaukee clearly bring income into the city when they use the port facilities. It is also true that shippers "inside" Milwaukee bring income into the city in the same way. If the other party to the transaction pays the shipping costs through the port, the shipper will include them in the price he quotes to the other party. In either case, the port revenues are primary income.[18]

Until recently, there has been no development of any regional multiplier for the Milwaukee area, and in any analysis of secondary income generated by initial expenditures, we were forced to rely on multipliers developed for the Chicago area. Even at the present time, when looking for a multiplier calculated specifically for the water transport industry, we find that the one which is probably most applicable to Milwaukee's environment is derived in a study of Chicago by Professor Irving Hoch, formerly a staff economist for the Chicago Area Transportation Study.[19] Hoch used the 1947 Bureau of Labor Statistics input-output tables for the fifty industries included in his model, and, among other things, he estimated the multiplier effects on household activity and investment, resulting from increased output in each industry. One of the industries was "water transport," for which he estimated a multiplier of 2.905.[20]

18. Treating Milwaukee as a "free city" emphasizes another important aspect of its economy. Milwaukee produces no food; it must "import" it from other areas, including the rest of Wisconsin and other states. To pay for its imports of food, Milwaukee must "export" to other areas. These exports may be either commodities (such as beer) or services provided by Milwaukee which persons elsewhere will pay for. The Milwaukee port falls into the latter category. In 1957, the Federal Reserve Bank of Chicago listed Milwaukee's harbor facilities (including both public and private) as one of four major export-earning services, along with the Northwestern Mutual Life Insurance Company, the repair shops of the Milwaukee Road, and the Braves baseball team.

19. Hoch, "A Comparison of Alternative Inter-Industry Forecasts for the Chicago Region," *Papers and Proceedings of the Regional Science Association*, V, 217–35.

20. Chicago is directly located on both the Great Lakes–Seaway route and the inland waterway system to the Gulf, and over one third of its 1961 tonnage was "internal." Also, Milwaukee's output is substantially more heavily concentrated in

In 1965, however, the Southeastern Wisconsin Regional Planning Commission (SEWRPC) published a study which, in part, calculated a multiplier for the southeastern Wisconsin region.[21] This multiplier relates changes in total regional income to changes in export income. The regional multiplier of 2.44 (the derivation of which is outlined in Appendix F) is slightly higher than the Milwaukee multiplier that was subsequently computed, in the same manner, by Kenneth J. Schlager, Chief Systems Enginner for the SEWRPC. This estimated general multiplier, for Milwaukee, of 2.33 should be roughly suitable for determining the effect of port income from export services on local income.[22] The estimated Milwaukee multiplier of 2.33 is used in column 3 of Table 9-5 while Hoch's "water transport" multiplier of 2.905 is used in column 4.

On the basis of the "water transport" multiplier of 2.905, total income generated by the port was about $64.1 million in 1963. This was 2.70 per cent of total Milwaukee County income and 2.36 per cent of SMSA income. Using the Milwaukee multiplier of 2.33, total port-generated income was about $51.4 million (2.17 per cent of county income and 1.89 per cent of income in the SMSA). All of these results must be regarded as rough approximations, but they do suggest the range within which the true figures probably lie. It may be said with some confidence that the shipping activities at the Port of Milwaukee are the ultimate source of about 2 per cent of all income received by residents of the Milwaukee SMSA.

---

manufacturing (39 per cent of the Milwaukee labor force in 1960 was in manufacturing, as compared with 33 per cent in Chicago, according to the U.S. Bureau of the Census, *County and City Data Book*). These factors suggest that the true multiplier for Milwaukee's water transport industry may perhaps be somewhat lower than Chicago's.

21. SEWRPC, *Technical Record*, II, no. 3, pp. 9–13; reprinted in Appendix F.

22. This general multiplier would not be suitable in determining the effect of port investment on the community. Further computations, based on the construction industry as the primary supplier of port facilities, were made by Schlager in order to determine the investment multiplier of 2.55.

(Investment multiplier $= I = 1/1 - ak$)

$a =$ income created per dollar of local construction industry sales

$k =$ consumption factor for construction industry

Raw material purchases per sales dollar $= 0.51$; regional share of raw material purchases $= 0.25$

$1 - a = (0.51)(0.75) = 0.38$

$a = 0.62, k = 0.98$

Therefore, $I = 1/1 - ak$
$= 1/1 - (0.62)(0.98)$
$= 2.55$

One important source of income from cargo shipping has been left out of Table 9-5: the expenditures by ships using the Municipal Mooring Basin in the winter. The secretary of the Lake Carriers' Association estimated in 1952 that each ship laid up in a port during the winter spent from $10,000 to $20,000 for supplies and repairs.[23] The Milwaukee Municipal Mooring Basin handles about thirty ships each winter, oper-

TABLE 9-6

EMPLOYMENT GENERATED BY PORT ACTIVITIES,
MILWAUKEE SMSA, 1963

Unit of measure	Direct employment	% of all units SMSA	Total employment (k = 2.905)	% of all units SMSA	Total employment (k = 2.33)	% of all units SMSA
Number of families, SMSA	3,156	1.04	9,168	3.02	7,353	2.42
Number of male civilian members of labor force, SMSA	4,106	1.25	11,928	3.64	9,567	2.92

Source: Table 9-5 and U.S. Bureau of the Census, *United States Census of Population, 1960, Final Report, PC(1) — 51C*.

ating at close to its capacity. Direct income generated from the mooring basin can, therefore, be estimated at between $300,000 and $600,000 per year, which, if anything, is probably a conservative estimate for the present time. Using the multiplier of 2.905, total income from this source would be between $871,500 and $1,743,000 per year; using the 2.33 multiplier, annual income would be between $699,000 and $1,398,000.

The impact of port activities can perhaps be shown more forcefully in terms of employment instead of income. The port's effect on employment can be estimated in several ways; two common measures are used in Table 9-6. The 1960 census calculated median family income for the Milwaukee SMSA as $6,995.[24] On the basis of that figure, port activities directly provided income for 3,156 typical Milwaukee area families (1.04 per cent of all 303,887 families in the SMSA). Taking into account the multiplier effects of the expenditures by these families, port activities were the ultimate source of income for 9,168 families (3.02 per cent)

23. Cited in Hamming, *The Port of Milwaukee*, p. 66.
24. U.S. Bureau of the Census, *United States Census of Population, 1960, Final Report PC(1) — 51C*, p. 51-223.

using Hoch's "water transport" multiplier, or for 7,353 families (2.42 per cent) using the Milwaukee multiplier.

Another estimate can be made on the basis of the total male civilian labor force instead of families. The census estimated median income for employed male civilians at $5,377.[25] Using this income, the port directly

TABLE 9-7

REVENUE FROM CROSS-LAKE PASSENGER SERVICE, MILWAUKEE, 1963

City*	Number traveling	Revenue per unit	Total direct income
Muskegon (Passengers)	96,712	$2.90	$280,464.80
Muskegon (Autos)	27,632	4.50	124,344.00
Ludington (Passengers)	104,849	2.50	262,122.50
Ludington (Autos)	29,957	4.50	134,806.50
Total			$801,737.80

Employment from total direct income (families)	Employment from total direct income (civilian male workers)	Total income (k = 2.33)	Employment (families)	Employment (male) workers)
115	149	$1,868,049.07	267	347

Total income (k = 2.905)	Employment (families)	Employment (male workers)
$2,329,048.31	333	433

Source: U.S. Army Corps of Engineers, *Waterborne Commerce of the United States*, Annual Report, 1963.
*Service between Milwaukee and listed city.

provided income for 4,106 members of the male civilian labor force (1.25 per cent of the total force of 327,851); taking into account the multiplier effects, the port provided income for 11,928 members (3.64 per cent) if the multiplier is 2.905, or 9,567 members (2.92 per cent) if the multiplier is 2.33. The Municipal Mooring Basin provides employment for additional workers and income for their families; with a multiplier of 2.905, it supports 125 to 250 families.

There is yet another important form of port traffic to be evaluated:

25. *Ibid.*, p. 51-208.

the cross-lake passenger travel to Muskegon and Ludington. Table 9-7 presents an estimate of the income generated by the "Milwaukee Clipper" (to Muskegon) and the Chesapeake & Ohio car ferry passenger service (to Ludington). In measuring revenue per passenger, the one-way fare charged by each line has been used, attributing half of the fare revenue to Milwaukee. The statistics of the U.S. Army Corps of Engineers list only the number of passengers handled at each port, without providing a breakdown by port of origin or destination; since the fares to the two ports are not identical, it has been necessary to allocate the total number of passengers among them. Fortunately, Muskegon has only one passenger service, that to Milwaukee; the number of passengers it handles, therefore, necessarily is the number handled by the "Clipper" in Milwaukee.[26] Subtracting that number from the total for Milwaukee gives the number handled by the Chesapeake & Ohio.

Both lines also carry passengers' automobiles. The normal ratio of autos to passengers is usually about one for every 3.5 passengers.[27] This ratio suggests that the "Clipper" probably handled over 27,000 cars and the Chesapeake & Ohio nearly 30,000. Once again, half of the one-way fare has been taken to measure the income generated in Milwaukee from this traffic. Thus the passenger traffic brings in directly about $800,000 per year, providing income for 115 families or 149 male workers; multiplier effects raise the total to approximately $2,000,000 and 300 families.

Since the car ferries serve a large number of non-Milwaukee tourists, it is reasonable to assume that the money spent by these tourists in Milwaukee is also port-generated income. However, no useable estimates of average tourist spending have been developed, and the cross-lake traffic also includes native Milwaukeeans; therefore, no estimate of this form of income has been attempted. It would probably raise the totals in Table 9-7 substantially if it were included.

An additional type of income generated by the Port of Milwaukee is related to private and public investment expenditure on construction and improvement of port facilities. It has been reasonably estimated that

26. The Grand Trunk Western car ferry also provides passenger service to Muskegon, but its traffic is very small, since it does not carry passengers' automobiles. Hamming reported that the Grand Trunk's passenger traffic fell sharply after World War II when the "Clipper" inaugurated direct cross-lake round-trip service; by 1950 the Grand Trunk ferry handled only 1,500 passengers (*The Port of Milwaukee*, p. 83), and it has not rebounded since 1950. Attributing its passenger traffic to the "Clipper" thus introduces only a very small error into the results.

27. Milwaukee, Board of Harbor Commissioners, *1962 Port Brochure*, p. 17.

combined public and private investment in the port has been about $5,000,000 annually in recent years.[28] When we apply the investment multiplier of 2.55 [29] to this figure, we see that port investment creates approximately $12,750,000 in income annually for the community. This means an additional 2,371 jobs can be added to those already listed as attributable to port operations.

It should be stressed that these measures of employment are not merely statistical abstractions with no counterpart in the real world. The jobs do exist. "Hundreds of longshoremen are lucratively employed. The revival of the export grain trade has created new work for grain trimmers, elevator employees, railroads, and truckers. Where one vessel agency existed in Milwaukee in 1946, there were thirteen agencies in 1961, and more are on the way. New opportunities, both for individuals and for management, have appeared in the fields of warehousing, marine insurance, banking, cargo surveying, customs brokerage, freight forwarding, ship repairs, chandlery, and other skills and occupations." [30] Even in 1952, Hamming estimated that "harbor maintenance and vessel traffic form the basis for a number of local enterprises whose eixstence is wholly or in part supported by harbor activities and provide employment directly for at least 500 people. Two marine contract companies are engaged in dredging. . . . Several industries manufacture parts and accessories for outfitting all types of vessels. Two local concerns supply many of the bulk freighters with meats and groceries while two other enterprises cater to ship's laundry service. . . . One firm, which has been in the ship chandler's business for more than 100 years, carries a complete stock of marine supplies and specializes in the manufacture of sails and canvas. It employs about 100 persons." [31]

One other source of employment, probably the oldest in Milwaukee's history, should be mentioned. In 1963 Milwaukee commercial fishermen reported 1,283 tons for their annual catch. The figure appears in Table 4-3 under "local." No estimate of income from commercial fishing is available, but Hamming estimated that the fishing industry in 1952 pro-

28. Private investment questionnaire.

29. As seen in n. 22, above, the nature of the construction industry necessitates the computation of a special investment multiplier in order to relate investment expenditures to income. Because of the construction industry's relatively high consumption function, the investment multiplier exceeds the general Milwaukee multiplier.

30. Milwaukee, Board of Harbor Commissioners, *Impact of the Milwaukee Port*, pp. 8–9.

31. Hamming, *The Port of Milwaukee*, pp. 65–66.

vided a livelihood for "about 25 families." [32] The catch then was only about 200 tons. If commercial fishing is assumed to provide constant returns to scale for fishermen, some 150 families earned their living directly from that industry in 1963.

At first glance, income and employment benefits of the magnitude of 2 to 4 per cent may not appear to be very important. Again it should be pointed out that these figures represent only the most easily measured returns from port activities. It is not possible to estimate the transport cost savings that the industry and individuals have reaped from the existence of the port. In 1947 the Army Corps of Engineers estimated that, over the whole country, waterborne freight moves at an average saving of $3.68 per ton over other modes of carriage.[33] For Milwaukee, the district engineer estimated in 1960 that transport savings attributable to the deepening of the harbor to Seaway draft, *by itself*, would result in annual savings of about 93 cents per ton of general cargo [34] and in savings on various bulk commodities ranging from nothing at all to 54 cents per ton, depending on the commodity, its origin or destination, and the type of vessel used.[35]

These figures are offered for illustrative purposes only; this study does not attempt to offer precise estimates of any sort for transport cost savings. Nor does it attempt to measure the impact of the port on Milwaukee and Wisconsin industrial and agricultural employment. However, estimates can be developed for the export traffic, which is only about 6 per cent of the total.

The U.S. Department of Agriculture estimated that, in 1963, exports of Wisconsin farm products provided jobs for 16,100 farm workers.[36] Similarly, we can estimate that 1963 exports of manufactured products provided jobs for 54,080 industrial workers and that exports attributable to workers in "other occupations" provided 13,053 jobs.[37] These latter estimates are based on the 1960 Department of Commerce export

32. *Ibid.*, p. 67.

33. U.S. House Committee on Harbor and River Improvement, *A Report upon the Improvement of Rivers and Harbors in the Jacksonville, Florida, District,* cited in Durr, "Economic Importance of the Port of Miami," *Miami Economic Research,* VIII, no. 4, p. 2.

34. U.S. Army Engineer District, *Milwaukee Interim Report,* p. B-4.

35. *Ibid.*, Appendix B; each commodity is treated in a separate group of tables.

36. Tontz and Angelidis, "U.S. Agricultural Export Shares by Regions and States," *Foreign Agricultural Trade of the United States,* Nov.–Dec., 1964, Table 3, p. 28.

37. "Other occupations" include mining, wholesale trade, transportation, finance, construction, and service industries.

study for Wisconsin and a companion study by the Bureau of Labor Statistics.[38] By relating the 1960 Bureau of Labor Statistics estimate of jobs provided by manufactured exports to total manufactured export production in 1960, we are able to derive a ratio that should be quite stable in the short run.[39] We can then apply this ratio to the 1963 manufactured export figure in order to estimate the number of jobs provided by export production in 1963.[40] Also, since "other occupations" produced exports equal to 18.6 per cent of the manufactured and farm export total in 1960,[41] a study by the Southeastern Wisconsin Regional Planning Commission indicates that we would not be far off by assuming this ratio to be approximately equal in 1963.[42]

In Table 6-2 it was estimated that 31 per cent of the state's agricultural exports were shipped from Milwaukee; the average for other manufacturing industries, not shown in that table, can be calculated as 7 per cent. Using these percentages to estimate employment due to exports and treating other occupations as exporting through Milwaukee in the same percentage as manufacturing, it appears that about 4,991 farm workers, 3,786 employees in manufacturing, and 914 in other occupations were employed in producing exports shipped via the Port of Milwaukee.[43]

38. These works have already been quoted frequently in earlier chapters, see pp. 14 and 64, respectively.

39. Logically this ratio should decrease slightly as production increases because advancing technology will enable a greater output per worker. Over as short a period as three years, however, any decrease in the ratio would probably be quite negligible, and it simplifies our analysis to assume a constant relationship over this relatively short period.

40. Manufactured exports in 1960 were valued at $385.4 million. By 1963 the value had risen to $500.2 million. U.S. Bureau of the Census, *Survey of the Origin of Exports of Manufactured Products, 1963*, Current Industrial Reports, Table 1, p. 2. The U.S. Bureau of Labor Statistics estimated that 41,000 jobs were provided by Wisconsin's manufactured exports in 1960. See *Domestic Employment Attributable to U.S. Exports, 1960*, supplement.

41. *Ibid.*

42. SEWRPC, "Land Use-Transportation Study," in *Inventory Findings, 1963*, I, 34, Table 15. Actually, this estimate will most likely be a little low, since construction, finance, and service industries have been growing in recent years at the expense of manufacturing and farming.

43. The point has already been made in Chapter 6 that Table 6-2 overstates the share of Wisconsin exports moving through Milwaukee, since firms in many other states also use the port. This fact does not invalidate the calculations in the text, however, since workers in these other states were employed to make the goods actually shipped. Therefore, while the calculation overstates the number of *Wisconsin* workers, it is a reasonable estimate of the number of workers for the whole

The income received by these workers can also be estimated, again using the 1960 census. Income distributions and median incomes are included for each of six male occupational classes.[44] Two of these are categories of farm workers; the other four comprise all persons in manufacturing and other occupations, except mining. If it is assumed that the persons who produced for Milwaukee export were divided among these classes in the same proportions as all state employment, then the total income of these persons can readily be calculated. On that basis, Milwaukee's agricultural exports produced $10,526,019 in farm workers' income; manufactures generated $20,315,676, and other occupations $4,904,524.[45] Total income from Milwaukee exports was $35,746,219.

Total Wisconsin employment in agriculture was 258,000 in 1963;[46] total manufacturing employment was 462,154.[47] Therefore, an estimated 6.2 per cent of Wisconsin farm workers owed their jobs to exports, and 11.7 per cent of employees in manufacturing similarly produced for export. Again using Table 6-2 as a basis for calculation, an estimated 1.92 per cent of all farm workers in the state and 0.82 per cent of all industrial workers produced for export shipment via Milwaukee, though it should be remembered that these percentages are maxima and substantially overstate the actual number of Wisconsin workers so engaged.[48]

This study does not claim that 9,691 workers would have been unemployed if the Milwaukee port did not exist; some of the goods exported would have gone via other routes in the absence of the port. But the application of basic economic theory tells us that the port played an important part. Foreigners would not have purchased their goods from Wis-

United States, and is so treated in the text. The survey questionnaire of Wisconsin exporters' routes (see Chapter 6) estimated that Wisconsin manufacturers actually ship about 6 per cent of their exports via Milwaukee (Table 6-4). Using this figure, 3,245 manufacturing workers and 783 in other occupations produced for Milwaukee's export traffic.

44. U.S. Bureau of the Census, *United States Census of Population, 1960, Final Report PC (1) — 51C*, Table 68.

45. The estimates for manufacturing and other occupations are based on the 7 per cent figure. If 6 per cent is used, in accordance with Table 6-4, manufacturing income was $17,411,597; income from other occupations was $4,202,544; total income was $32,140,160.

46. Department of Agriculture figures cited in Tontz and Angelidis, "U.S. Agricultural Export Shares by Regions and States," *Foreign Agricultural Trade of the United States*, Nov.–Dec., 1964.

47. U.S. Department of Commerce, *1963 Census of Manufactures*, Area Series, Wisconsin, Preliminary Report (Washington, D.C., n.d.), Table 1, p. 1.

48. On the basis of Table 6-4, 0.6 per cent of Wisconsin manufacturing employees produced exports that were shipped via Milwaukee.

consin firms if these companies did not sell at prices at least as low as any other producer; "prices" in this sense include the costs of transportation.[49] As long as there is any elasticity in the demand curves for Milwaukee and Wisconsin products, cheaper transport means greater sales and greater employment. It also means that Milwaukee and Wisconsin industries are able to sell their output over a wider area.[50]

The same considerations apply equally to domestic traffic. Milwaukee industries do not ship through the port to other U.S. ports,[51] and probably only the brewers and industries using steel receive any significant amount of their raw material via water, but the coal and petroleum products which dominate port traffic are used as fuel by industry as well as by individuals. The fact that water transport is available means that many industries can get their fuel cheaper than they otherwise could, and because fuel costs are a cost of production, their products can also be sold at lower prices than otherwise. Additional industrial workers in Milwaukee can therefore be considered as owing their jobs to the port. The precise magnitude, or even a rough approximation, cannot be estimated; the data simply are not available. But economic theory and economic history both tell us that such industrial port-dependent jobs did and do exist.

Hamming concluded that "the availability of cheap fuels (by water) and rate equalization with Chicago (principally because of the car ferry service) have been important factors in the industrialization of Milwaukee."[52] This study supports his conclusion.

Table 9-8 summarizes the findings made in this chapter, regarding income and employment, with the appropriate multipliers applied where

49. In fact, we can go further. If any export industries are perfectly competitive domestically (meaning that all United States firms in the industry have the same per-unit production costs), then transport costs become absolutely decisive in determining which firm wins the foreigner's order. We do not claim that all or any Wisconsin exporters are in such industries, but it may be noted that agriculture has traditionally been cited as an example of a competitive industry.

50. Transport costs have long been recognized as a major factor in determining the extent of a market. See, for example, Alfred Marshall's famous definition of a market in *Principles of Economics*, p. 325: "Thus the more nearly perfect a market is, the stronger is the tendency for the same price to be paid for the same thing at the same time in all parts of the market; but of course if the market is large, allowance must be made for the expense of delivering the goods to different purchasers; each of whom must be supposed to pay in addition to the market price a special charge on account of delivery."

51. This statement does not include "Interlake Car Ferry" shipments.

52. Hamming, *The Port of Milwaukee*, p. 149.

applicable. Following the procedure used throughout the chapter, Table 9-8 presents figures arrived at with the use of both the "water transport" and the Milwaukee multipliers.

When the total income and employment generated by these various port-related operations are viewed as a whole, it becomes evident that the port is a significant factor in both the day-to-day functioning and the development of the community. The totals in Table 9-8 represent a figure

TABLE 9-8

INCOME AND EMPLOYMENT RELATED TO PORT OPERATIONS, MILWAUKEE, 1963

| | $k = 2.33$ | | $k = 2.905$ | |
	Income	Employment (male workers)	Income	Employment (male workers)
Foreign and domestic shipping services	$51,441,000	9,567	$64,136,000	11,928
Mooring basin operation*	1,000,000	186	1,200,000	223
Passenger service	1,868,000	347	2,329,000	433
Fishing*	2,333,000	433	2,905,000	540
Farm exports†	10,526,019	4,991	10,526,019	4,991
Manufactured exports†	20,315,676	3,786	20,315,676	3,786
Other exports†	4,904,524	914	4,904,524	914
Investment ($k = 2.55$)	12,750,000	2,371	12,750,000	2,371
Total‡	$105,137,000	22,595	$119,066,000	25,186

Figures have been rounded.

*Estimated.

†Export figures are only for that part of total production that is shipped through the Port of Milwaukee. No multiplier has been applied.

‡As stated in the text, a considerable amount of port-generated income cannot be estimated. As a result, this total figure is not all inclusive, but merely a rough indication of the port's impact.

equal to about 8 per cent of the total employment in the Milwaukee SMSA, or nearly 2 per cent of all the employment in the state of Wisconsin. Nevertheless, even these figures may underestimate the port's true significance. As was stated above, there are various port-generated benefits that cannot be readily estimated in absolute terms. For example, it would be next to impossible to evaluate the importance of the availability of inexpensive fuels for industrial and personal consumption. Similarly, no attempt has been made to compute the port's value as an incentive to industrial development, or as a source of tourist trade. Finally, what value can we attach to the port's contribution to overcoming Milwaukee's geographical disadvantage of being located off the nation's major land transportation routes?

In conclusion, we can accurately say that the Port of Milwaukee is certainly a major asset to the entire community, that it is destined to play a major role in future development, and, to the extent that it develops revenue from outside the area, its significance will be multiplied and extended to include an area far exceeding those interests directly dependent on port operations.

10

SUMMARY AND CONCLUSIONS

THE St. Lawrence Seaway–Great Lakes navigation route, which opened on April 15, 1959,[1] has been a significant influence on foreign trade in recent years. While it has generally stimulated shipping at all Great Lakes ports, it came at a particularly opportune moment for Milwaukee. Since the Seaway's opening, overseas traffic with Great Lakes ports has grown substantially, though the lake ports have long had a very substantial interlake trade with Canada in bituminous coal, newsprint, and grain. In recent years, this bulk Canadian traffic has tended to obscure the growth of overseas traffic in foreign trade statistics, especially since coal traffic has recently been declining. In the first season of Seaway operation, the Great Lakes increased its export tonnage by 25 per cent and export value by 67 per cent. A substantial growth in general cargo exports is the primary reason for this growth in value (general cargo commodities being generally more valuable than bulk commodities) as well as one of the major components of the new Seaway commerce of the lake ports, including Milwaukee. General cargo exports were five times the 1958 level by 1963, and general cargo imports have also experienced impressive growth.

Despite this rapid growth rate, the Great Lakes ports are still shipping only about 7 per cent of the manufactured exports of their hinterlands. The primary reasons for this small percentage are infrequency of sailings, the seasonal nature of the Seaway, lack of sailings to particular destinations, lack of facilities at lake ports which are available at Gulf or Atlantic ports, and the paucity of U.S.-flag ships on the Great Lakes.

1. The "official" opening date was June 26, 1959.

If these obstacles can be overcome, it is obvious that the hinterlands of the Great Lakes represent a virtually untapped source of future growth.

As a group, the Great Lakes ports have experienced a growth in their relative share of total U.S. overseas shipping in terms of both tonnage and value. Value has grown more significantly than tonnage, but foreign traffic at Great Lakes ports is still primarily bulk in nature despite the Seaway's impetus to general cargo. Of the bulk imports, iron ore, brought from Labrador, owes its notable growth record to the opening of the St. Lawrence route.

Milwaukee's shipping traffic dates from the early eighteenth century, and, like other Great Lakes ports, it was dominated by bulk cargoes until the Seaway's operation. Domestic bulk commodity receipts, notably coal and petroleum products, and the cross-lake car ferry traffic with Muskegon and Ludington accounted for the major portion of the port's activity. Coal receipts have been decreasing for many years, however, and petroleum products, which went from nothing in 1936 to 2.5 million tons in 1961, suffered a sharp decline in 1962 with the opening of the pipeline between Milwaukee and Chicago. The waterborne commerce volume of approximately 8,370,000 short tons in 1961 fell to 6,725,000 short tons in 1962, and then to 6,381,000 short tons in 1964, the lowest point since 1940. This regression can be entirely accounted for by the loss of petroleum traffic to the pipeline. This reduction in domestic tonnage is not really of any serious consequence, however, since the pipeline company uses the port's storage facilities and is required to make payments to the port in lieu of wharfage fees. As a result, municipal port revenues were only slightly affected by the drop in waterborne petroleum traffic.

As long as Milwaukee maintains rail-rate parity with Chicago, a reduction in domestic tonnage is not too serious; the port's basic attractions will remain, and it is probable that new domestic commerce will eventually develop to fill the gap. Rail-rate parity can be largely attributed to the car ferry operations and facilities, a unique feature of the Port of Milwaukee and some other Lake Michigan ports. The car ferries handle over 25 per cent of Milwaukee's lake tonnage, and this shortened route keeps rail rates to the Atlantic seaboard equal to rates from Chicago. This rate parity, created by the ferries, exists even if goods are carried overland by rail rather than across the lake. The ferry service thus goes far toward overcoming a handicap that Milwaukee has had for over a century: it is not located on the major land transport routes of the nation.

However, since bulk commodities and car ferry traffic do not seem likely to take up the slack in the near future, Milwaukee's prospects for regaining its recent tonnage levels and attaining future growth depend largely on the Seaway traffic that it can generate. The port's volume of foreign shipping has grown impressively since the Seaway's opening, and over 60 per cent of the record 1961 foreign tonnage was in trade with overseas ports. It appears very likely that Milwaukee will be one of the leading Great Lakes ports in terms of overseas traffic, including general cargo.

Milwaukee's lake vessel receipts are a hundred times its lake vessel shipments. With continued expansion of general cargo traffic in the future, this margin should decline.

In 1856, Milwaukee became the first Great Lakes port to trade directly with Europe, but it was not until 1933 that the first regularly scheduled sailings began. Between World War II and 1964, the number of ocean lines serving Milwaukee increased from 2 to 48, and in 1964 there were 439 ocean-bound sailings from the port. Although this has been an impressive and steady growth, it is still a very small total when compared with major coastal ports, such as New York and Baltimore. Much additional expansion will be necessary before the Port of Milwaukee can become an effective competitor for even Wisconsin and Milwaukee products.

In addition to the obstacles already mentioned, two more should be added. First, it is likely that many foreign buyers simply may not know of the availability of service via Milwaukee, or may be misinformed as to the speed or frequency. Since a large number of foreign buyers specify the routes to be used for their purchases, Milwaukee can perhaps speed up the process of adjustment to the new Seaway route by vigorous promotion abroad, and, in fact, the port is engaged in substantial promotional activity at this very time.

Nevertheless, Canada still remains Milwaukee's chief foreign trade partner; barley and newsprint being the major import commodities and corn the primary export. However, the port is handling an increasing quantity of machinery and relief commodity exports. Western and southern Europe provide the major market for the former, and the underdeveloped nations of the world receive the bulk of the latter. These relief exports are doubly important to the port, since they serve as a base export commodity for sailings to all parts of the world. They have unquestionably played a major role in the development of trade between Milwaukee and the nations of Asia and Africa.

The second additional obstacle is the port's heavy dependence upon this government relief cargo as a base for overseas general cargo exports. Over the years, this traffic has become increasingly erratic, and since

1961 the Great Lakes ports, as a group, have lost a good portion of their total share to the Gulf ports as the result of a still smoldering "rate war." This stiff competition from the Gulf ports has centered around grain and flour exports from the Kansas-Nebraska area. It began in 1961 when the railroads serving the Gulf introduced the first of several rate cuts for this commodity. The rail lines serving the Great Lakes subsequently matched the initial cut and fought later rate reduction efforts before the ICC. Although a portion of the pre-1961 traffic was regained, this conflict was not beneficial to Great Lakes growth efforts. As was pointed out earlier, a large volume of commercial shipping depends upon the availability of sailings made possible by some base commodity such as relief cargoes. Although the potential opportunity to substitute locally produced machinery and other manufactured goods for relief cargo does exist, any development in this direction will undoubtedly be relatively slow, and in the meantime the availability of government shipments as an export base remains a crucial problem.

These obstacles are formidable, but Milwaukee does have several advantages which help to overcome them. In its competition with other Great Lakes ports, it has rate advantages over Duluth-Superior and more frequent service than that port, making it an effective competitor of the Lake Superior port in Minnesota and Iowa as well as in northern Wisconsin. Its more important rival for overseas trade is likely to be Chicago. Milwaukee's hinterland to the south, based on class freight rates, ends at the Wisconsin state line; but it enjoys equalized commodity rates with Chicago from many points in central and southern Illinois, and its effective hinterland appears to include all of that state. It has facilities for heavy-lift shipments that many other lake ports cannot match.

Ships that serve Chicago can also stop at Milwaukee with a very slight loss of additional time for loading, and we have seen that Milwaukee accounts for a larger share of each ship's total cargo than it did in the past. Milwaukee is closer to overseas ports than is Chicago, though its margin is very small in miles. The importance of this fact lies not in any savings in shipping costs, but in savings in time. Possibly Milwaukee can eventually utilize this water transport advantage as effectively as Chicago has used its edge in railroad service.

Milwaukee was a port before it was a city, and the port has had a strong impact on the city since the first white men arrived. Early settlers such as Byron Kilbourn recognized the importance of the port when they sought to dig a canal from Milwaukee to the Rock River, which would have linked the Great Lakes and the Mississippi River system if it had been completed. Even without the canal and without any port improvements at all, Milwaukee handled over 1,000 tons of lead four years before it was incorporated as a city.

Federal government expenditures on the port began in 1838, and over $50,000 of federal money had been spent in harbor improvements by 1846, the year Milwaukee became a city. Local government investment began in 1854, eight years later, and has been a permanent part of the municipal budget ever since (except in 1858 and 1859). The city has $20,000,000 invested in the fixed assets of the port and has paid an additional $3.6 million to date in interest on the capital borrowed to finance some of its investment, as well as $2.9 million for maintenance dredging and docking. Combining these figures with another $7.3 million for other maintenance and operational expenses, we get a total of $33.8 million in total municipal expenditures. In return, the city has derived $11.7 million in total operating income, and the city, county, and state have received about $3.2 million in real estate taxes on publicly owned harbor land. Recent surplus and tax revenues suggest strongly that the port will continue to enjoy a substantial annual return on its invested capital. The port and city have also been the recipients of substantial capital gains on original investments which have appreciated to $32,507,359 as of December 31, 1962.

The port has also produced income for individuals. When we consider all of the income sources analyzed in Chapter 9 (shipping services, mooring basin operation, passenger service, export production, fishing, and harbor investment), we see that about 2 per cent of all Wisconsin employment, or about 8 per cent of Milwaukee area employment, is either directly or indirectly attributable to the port.

In addition, the availability of water transport and its inherent transportation cost savings is certainly a potential inducement to industrial location and development. Although the determination of any absolute value attributable to this latter benefit may be indeterminate, or at best very vague, its existence should be recognized along with the more quantitatively measurable benefits. It is impossible to estimate how much of the area's total income would not have accrued in the absence of the Milwaukee port, but it is certain that at least some fraction of port-generated income was created only because of the existence of this relatively inexpensive transportation facility.

It is equally difficult to estimate the benefits that have accrued as a result of savings in transportation costs. If the U.S. Army Corps of Engineers' estimate in 1947 of $3.68 per waterborne ton is accepted in the absence of anything better, Milwaukee's port facilities were partly responsible for about $23.5 million in transportation cost savings in 1964 alone, or nearly $300 million over the last ten year period (1955–64).

Perhaps one-third to one-half of the sum might be attributed to the port facilities at Milwaukee; the remainder would be attributed to the shipping or receiving port plus other factors. Whatever their true magnitude may be, these savings have surely been important factors in the industrialization and growth of the city of Milwaukee.

This study has been primarily analytical, but in the course of it a few possible policy recommendations have suggested themselves, and in conclusion these recommendations are briefly enumerated.

At present, the port's best growth prospects appear to lie in the development of its overseas Seaway shipping, particularly in general cargo traffic, which produces greater income for the area than do bulk commodities. The two most important components have been government relief cargo and machinery; both commodities are produced in large quantities in Milwaukee and in Wisconsin. In the long run, the surest growth would undoubtedly come from increased exports of machinery, of which the port now handles very little, compared to its possibilities. A few Wisconsin firms accounted for a great share of the port's total export tonnage in this category, and intensive work to attract these shippers might yield great dividends. But while cargo ships will go where the cargo is (in the long run), it will be far easier to attract the cargo if regular shipping services are assured, and having shipments of government cargoes available is probably the most certain way of obtaining that regular service.

A special subcommittee of the U.S. Senate Committee on Commerce has studied this problem and has made several recommendations which this study supports.[2] The four major recommendations of the Senate subcommittee are as follows: (1) Continued development of Great Lakes–Seaway facilities, including a lengthening of the Seaway shipping season and the deepening of all major harbors and channels to the 27-foot Seaway capacity. The Port of Milwaukee is currently undergoing a major dredging operation and will have full Seaway capacity during the 1967 shipping season. (2) The promotion of the use of the Great Lakes by U.S.-flag ships through a revamping of the cargo preference laws. A Defense Department shipment may not leave a port in a foreign-flag ship if there is a U.S.-flag ship available at any port in the same administrative district. As long as the cargo preference laws group the Great Lakes and North Atlantic into a single administrative jurisdiction, sailings of U.S.-flag ships to the Great Lakes will be deterred and the uneconomic practice of transporting cargoes overland from the Midwest to the At-

---

2. U.S. Senate, *Great Lakes–St. Lawrence Seaway Transportation*, Report of a Special Subcommittee of the Committee on Commerce.

lantic coast will be continued. (3) A revamping of Section 22 of the Interstate Commerce Act so as to end railroad discrimination against lake ports. Under Section 22, the railroads are currently permitted to grant special rates for government shipments. This enables them to openly and legally discriminate against lake ports by offering lower rates from the Midwest to Atlantic ports than from the Midwest to Great Lakes ports — a practice that may be economically beneficial to certain railroad corporations, but certainly detrimental to the economy of the entire Great Lakes area. (4) An expansion of the information and promotion program of the Seaway Development Corporation. These promotional functions of the Seaway Corporation should be encouraged by the Department of Commerce and be included as part of the Seaway Corporation's annual budget, so that the funds expended come from tolls alone and not from appropriated moneys. The study also suggested that the Seaway amortization period be extended from fifty to one hundred years and that the interest rate be established at 2 per cent.

The Milwaukee Board of Harbor Commissioners and its staff recognize that the port's best growth prospect appears to lie in the development of its overseas Seaway shipping. They have sought ways to assure a reasonable steady flow of government cargo, but the problem has certainly not been solved,[3] and there is no guarantee that the Senate subcommittee's recommendations will be adopted. The only other approach that appears to be promising would be an intensive educational and promotional campaign in Europe and elsewhere (preferably in concert with other Great Lakes ports that find themselves in a similar situation), aimed at the buyers who choose their own shipping routes; the Port of Milwaukee has already made an independent start on this.

The Port of Milwaukee's commerce has received several setbacks more or less simultaneously (the relief cargo "rate war," the decline in petroleum products shipments, and the depletion of scrap iron and steel shipments), but the problem appears to have found a solution in the continued development of overseas commerce. In the long run, it seems quite obvious that the port's growth prospects depend on its ability to utilize the St. Lawrence Seaway.

3. The importance of relief cargo as a base stands out most clearly in connection with Milwaukee's exports to Asia and Africa; for nearly every country that Milwaukee traded with, government relief cargo provided most of the tonnage, and machinery exports provided the remainder. The growing industrialization of these areas should offer expanding markets for Milwaukee manufacturers and opportunity for the port, if it can establish the necessary frequency of service.

APPENDIXES
SELECTED REFERENCES
INDEX

APPENDIX A

PORT OF MILWAUKEE,
IMPORTS BY ORIGIN AND COMMODITY, 1963

Country	No.	Commodity*	Dollars	Total	Short tons	Total
CANADA	102	Barley and Rye	6,323,490		118,097	
	450	Standard Newsprint Pap	6,941,703		55,380	
	457	Paper Related Prod Nec†	3,807		28	
	553	Salt	220,492		35,905	
	601	Pig Iron	339,397		6,231	
	602	Iron and Steel Scrap	33,993		753	
	609	Rolled & Fin Steel Mill Prod	2,119,327		18,588	
	796	Vehicles and Parts Nec	1,173		‡	
				15,983,382		234,982
SWEDEN	018	Meat & Prod Nec	49,270		93	
	047	Fish & Prod Nec	6,747		16	
	060	Hides and Skins Raw	30,970		72	
	065	Leather	102			
	138	Prepared Fruits	486		2	
	185	Molasses Ed & Sugar Prod	4,821		9	
	190	Dis Spirits Liq & Wines	140			
	205	Rubber Tires Tubes	2,217		3	
	320	Cotton Manufactures	1,183			
	350	Wood Semi & Mfrs.	2,400			
	381	Man-Made Fibers and Mfrs	257			
	421	Wood Mfrs Nec	3,004		2	
	441	Wood Pulp	173,954		2,011	
	457	Paper Related Prod Nec	24,677		182	
	530	Glass & Glass Products	2,358		3	
	547	Clay Prods Nec	810		1	
	606	Tools & Basic Hardware	40,974		16	
	609	Rolled & Fin Steel Mill Prod	22,164		44	
	612	Metal Mfrs & Parts Nec	3,030		1	
	700	Elect Mach & Appar	1,868		3	
	730	Machine Tools & Parts	22,615		17	
	740	Text Sew & Shoe Mach & Part	32,145		9	
	745	Mach and Parts Nec	350			
	783	Merchant Vessels & Parts	1,650		1	
	790	Aircraft & Parts	880			
	796	Vehicles & Parts Nec	756		1	

157

APPENDIX A (*continued*)

Country	No.	Commodity*	Dollars	Total	Short tons	Total
	900	Commodities Nec	1,890		15	
	920	U.S. Articles Returned	7,209		5	
				438,927		2,502
NORWAY	037	Cheese	1,963		3	
	047	Fish & Prod Nec	363,080		556	
	049	Shellfish and Prod	9,318		6	
	060	Hides and Skins Raw	1,635		3	
	095	Animal Prod Ined Nec	42,562		300	
	109	Flour & Grain Pres Nec	7,335		25	
	130	Fruits Fr or Fzn	1,493		5	
	138	Prepared Fruits	555		1	
	207	Rubber Mfrs Nec	1,692		1	
	297	Veg Prod Ined Nec	4,822		90	
	350	Wool Semi & Mfrs	4,267			
	421	Wood Mfrs Nec	2,439		1	
	457	Paper Related Prod Nec	2,683		19	
	526	Stone & Mfrs Nec	3,286		46	
	547	Clay Products Nec	6,569		7	
	555	Nonmet Min & Mfrs Nec	25,031		368	
	603	Iron-Steel Semi-Fin Prod	209,129		2,261	
	607	House, Kitch, & Hosp Utensils	1,742		2	
	612	Metal Mfrs Nec	11,995		2	
	632	Copper-Base Alloy Semifab	16,121		34	
	700	Elec Mach & Appar	2,553		2	
	730	Machine Tools & Parts	7,022		1	
	783	Merchant Vessels and Parts	7,853		4	
	796	Vehicles and Parts Nec	1,603		1	
	829	Industrial Chemicals	9,682		25	
	900	Commodities Nec	6,409		1	
	920	U.S. Articles Returned	1,005			
				753,844		3,767
DENMARK	018	Meat & Prod Nec	27,157		45	
	037	Cheese	6,207		8	
	047	Fish & Prod Nec	8,427		30	
	049	Shellfish & Prod	1,821			
	060	Hides and Skins Raw	3,451		8	
	065	Leather and Mfrs	2,852		1	
	075	Furs and Mfrs	238			
	095	Animal Prod Ined Nec	120,350		25	
	190	Dis Spirits Liq & Wine	54,717		116	
	207	Rubber Mfrs Nec	14,000		15	
	260	Seeds Except Oilseeds	117,274		223	

APPENDIX A (*continued*)

Country	No.	Commodity*	Dollars	Total	Short tons	Total
	320	Cotton Manufactures	2,009			
	335	Veg Fiber Semi & Mfrs Nec	966,794		3,157	
	350	Wool Semi & Mfrs	9,550		2	
	413	Lumber & Shingles	2,971		27	
	421	Wood Mfrs Nec	21,231		13	
	457	Paper Related Prod Nec	916			
	530	Glass and Glass Products	158			
	547	Clay Prod Nec	456			
	607	House, Kitch, & Hosp Utensils	1,753		1	
	612	Metal Mfrs & Parts Nec	2,477		2	
	700	Elect Mach & Appar	18,633		30	
	740	Text Sew & Shoe Mach & Parts	2,624		1	
	745	Mach and Parts Nec	1,143		1	
	770	Agric Mach and Parts	25,804		8	
	829	Industrial Chemicals	6,480		3	
	860	Misc Chemical Prod	447		1	
	900	Commodities Nec	16,386		9	
	920	U.S. Articles Ret	3,040			
				1,439,366		3,729
UNITED KINGDOM	047	Fish and Products Nec	547		3	
	060	Hides and Skins Raw	5,950		6	
	065	Leather and Mfrs	115,222		34	
	075	Furs and Mfrs	118			
	109	Flour & Grain Prep Nec	294			
	136	Fruit Juices	11,691		32	
	138	Prepared Fruits	33,263		62	
	167	Coc Choc Cof & Tea Nec	910		3	
	185	Molasses Ed & Sugar Prod	7,995		20	
	190	Dis Spirits Liq & Wines	1,190,365		1,495	
	203	Rubber Scrap	1,662		8	
	260	Seeds Except Oilseeds	231			
	285	Tobacco Manufactured	143			
	320	Cotton Manufactures	1,119			
	335	Veg Fiber Semi & Mfrs Nec	203,122		683	
	350	Wool Semi & Mfrs	11,905		1	
	381	Man-Made Fibers & Mfrs	441			
	390	Textile Prod Nec	34,387		80	
	421	Wood Mfrs Nec	1,694		1	
	457	Paper Related Prod Nec	24,232		32	
	523	Building Cement	102			
	530	Glass & Glass Products	10,887		50	
	543	Brick & Tile	11,501		49	

APPENDIX A (*continued*)

Country	No.	Commodity*	Dollars	Total	Short tons	Total
	547	Clay Products Nec	9,795		6	
	555	Nonmet Min & Mfrs Nec	3,555		14	
	606	Tools & Basic Hardware	967			
	607	House, Kitch, & Hosp Utensils	2,623		1	
	608	Iron and Steel Pipe	85,457		622	
	609	Rolled & Fin Steel Mill Prod	88,957		328	
	612	Metal Mfrs & Parts Nec	42,079		30	
	614	Chrome	19,034		13	
	618	Alum Metal Crude	1,412		2	
	624	Copper Semi Fab Forms	2,087		2	
	652	Nickel Ore Conc Scrap	227,657		36	
	690	Precious Metals Mfrs	1,800		1	
	700	Elec Mach & Appar	57,376		40	
	710	Engines Turb Parts Nec	39,965		30	
	730	Machine Tools and Parts	513,064		202	
	745	Mach and Parts Nec	68,367		38	
	770	Agric Mach and Parts	419,452		514	
	780	Auto Truck & Bus Exc Parts	13,152		13	
	782	Auto Truck and Bus Parts	227,068		154	
	783	Merchant Vessels & Parts	18,952		9	
	796	Vehicles and Parts Nec	75,818		50	
	805	Coal-Tar Products	2,520		1	
	810	Medicinal & Pharm Prep	45,971		10	
	829	Industrial Chemicals	7,846		22	
	848	Pigments Paints & Varnish	2,594		10	
	860	Misc Chemical Prod	97,361		182	
	900	Commodities Nec	39,503		49	
	920	U.S. Articles Returned	30,663		12	
				3,812,876		4,950
IRELAND	109	Flour & Grain Prep Nec	3,333		19	
	190	Dis Spirits Liq & Wines	9,264		10	
	297	Veg Prod Ined Nec	17,564		36	
	547	Clay Prod Nec	950			
				31,111		66
NETHERLANDS	018	Meat & Prod Nec	46,254		40	
	047	Fish & Prod Nec	16,774		65	
	060	Hides and Skins Raw	584,614		1,183	
	065	Leather & Mfrs	6,079		3	
	095	Animal Prod Ined Nec	78,071		149	
	125	Veg & Prep Nec	73,806		428	
	136	Fruit Juices	1,057		1	
	167	Coc Choc Cof & Tea Nec	16,425		40	
	170	Spices	2,998		9	

APPENDIX A (*continued*)

Country	No.	Commodity*	Dollars	Total	Short tons	Total
	185	Molasses Ed & Sugar Prod	12,242		10	
	190	Dis Spirits Liq & Wines	12,421		51	
	207	Rubber Mfrs Nec	1,391		3	
	236	Oil Seeds Nec	3,415		17	
	250	Veg Dyeing Tanning Mat	1,454		10	
	260	Seeds Except Oilseeds	366,404		666	
	285	Tobacco Manufactured	46,814		28	
	297	Veg Prod Ined Nec	3,662		3	
	320	Cotton Manufactures	326			
	335	Veg Fiber Semi & Mfrs Nec	485,729		1,299	
	390	Textile Prod Nec	28,343		75	
	421	Wood Mfrs Nec	368			
	457	Paper Related Prod Nec	37,718		104	
	547	Clay Products Nec	481			
	609	Rolled & Fin Steel Mill Prod	6,470		62	
	700	Elect Mach & Appar	6,941		2	
	745	Mach and Parts Nec	12,617		7	
	770	Agric Mach and Parts	36,851		33	
	796	Vehicles and Parts Nec	2,323		3	
	829	Industrial Chemicals	6,762		41	
	900	Commodities Nec	2,044		1	
	920	U.S. Articles Returned	18,127		33	
				1,918,981		4,363
BELGIUM	205	Rubber Tires & Tubes	3,097		3	
	335	Veg Fiber Semi & Mfrs Nec	207,383		622	
	445	Paper Base Stocks Nec	3,720		5	
	526	Stone & Mfrs Nec	3,876		44	
	530	Glass & Glass Products	42,407		287	
	555	Nonmet Min & Mfrs Nec	5,559		24	
	603	Iron-Steel Semi Fin Prod	95,544		1,038	
	606	Tools & Basic Hardware	15,506		97	
	607	House, Kitch & Hosp Utensils	253			
	608	Iron & Steel Pipe	5,552		40	
	609	Rolled & Fin Steel Mill Prod	590,490		3,837	
	612	Metal Mfrs and Parts Nec	11,154		28	
	618	Alum Metal Crude	20,092		40	
	624	Copper Semifab Forms	22,985		37	
	642	Lead & Lead-Base Alloys	2,003		11	
	730	Machine Tools and Parts	96,888		9	
	780	Auto Truck & Bus Exc Parts	2,000		2	
	796	Vehicles & Parts Nec	455		1	
	829	Industrial Chemicals	7,574		24	
	920	U.S. Articles Returned	6,550		31	
				1,143,088		6,179

APPENDIX A (*continued*)

Country	No.	Commodity*	Dollars	Total	Short tons	Total
FRANCE	037	Cheese	20,025		26	
	060	Hides and Skins Raw	365,061		566	
	065	Leather and Mfrs	25,497		8	
	095	Animal Prod Ined Nec	40,191		110	
	125	Veg and Prep Nec	495		1	
	136	Fruit Juices	2,951		14	
	138	Prepared Fruits	17,982		38	
	190	Dis Spirits Liq & Wines	351,047		501	
	207	Rubber Mfrs Nec	3,880		3	
	250	Veg Dyeing Tanning Mat	5,374		39	
	260	Seeds Except Oilseeds	18,100		22	
	320	Cotton Manufactures	14,742		3	
	350	Wool Semi & Mfrs	5,215		1	
	381	Man-Made Fibers & Mfrs	2,255			
	390	Textile Prod Nec	709			
	408	Wood Unmfrd Nec	42,600		35	
	421	Wood Mfrs Nec	1,313			
	530	Glass & Glass Products	11,390		60	
	547	Clay Products Nec	855			
	555	Nonmetal Min & Mfrs Nec	3,329		76	
	607	House, Kitchen, Hosp Utensils	7,604		11	
	608	Iron and Steel Pipe	10,641		82	
	609	Rolled & Fin Steel Mill Prod	35,389		501	
	612	Metal Mfrs & Parts Nec	700			
	618	Alum Metal Crude	80,800		199	
	624	Copper Semi-Fab Forms	12,329		12	
	632	Copper-Base Alloy Semi	6,749		12	
	700	Elec Mach & Appar	22,422		6	
	710	Engines Turb Parts Nec	8,425		4	
	730	Machine Tools & Parts	37,290		12	
	770	Agric Mach & Parts	30,482		11	
	780	Auto Truck & Bus Exc Parts	26,847		30	
	782	Auto Truck & Bus Parts	7,546		7	
	796	Vehicles & Parts Nec	26,252		14	
	829	Industrial Chemicals	1,028		5	
	900	Commodities Nec	725,122		48	
	920	U.S. Articles Returned	60,533		92	
				2,033,170		2,549
WEST GERMANY	037	Cheese	6,670		12	
	060	Hides and Skins Raw	252,415		451	
	065	Leather and Mfrs	8,157		2	
	075	Furs & Mfrs	144			
	095	Animal Prod Ined Nec	50,337		215	

APPENDIX A (*continued*)

Country	No.	Commodity*	Dollars	Total	Short tons	Total
	136	Fruit Juices	968		4	
	170	Spices	281			
	185	Molasses Ed & Sugar Prod	495		1	
	190	Dis Spirits Liq & Wines	250,247		1,299	
	195	Beverages Sirups Nec	413		2	
	205	Rubber Tires Tubes	4,117		4	
	207	Rubber Mfrs Nec	4,538		5	
	260	Seeds Except Oilseeds	168		1	
	335	Veg Fiber Semi & Mfrs Nec	19,350		60	
	350	Wool Semi & Mfrs	5,370		1	
	381	Man-made Fibers & Mfrs	2,784		1	
	421	Wood Mfrs Nec	35,804		33	
	457	Paper Related Prod Nec	16,749		16	
	530	Glass & Glass Products	71,694		142	
	543	Brick & Tile	379		6	
	547	Clay Products Nec	8,568		8	
	555	Nonmet Min & Mfrs Nec	1,346			
	603	Iron-Steel Semifin Prod	24,945		220	
	605	Iron-Steel Cast & Forging	1,563		1	
	606	Tools & Basic Hardware	4,558		1	
	607	House, Kitch, Hosp Utensils	1,360		1	
	608	Iron and Steel Pipe	3,489		23	
	609	Rolled & Fin Steel Mill Prod	140,000		1,333	
	612	Metal Mfrs & Parts Nec	231,831		289	
	618	Alum Metal Crude	29,263		55	
	624	Copper Semifab Forms	101,745		100	
	632	Copper-Base Alloy Semi	75,568		67	
	652	Nickel Ore Conc Scrap	6,339		3	
	690	Precious Metals Mfrs	2,893		1	
	700	Elect Mach & Appar	214,862		102	
	710	Engines Turb Parts Nec	6,918		20	
	730	Machine Tools and Parts	269,872		122	
	740	Text Sew & Shoe Mach & Part	20,032		7	
	745	Mach and Parts Nec	381,273		165	
	770	Agric Mach and Parts	43,100		61	
	780	Auto Truck & Bus Exc Parts	2,777		1	
	782	Auto Truck and Bus Parts	435			
	783	Merchant Vessels & Parts	1,882			
	786	Railway Locomotive & Parts	800		8	
	796	Vehicles and Parts Nec	9,978		11	
	805	Coal-Tar Products	1,765		2	
	829	Industrial Chemicals	41,383		166	
	859	Fertilizer & Material Nec	5,396		202	
	860	Misc Chemical Prod	1,466		2	

APPENDIX A (*continued*)

Country	No.	Commodity*	Dollars	Total	Short tons	Total
	900	Commodities Nec	165,627		85	
	920	U.S. Articles Returned	133,665		97	
				2,665,787		5,404
EAST GERMANY	848	Pigments Paints & Varnish	13,003	13,003	46	46
AUSTRIA	065	Leather and Mfrs	55,245		25	
	075	Furs and Mfrs	174			
	190	Dis Spirits Liq & Wines	337			
	320	Cotton Mfrs	697			
	350	Wool Semi & Mfrs	2,431			
	421	Wood Mfrs Nec	604		10	
	530	Glass & Glass Products	327			
	547	Clay Prod Nec	152			
	609	Rolled & Fin Steel Mill Prod	307			
	612	Metal Mfrs & Parts Nec	21,920		19	
	700	Elect Mach & Appar	7,103		1	
	730	Machine Tools and Parts	10,521		7	
	900	Commodities Nec	1,163			
				100,981		62
CZECHO-SLOVAKIA	190	Dis Spirits Liq & Wines	936	936	3	3
HUNGARY	190	Dis Spirits Liq & Wines	695	695	2	2
SWITZERLAND	060	Hides and Skins Raw	12,746		17	
	065	Leather and Mfrs	32,061		8	
	095	Animal Prod Ined Nec	116,137		16	
	136	Fruit Juices	1,781		8	
	167	Coc Choc Cof & Tea Nec	352			
	185	Molasses Ed & Sugar Prod	548		1	
	190	Dis Spirits Liq & Wines	2,395		5	
	207	Rubber Mfrs Nec	2,164		1	
	320	Cotton Manufactures	9,971		1	
	350	Wool Semi & Mfrs	3,789			
	421	Wool Mfrs Nec	628			
	457	Paper Related Prod Nec	5,534		8	
	530	Glass & Glass Products	269			
	555	Nonmet Min & Mfrs Nec	8,266		5	
	607	House, Kitch & Hosp Utensils	323			
	608	Iron & Steel Pipe	5,589		35	
	612	Metal Mfrs & Parts Nec	8,759		8	

APPENDIX A (*continued*)

Country	No.	Commodity*	Dollars	Total	Short tons	Total
	624	Copper Semi-Fab Forms	8,595		6	
	632	Copper-Base Alloy Semi	6,787		13	
	700	Elect Mach & Appar	653		1	
	730	Machine Tools & Parts	43,562		4	
	740	Text Sew & Shoe Mach & Part	6,438		2	
	745	Mach and Parts Nec	74,714		36	
	805	Coal-Tar Products	6,534			
	829	Industrial Chemicals	415			
	900	Commodities Nec	24,285		3	
				383,295		180
FINLAND	037	Cheese	910		1	
	060	Hides & Skins Raw	132			
	381	Man-Made Fibers & Mfrs	2,594		2	
	457	Paper Related Prod Nec	17,036		197	
	900	Commodities Nec	12,925			
				33,597		202
POLAND	190	Dis Spirits Liq & Wines	758		3	
	260	Seeds Except Oilseeds	18,040		44	
	421	Wood Mfrs Nec	1,502			
	900	Commodities Nec	250		1	
				20,550		48
SPAIN	065	Leather & Mfrs	4,730			
	138	Prepared Fruits	81,806		266	
	190	Dis Spirits Liq & Wines	20,390		36	
	207	Rubber Mfrs Nec	108			
	350	Wool Semi & Mfrs	2,779		1	
	390	Textile Prod Nec	997		1	
	421	Wood Mfrs Nec	5,824		1	
	526	Stone & Mfrs Nec	2,942		57	
	547	Clay Products Nec	719		2	
	607	House, Kitch, Hosp Utensils	234			
	612	Metal Mfrs & Parts Nec	146			
	618	Alum Metal Crude	18,435		35	
	900	Commodities Nec	2,530			
				143,357		401
PORTUGAL	047	Fish & Prod Nec	2,954		4	
	190	Dis Spirits Liq & Wines	24,609		63	
	335	Veg Fiber Semi & Mfrs Nec	167,071		519	
	350	Wool Semi & Mfrs	353			
	526	Stone & Mfrs Nec	5,612		155	
	547	Clay Products Nec	1,140		8	
				201,739		750

APPENDIX A (*continued*)

Country	No.	Commodity*	Dollars	Total	Short tons	Total
ITALY	037	Cheese	59,686		58	
	060	Hides and Skins Raw	222,750		290	
	065	Leather and Mfrs	26,844		5	
	095	Animal Prod Ined Nec	987			
	109	Flour & Grain Prep Nec	1,716		7	
	138	Prepared Fruits	24,882		146	
	140	Nuts & Preparations	1,700		1	
	190	Dis Spirits Liq & Wines	558,823		1,108	
	207	Rubber Mfrs, Nec	1,187			
	250	Veg Dyeing Tanning Mat	4,145		8	
	320	Cotton Manufactures	3,948		1	
	335	Veg Fiber Semi & Mfrs Nec	1,059			
	350	Wool Semi & Mfrs	37,783		5	
	381	Man-made Fibers & Mfrs	1,767			
	390	Textile Prod Nec	3,027			
	421	Wood Mfrs Nec	23,685		7	
	457	Paper Related Prod Nec	167			
	526	Stone & Mfrs Nec	135,436		1,264	
	530	Glass & Glass Products	9,306		12	
	543	Brick and Tile	4,837		48	
	547	Clay Products	17,513		15	
	554	Sands Grav Crushed Rock	493		34	
	555	Nonmet Min & Mfrs Nec	7,970		33	
	607	House, Kitch, Hospt Utensils	2,664		1	
	612	Metal Mfrs & Parts Nec	78,125		91	
	618	Alum Metal Crude	22,854		42	
	690	Precious Metals Mfrs	135			
	700	Elect Mach & Appar	29,448		7	
	710	Engines Turb Parts Nec	2,500			
	796	Vehicles and Parts Nec	354,154		165	
	860	Misc Chemical Prod	463		1	
	900	Commodities Nec	92,629		124	
	920	U.S. Articles Returned	12,747		4	
				1,745,430		3,481
YUGOSLAVIA	190	Dis Spirits Liq & Wines	2,899		11	
	421	Wood Semi & Mfrs	5,950		17	
	526	Stone & Mfrs Nec	957		21	
	600	Iron Ore & Conc	262		61	
	642	Lead & Lead-Base Alloys	13,964		82	
				24,032		193
GREECE	190	Dis Spirits Liq & Wines	13,555		16	
	350	Wool Semi & Mfrs	1,554			
	547	Clay Products Nec	1,243		7	
				16,352		23

APPENDIX A (*continued*)

Country	No.	Commodity*	Dollars	Total	Short tons	Total
ISRAEL	190	Dis Spirits Liq & Wines	3,749		14	
	900	Commodities Nec	4,000			
				7,749		14
SAUDI ARABIA	920	U.S. Articles Returned	738			
				738		
INDIA	335	Veg Fiber Semi & Mfrs Nec	1,026		17	
	421	Wood Mfrs Nec	127			
	607	House Kitch Hosp Utensils	517			
				1,670		18
BURMA	413	Lumber & Shingles	643		3	
				643		3
THAILAND	125	Veg & Prep Nec	7,611		98	
	200	Rubber Crude Allied Gum	513,405		1,092	
	326	Sisal & Jute Unmanfd	70,780		641	
				591,796		1,832
CAMBODIA	200	Rubber Crude Allied Gum	5,130		11	
				5,130		11
FEDERATION OF MALAYA	138	Prepared Fruits	45,621		252	
	200	Rubber, Crude Allied Gum	292,484		578	
	665	Tin Metal Crude	127,159		66	
				465,264		896
SINGAPORE	300	Cotton Unmanufactured	15,317		11	
				15,317		11
INDONESIA	200	Rubber Crude Allied Gum	2,345		6	
				2,345		6
PHILIPPINE REPUBLIC	140	Nuts and Preparations	55,208		250	
	413	Lumber and Shingles	20,606		164	
	416	Wood Containers Plywood	21,744		219	
				97,558		633
SOUTH KOREAN REPUBLIC	920	U.S. Articles Returned	2,456		10	
				2,456		10

APPENDIX A (continued)

Country	No.	Commodity*	Dollars	Total	Short tons	Total
HONG KONG	207	Rubber Mfrs Nec	1,784		2	
	310	Cotton Semi-manufactured	9,701		76	
	390	Textile Prod Nec	86,659		87	
	421	Wood Mfrs Nec	3,707		2	
	606	Tools & Basic Hardware	1,023		1	
	700	Elec Mach & Appar	2,069		2	
	796	Vehicles and Parts Nec	12,268		11	
				117,211		181
TAIWAN	125	Veg & Prep Nec	413,898		449	
	138	Prepared Fruits	19,128		98	
	920	U.S. Articles Returned	165,780		708	
				598,806		1,254
JAPAN	047	Fish & Prod Nec	93,692		167	
	049	Shellfish and Prod	56,561		65	
	065	Leather & Mfrs	481			
	095	Animal Prod Ined Nec	53,175		331	
	138	Prepared Fruits	58,886		181	
	190	Dis Spirits Liq & Wine	4,629		13	
	205	Rubber Tires & Tubes	20,103		24	
	207	Rubber Mfrs Nec	2,318		2	
	320	Cotton Manufactures	24,003		10	
	326	Sisal & Jute Unmfd	3,752		29	
	350	Wool Semi & Mfrs	768		2	
	390	Textile Prod Nec	1,245			
	413	Lumber and Shingles	26,862		72	
	416	Wood Containers Plywood	3,581		20	
	421	Wood Mfrs Nec	42,709		67	
	530	Glass & Glass Products	797		1	
	543	Brick and Tile	35,203		174	
	547	Clay Products Nec	9,503		20	
	555	Nonmet Min & Mfrs Nec	27,493		84	
	603	Iron & Steel Semi-Fin Prod	54,733		604	
	606	Tools & Basic Hardware	58,411		378	
	608	Iron & Steel Pipe	84,264		80	
	609	Rolled & Fin Steel Mill Prod	112,996		351	
	612	Metal Mfrs & Parts Nec	22,954		86	
	624	Copper Semi-Fab Forms	563		1	
	632	Copper Base Alloy Semi	22,480		30	
	700	Elect Mach & Appar	10,888		3	
	730	Machine Tools & Parts	71,488		75	
	745	Mach and Parts Nec	31,414		35	
	770	Agricul Mach & Parts	610		1	
	796	Vehicles and Parts Nec	10,085		10	

APPENDIX A (*continued*)

Country	No.	Commodity*	Dollars	Total	Short tons	Total
	900	Commodities Nec	15,032		13	
	920	U.S. Articles Returned	16,939		145	
				978,618		3,075
NEW ZEALAND	095	Animal Prod Ined Nec	86,688		5	
				86,688		5
AUSTRALIA	095	Animal Prod Ined Nec	25,000		2	
	682	Other Non-Ferrous Ores	47,694		665	
				72,694		668
ALGERIA	190	Dis Spirits Liq & Wines	368		1	
				368		1
FRENCH EQUATORIAL AFRICA	220	Drugs Crude	20,281		2	
				20,281		2
NIGERIA	355	Veg Fibers Semi & Mfr Nec	1,329		4	
				1,329		4
MADEIRA	190	Dis Spirits Liq & Wine	685		2	
				685		2
BELGIAN CONGO	200	Rubber Crude & Allied Gum	24,630		50	
				24,630		50
REPUBLIC SOUTH AFRICA	900	Commodities Nec	441			
				441		
GRAND TOTAL				35,996,916		282,558

Source: Chicago Association of Commerce and Industry, Research and Statistics Division, *U.S. Great Lakes Ports Monthly Statistics for Overseas and Canadian Waterborne Traffic*, 1963, Monthly Data. Place names are given as in source.

Figures have been rounded.

*Commodities are classified according to schedule T. Wording of description of commodities differs slightly from description in Tables 4-3 and 5-5 because of the difference in source.

†Not elsewhere classified.

‡Tonnage figures have been omitted where there was less than one ton.

APPENDIX B

PORT OF MILWAUKEE,
EXPORTS BY DESTINATION AND COMMODITY, 1963

Country	No.	Commodity*	Dollars	Total	Short tons	Total
CANADA	100	Corn	6,320,705		142,473	
	103	Wheat	542,987		7,507	
	109	Flour & Grain Prep Nec†	236,264		6,218	
				7,099,956		156,198
EL SALVADOR	035	Dried Milk	46,810		276	
	107	Wheat Flour Semolina	4,529		77	
				51,339		353
HONDURAS	035	Dried Milk	45,716		254	
				45,716		254
JAMAICA	035	Dried Milk	85,226		501	
	109	Flour & Grain Prep Nec	88,389		998	
	127	Veg & Prep Nec	93,875		148	
	742	Other Indus Mach & Parts	566,596		590	
				834,086		2,238
DOMINICAN REPUBLIC	035	Dried Milk	77,753		433	
	109	Flour & Grain Prep Nec	72,120		791	
	127	Veg & Prep Nec	236,265		306	
	190	Dis Spirits Liq & Wine	3,886		28	
	742	Other Indus Mach & Parts	8,017		1	
				398,041		1,559
HAITI	035	Dried Milk	37,362		222	
	109	Flour & Grain Prep Nec	12,492		168	
	127	Veg & Prep Nec	21,189		42	
				71,043		432
TRINIDAD	901	Gen Misc Commodity Nec	10,030		17	
				10,030		17
GREATER ANTILLES	123	Veg & Prep Canned	1,260		5	
				1,260		5

APPENDIX B (*continued*)

Country	No.	Commodity*	Dollars	Total	Short tons	Total
FRENCH WEST INDIES	787	Auto Truck & Access	2,794	2,794	2	2
COLOMBIA	107	Wheat Flour Semolina	29,292		425	
	109	Flour & Grain Prep Nec	51,538		723	
	127	Veg & Prep Nec	438,431		737	
	787	Auto Truck & Access	3,690	522,951	4	1,889
VENEZUELA	035	Dried Milk	55,087		327	
	109	Flour & Grain Prep Nec	77,706		998	
	611	Metal Manufactures Nec	26,201		33	
	701	Elec Mach & App	3,305		3	
	742	Other Indus Mach & Part	329,350	491,649	89	1,450
BRAZIL	035	Dried Milk	572,299		3,904	
	109	Flour & Grain Prep Nec	74,192		1,007	
	127	Veg & Prep Nec	192,730		399	
	606	Tools & Basic Hardware	525		‡	
	731	Machine Tools	73,500	913,246	117	5,427
URUGUAY	035	Dried Milk	8,060	8,060	48	48
ARGENTINA	611	Metal Manufactures Nec	41,884		62	
	722	Construct & Rel Mach	800			
	742	Other Indus Mach & Part	64,121		45	
	770	Agric Mach & Parts	6,684		6	
	787	Auto Truck & Access	172,542	286,031	283	395
SWEDEN	013	Canned Meat	30,597		29	
	060	Hides & Skins Raw	27,729		97	
	065	Leather and Mfrs	9,695		12	
	100	Corn	2,470		12	
	109	Flour & Grain Prep Nec	41,171		509	
	123	Veg & Prep Canned	23,820		89	
	127	Veg & Prep Nec	18,735		74	
	297	Veg Prod Ined Nec	3,608		22	
	540	Clays and Earths	20,335		799	
	555	Nonmet Min Nec	76,633		916	
	606	Tools & Basic Hardware	4,541			
	611	Metal Manufactures Nec	7,138		2	

APPENDIX B (*continued*)

Country	No.	Commodity*	Dollars	Total	Short tons	Total
	622	Refined Copper Crude	134,646		224	
	701	Elec Mach & Apparatus	60,265		76	
	710	Engines Turb & Parts Nec	855,171		536	
	722	Construct & Rel Mach	317,263		250	
	731	Machine Tools	178,833		38	
	742	Other Indus Mach & Part	99,646		23	
	770	Agric Mach & Parts	62,761		63	
	785	Merchant Vessels	7,372		3	
	787	Auto Truck & Access	210,674		118	
	837	Syn Resins Ex Fin Form	15,634		67	
	844	Chemical Spec Nec	5,460		9	
	901	Gen Misc Commodity Nec	14,400		6	
				2,228,597		3,976
NORWAY	017	Meat & Prod Nec	1,783		5	
	060	Hides & Skins Raw	18,443		83	
	109	Flour & Grain Prep Nec	635		1	
	123	Veg & Prep Canned	1,055		4	
	606	Tools & Basic Hardware	559			
	607	House, Kitch, Hosp Utensils	2,295		1	
	611	Metal Manufactures Nec	8,738		5	
	701	Elec Mach & Appar	688			
	710	Engines Turb & Parts Nec	299,218		186	
	722	Construct & Rel Mach	593,523		396	
	742	Other Indus Mach & Parts	232,305		33	
	770	Agric Mach & Parts	28,582		15	
	781	Auto Trucks Exc Parts	194,954		146	
	787	Auto Truck & Access	2,182		1	
	844	Chemical Spec Nec	1,288		6	
	901	Gen Misc Commodity Nec	1,088			
				1,387,336		882
DENMARK	017	Meat & Prod Nec	1,312		3	
	035	Dried Milk	13,110		110	
	123	Veg & Prep Canned	616		3	
	127	Veg & Prep Nec	800		2	
	185	Molasses Edib & Sugar Prod	1,879		6	
	320	Cotton Manufactures	567			
	475	Paper Related Prod Nec	20,938		116	
	540	Clays & Earths	4,124		151	
	555	Nonmet Min Nec	588		5	
	606	Tools & Basic Hdwe	3,263		6	
	710	Engines Turb & Parts Nec	169,871		114	
	722	Construct & Rel Mach	1,910		1	
	742	Other Indus Mach & Part	45,172		13	

APPENDIX B (*continued*)

Country	No.	Commodity*	Dollars	Total	Short tons	Total
	770	Agric Mach & Parts	14,386		10	
	787	Auto Truck & Access	10,132		7	
	837	Syn Resins Ex Fin Form	3,744		18	
	844	Chemical Spec Nec	560		1	
				292,972		567
UNITED KINGDOM	010	Meat Fresh or Fzn	14,300		32	
	017	Meat & Prod Nec	25,350		22	
	020	Animal Oils & Fats Edib	313,312		1,579	
	060	Hides and Skins Raw	2,592		35	
	065	Leather and Mfrs	16,977		120	
	100	Corn	218,736		4,990	
	109	Flour & Grain Prep Nec	660		1	
	123	Veg & Prep Canned	36,636		177	
	127	Veg & Prep Nec	44,682		139	
	150	Veget Oils Fats Edible	3,255		11	
	207	Rubber Manufactures Nec	1,351			
	390	Textile Prod Nec	3,510		4	
	416	Wood Contain Plywood	48,277		218	
	421	Wood Manufactures Nec	8,391		4	
	475	Paper Related Prod Nec	35,252		111	
	517	Lub Oils & Greases	128			
	530	Glass & Glass Products	1,862		2	
	540	Clays & Earths	1,210		30	
	555	Nonmet Min Nec	50,993		157	
	606	Tools & Basic Hardware	13,689		5	
	609	Roll & Fin Steel Mill Prod	7,333		23	
	611	Metal Manufactures Nec	244,158		474	
	622	Refined Copper Crude	201,464		336	
	632	Copper-Base Alloy Semi	6,664		7	
	662	Tin Ore Conc Scrap	82,296		178	
	701	Elec Mach & App	586,763		232	
	710	Engines Turb & Parts Nec	511,979		290	
	722	Construct & Rel Mach	166,874		113	
	731	Machine Tools	1,182,582		514	
	742	Other Indus Mach & Part	718,999		282	
	770	Agric Mach & Parts	177,997		148	
	781	Auto Trucks Exc Parts	46,747		32	
	787	Auto Truck & Access	209,671		131	
	796	Vehicles & Parts Nec	2,480		1	
	844	Chemical Spec Nec	134,185		64	
	901	Gen Misc Commodity Nec	137,124		255	
				5,258,479		10,716

APPENDIX B (*continued*)

Country	No.	Commodity*	Dollars	Total	Short tons	Total
IRELAND	100	Corn	233,075		5,306	
	123	Veg & Prep Canned	765		2	
	185	Molasses Edib & Sugar Prod	5,762		18	
	475	Paper Related Prod Nec	21,866		24	
	606	Tools & Basic Hardware	2,108		1	
	611	Metal Manufactures Nec	29,413		64	
	701	Elec Mach & Appar	10,158		5	
	742	Other Indus Mach & Parts	2,720		1	
	770	Agric Mach & Parts	15,603		15	
	901	Gen Misc Commodity Nec	2,666		2	
				324,136		5,438
NETHERLANDS	010	Meat Fresh or Fzn	133,536		317	
	017	Meat & Prod Nec	7,429		16	
	035	Dried Milk	410,728		3,224	
	060	Hides and Skins Raw	233,574		1,039	
	065	Leather and Mfrs	3,541		13	
	100	Corn	440,702		10,431	
	102	Barley and Rye	110,775		2,799	
	103	Wheat	82,252		1,103	
	107	Wheat Flour Semolina	41,033		598	
	110	Animal Feeds Nec	124,638		3,162	
	123	Veg & Prep Canned	1,623		5	
	185	Molasses Edib & Sugar Prod	5,525		18	
	235	Oilseeds Nec	18,012		126	
	260	Seeds Except Oilseeds	11,388		7	
	297	Veg Prod Ined Nec	5,910		267	
	390	Textile Prod Nec	55,632		135	
	400	Logs	580		2	
	475	Paper Related Prod Nec	658		1	
	517	Lub Oils & Greases	676			
	555	Nonmet Min Nec	8,893		49	
	606	Tools & Basic Hardware	39,787		10	
	607	House, Kitch, Hosp Utensils	7,722		3	
	611	Metal Manufactures Nec	397,249		656	
	622	Refined Copper Crude	135,688		226	
	632	Copper-Base Alloy Semi	37,449		37	
	701	Elec Mach & App	51,858		58	
	710	Engines Turb & Parts Nec	141,174		71	
	722	Construct & Rel Mach	558,962		496	
	731	Machine Tools	104,410		18	
	740	Tex Sew Shoe Mach & Parts	30,892		2	
	742	Other Indus Mach & Parts	355,325		156	
	770	Agric Mach & Parts	16,708		24	
	781	Auto Trucks Exc Parts	27,262		14	

APPENDIX B (*continued*)

Country	No.	Commodity*	Dollars	Total	Short tons	Total
	785	Merchant Vessels	2,000			
	787	Auto Truck & Access	175,830		106	
	796	Vehicles & Parts Nec	6,610		2	
	837	Syn Resins Ex Fin Form	5,262		19	
	844	Chemical Spec Nec	10,158		13	
	901	Gen Misc Commodity Nec	8,202		9	
				3,809,653		25,233
BELGIUM	010	Meat Fresh or Fzn	3,076		6	
	020	Animal Oils & Fats Edib	28,740		123	
	035	Dried Milk	11,438		69	
	065	Leather and Mfrs	1,945		10	
	098	Animal Prod Ined Nec	4,500		4	
	100	Corn	49,350		1,086	
	123	Veg & Prep Canned	1,789		5	
	185	Molasses Edib & Sugar Prod	37,606		109	
	260	Seeds Except Oilseeds	3,180		17	
	350	Wool Semi & Mfrs	12,484		49	
	390	Textile Prod Nec	28,804		95	
	475	Paper Related Prod Nec	226,426		696	
	551	Limestone Crushed	596		8	
	555	Nonmet Min Nec	12,591		120	
	606	Tools & Basic Hdwe	3,331		2	
	611	Metal Manufactures Nec	10,679		3	
	632	Copper-Base Alloy Semi	7,471		5	
	701	Elec Mach & App	68,853		77	
	710	Engines Turb & Parts Nec	80,871		56	
	722	Construct & Rel Mach	299,714		269	
	731	Machine Tools	70,690		42	
	740	Tex Sew Shoe Mach & Parts	9,075			
	742	Other Indus Mach & Part	80,891		36	
	770	Agric Mach & Parts	20,553		26	
	781	Auto Trucks Exc Parts	107,356		117	
	786	Railway Locomotives & Parts	660		2	
	787	Auto Truck & Access	1,048			
	796	Vehicles & Parts Nec	39,762		12	
	837	Syn Resins Except Fin Form	2,684		2	
	844	Chemical Spec Nec	3,862		8	
	901	Gen Misc Commodity Nec	76,886		62	
				1,306,911		3,119
FRANCE	010	Meat Fresh or Fzn	143,148		286	
	060	Hides and Skins Raw	10,590		29	
	065	Leather and Mfrs	53,610		63	
	123	Veg & Prep Canned	3,659		18	

APPENDIX B (*continued*)

Country	No.	Commodity*	Dollars	Total	Short tons	Total
	127	Veg & Prep Nec	40,175		226	
	185	Molasses Edib & Sugar Prod	74,822		225	
	260	Seeds Except Oilseeds	625			
	390	Textile Prod Nec	27,392		79	
	475	Paper Related Prod Nec	69,767		67	
	555	Nonmet Min Nec	12,210		132	
	606	Tools & Basic Hardware	654			
	611	Metal Manufactures Nec	79,440		191	
	701	Elec Mach & App	61,473		24	
	710	Engines Turb & Parts Nec	446,167		172	
	722	Construc & Rel Mach	620,683		562	
	731	Machine Tools	75,252		24	
	740	Tex Sew Shoe Mach & Parts	56,827		4	
	742	Other Indus Mach & Parts	757,140		351	
	770	Agric Mach & Parts	231,370		196	
	781	Auto Trucks Exc Parts	114,861		76	
	787	Auto Trucks & Access	6,956		3	
	810	Medic and Pharm Prep	972		1	
	837	Syn Resins Ex Fin Form	10,310		9	
	844	Chemical Spec Nec	3,324			
	901	Gen Misc Commodity Nec	88,760		12	
				2,990,187		2,750
WEST GERMANY	010	Meat Fresh or Fzn	12,785		39	
	017	Meat & Prod Nec	6,600		34	
	020	Animal Oils & Fats Edib	30,013		206	
	060	Hides and Skins Raw	169,475		936	
	098	Animal Prod Ined Nec	12,188		62	
	100	Corn	111,695		2,574	
	103	Wheat	83,338		1,728	
	123	Veg & Prep Canned	77,012		512	
	127	Veg & Prep Nec	1,154		6	
	185	Molasses Edible & Sugar Prod	39,574		123	
	190	Dis Spirits Liq & Wines	908		1	
	207	Rubber Manufactures Nec	770			
	390	Textile Prod Nec	56,097		124	
	400	Logs	27,186		160	
	421	Wood Manufactures Nec	2,200		4	
	475	Paper Related Prod Nec	19,540		19	
	555	Nonmet Min Nec	86,790		784	
	606	Tools & Basic Hdwe	2,112			
	611	Metal Mfrs Nec	442,728		944	
	632	Copper-Base Alloy Semi	3,764		4	
	652	Nickel Ore Conc Scrap	5,029		29	
	701	Elec Mach & App	18,973		3	

APPENDIX B (*continued*)

Country	No.	Commodity*	Dollars	Total	Short tons	Total
	710	Engines Turb & Parts Nec	93,487		49	
	722	Construct & Rel Mach	518,488		224	
	731	Machine Tools	129,372		34	
	742	Other Indus Mach & Parts	571,376		175	
	770	Agric Mach & Parts	201,470		155	
	781	Auto Trucks Exc Parts	151,405		100	
	787	Auto Truck & Access	11,531		7	
	793	Comm & Civil Aircraft	6,775		1	
	828	Other Indus Chem	1,688		1	
	844	Chemical Spec Nec	25,062		2	
	847	Pigments Paints & Varn	1,292		2	
	901	Gen Misc Commodity Nec	31,346		9	
				2,953,223		9,050
AUSTRIA	060	Hides and Skins Raw	10,233		35	
	710	Engines Turb & Parts Nec	3,663		3	
	722	Construct & Rel Mach	44,884		23	
	731	Machine Tools	1,144			
	742	Other Indus Mach & Parts	47,456		18	
				107,380		79
CZECHO-SLOVAKIA	020	Animal Oils & Fats Edible	651,784		3,222	
	080	Hides and Skins Raw	9,938		72	
				661,722		3,294
SWITZERLAND	010	Meat Fresh or Fzn	3,340		4	
	017	Meat & Prod Nec	1,500		4	
	039	Dairy Prod Nec	97,369		201	
	065	Leather and Mfrs	17,536		14	
	123	Veg & Prep Canned	840		4	
	297	Veg Prod Ined Nec	75,674		536	
	400	Logs	7,356		31	
	555	Nonmet Min Nec	1,982			
	606	Tools & Basic Hardware	2,520			
	611	Metal Mfrs Nec	59,069		130	
	701	Elec Mach & App	95,415		26	
	710	Engines Turb & Parts Nec	476,367		243	
	722	Construct & Rel Mach	74,699		44	
	731	Machine Tools	6,621		2	
	740	Tex Sew Shoe Mach & Part	12,670		1	
	742	Other Indus Mach & Part	30,433		8	
	770	Agric Mach & Parts	62,055		48	
	781	Auto Trucks Exc Parts	4,448		3	
	787	Auto Truck & Access	100,228		98	
	810	Medic & Pharm Prep	7,219		3	

APPENDIX B (*continued*)

Country	No.	Commodity*	Dollars	Total	Short tons	Total
	847	Pigments Paints & Varn	8,186		8	
	901	Gen Misc Commodity Nec	24,639		6	
				1,170,166		1,414
FINLAND	060	Hides & Skins Raw	7,590		31	
	123	Veg & Prep Canned	720		3	
	555	Nonmet Min Nec	3,102		34	
	606	Tools & Basic Hardware	514			
	710	Engines Turb & Parts Nec	12,356		7	
	722	Construct & Rel Mach	15,105		7	
	742	Other Indus Mach & Parts	1,561		1	
	770	Agric Mach & Parts	11,361		11	
	787	Auto Trucks & Access	4,550		5	
	837	Syn Resins Ex Fin Form	9,563		33	
	901	Gen Misc Commodity Nec	768		1	
				67,190		133
POLAND	035	Dried Milk	60,078		482	
	107	Wheat Flour Semolina	38,125		384	
				98,203		866
U.S.S.R.	742	Other Indus Mach & Parts	256,219		85	
				256,219		85
SPAIN	017	Meat & Prod Nec	5,599		19	
	060	Hides and Skins Raw	7,569		32	
	100	Corn	2,353,459		52,552	
	231	Soy Beans	1,010,847		11,619	
	320	Cotton Manufactures	965		7	
	701	Elec Mach & Appar	2,419		1	
	710	Engines Turb & Parts Nec	794			
	722	Construct & Rel Mach	196,913		162	
	742	Other Indus Mach & Part	517,190		234	
	770	Agric Mach & Parts	147,163		87	
	781	Auto Trucks Exc Parts	13,543		7	
	901	Gen Misc Commodity Nec	1,506		1	
				4,257,967		64,720
PORTUGAL	107	Wheat Flour Semolina	119,350		1,759	
	109	Flour & Grain Prep Nec	18,283		260	
	413	Lumber & Shingles	743		4	
	555	Nonmet Min Nec	5,303		23	
	710	Engines Turb & Parts Nec	1,309			
	722	Construct & Rel Mach	139,779		127	

APPENDIX B (*continued*)

Country	No.	Commodity*	Dollars	Total	Short tons	Total
	781	Auto Trucks Exc Parts	10,909		8	
	901	Gen Misc Commodity Nec	789		1	
				296,465		2,182
MALTA	123	Veg Prep & Canned	630		2	
				630		2
ITALY	035	Dried Milk	219,751		1,792	
	037	Cheese	305,235		1,163	
	039	Dairy Products Nec	109,907		386	
	060	Hides and Skins Raw	17,780		114	
	065	Leather & Mfrs	1,503			
	107	Wheat Flour Semolina	466,966		6,642	
	109	Flour & Grain Prep Nec	7,523		85	
	110	Animal Feeds Nec	1,986		30	
	123	Veg & Prep Canned	2,257		6	
	127	Veg & Prep Nec	206,515		417	
	185	Molasses Edib & Sugar Prod	5,525		18	
	320	Cotton Manufactures	4,281		42	
	350	Wool Semi & Mfrs	101,282		962	
	381	Man-Made Fibers and Mfr	4,512		41	
	390	Textile Prod Nec	600		1	
	400	Logs	25,179		134	
	475	Paper Related Prod Nec	671			
	555	Nonmet Min Nec	10,050		12	
	606	Tools & Basic Hardware	1,062			
	611	Metal Manufactures Nec	141,792		340	
	632	Copper-Base Alloy Semi	15,374		17	
	701	Elec Mach & App	6,308			
	710	Engines Turb & Parts Nec	326,744		109	
	722	Construct & Rel Mach	384,989		289	
	731	Machine Tools	591,679		155	
	742	Other Indus Mach & Part	1,201,565		583	
	770	Agric Mach & Parts	59,431		50	
	781	Auto Trucks Exc Parts	15,668		12	
	806	Other Chemical Prod	2,886		1	
	844	Chemical Spec Nec	2,337		1	
	901	Gen Misc Commodity Nec	6,156		2	
				4,247,514		13,404
YUGOSLAVIA	020	Animal Oils & Fats Edib	20,160		90	
	035	Dried Milk	1,165		7	
	107	Wheat Flour Semolina	65,406		863	
	390	Textile Prod Nec	73,060		38	
	400	Logs	6,989		31	

APPENDIX B (*continued*)

Country	No.	Commodity*	Dollars	Total	Short tons	Total
	742	Other Indus Mach & Parts	544,355		183	
	901	Gen Misc Commodity Nec	9,550		5	
				720,685		1,217
GREECE	010	Meat Fresh or Fzn	2,954		15	
	035	Dried Milk	54,755		339	
	103	Wheat	14,147		118	
	107	Wheat Flour Semolina	46,835		694	
	127	Veg & Prep Nec	70,000		117	
	390	Textile Prod Nec	264,365		139	
	611	Metal Mfrs Nec	1,767		6	
	701	Elec Mach & App	100,549		8	
	710	Engines Turb & Parts Nec	8,398		6	
	722	Construct & Rel Mach	854,344		918	
	731	Machine Tools	13,453		5	
	742	Other Indus Mach & Parts	258,090		85	
	770	Agric Mach & Parts	19,200		28	
	781	Auto Trucks Exc Parts	3,740		3	
	796	Vehicles & Parts Nec	1,206			
	844	Chemical Spec Nec	8,590		4	
	901	Gen Misc Commodity Nec	26,437		14	
				1,748,830		2,497
TURKEY	035	Dried Milk	271,718		1,516	
	103	Wheat	6,234		58	
	109	Flour & Grain Prep Nec	2,767		37	
	127	Veg & Prep Nec	5,015		8	
	606	Tools & Basic Hdwe	802			
	701	Elec Mach & App	596			
	710	Engines Turb & Parts Nec	651,816		436	
	722	Construct & Rel Mach	363,125		297	
	770	Agric Mach & Parts	379,849		403	
	787	Auto Trucks & Access	4,408		1	
				1,686,330		2,757
SYRIA	742	Other Indus Mach & Parts	660			
	810	Medic & Pharm Prep	4,725		3	
				5,385		3
CYPRUS	770	Agric Mach & Parts	15,575		9	
				15,575		9
LEBANON	107	Wheat Flour Semolina	226,101		2,295	
	150	Veg Oils & Fats Edible	610		2	
	190	Dis Spirits Liq Wine	5,115		27	

APPENDIX B (*continued*)

Country	No.	Commodity*	Dollars	Total	Short tons	Total
	390	Textile Prod Nec	59,930		31	
	701	Elec Mach & App	28,081		39	
	742	Other Indus Mach & Parts	14,572		8	
	781	Auto Trucks Exc Parts	20,179		14	
	796	Vehicles & Parts Nec	1,289			
	901	Gen Misc Commodity Nec	4,716			
				360,593		2,416
IRAQ	701	Elec Mach & App	9,872		11	
	770	Agric Mach & Parts	2,216		3	
				12,088		14
IRAN	035	Dried Milk	63,154		555	
	190	Dis Spirits Liq & Wine	9,149		48	
	607	House, Kitch, Hosp Utensils	25,672		14	
	611	Metal Mfrs Nec	7,795		2	
	701	Elec Mach & App	1,392		1	
	710	Engines Turb & Parts Nec	3,938		1	
	742	Other Indus Mach & Parts	4,389			
	781	Auto Trucks Exc Parts	36,583		28	
	796	Vehicles & Parts Nec	44,722		13	
				196,794		662
ISRAEL	010	Meat Fresh or Fzn	7,800		8	
	035	Dried Milk	88,274		498	
	060	Hides & Skins Raw	54,820		334	
	260	Seeds Except Oilseeds	1,710		1	
	350	Wool Semi & Mfrs	750		1	
	540	Clays & Earths	1,862		67	
	606	Tools & Basic Hdwe	1,866		1	
	701	Elec Mach & App	7,276		3	
	710	Engines Turb & Parts	28,494		11	
	731	Machine Tools	7,121		3	
	742	Other Indus Mach & Parts	322,874		159	
	770	Agric Mach & Parts	1,818		1	
	781	Auto Trucks Exc Parts	2,530		1	
	787	Auto Truck & Access	9,288		12	
	901	Gen Misc Commodity Nec	5,307		33	
				541,790		1,132
JORDAN	035	Dried Milk	8,198		45	
	701	Elec Mach & App	3,105		3	
	781	Auto Trucks Exc Parts	14,556		11	
	901	Gen Misc Commodity Nec	7,021		12	
				32,880		71

APPENDIX B (*continued*)

Country	No.	Commodity*	Dollars	Total	Short tons	Total
KUWAIT	107	Wheat Flour Semolina	78,676		1,568	
	722	Construct & Rd Mach	2,390		3	
	742	Other Indus Mach & Parts	6,390		4	
	781	Auto Trucks Exc Parts	71,479		53	
	785	Merchant Vessels	10,192		8	
	901	Gen Misc Commodity Nec	369,025		7	
				538,152		1,643
AFGHANISTAN	035	Dried Milk	3,031		167	
	039	Dairy Prod Nec	30,000		225	
	710	Engines Turb & Parts Nec	673			
				33,704		392
SAUDI ARABIA	107	Wheat Flour Semolina	6,000		100	
	701	Elec Mach & App	17,839		21	
	722	Construct & Rel Mach	5,600		3	
	810	Medic & Pharm Prep	6,750		1	
				36,189		125
ARABIA	701	Elec Mach & Apparatus	4,100		5	
	781	Auto Trucks Exc Parts	37,420		29	
				41,520		34
ADEN	035	Dried Milk	540		30	
				540		30
INDIA	035	Dried Milk	307,766		5,074	
	109	Flour & Grain Prep Nec	1,090		15	
	123	Veg & Prep Canned	532		1	
	127	Veg & Prep Nec	80,240		132	
	555	Nonmet Min Nec	2,572		12	
	606	Tools & Basic Hardware	5,449		16	
	609	Roll & Fin Steel Mill Prod	297,757		858	
	611	Metal Mfrs Nec	16,959		19	
	701	Elec Mach & App	302,329		118	
	722	Construct & Rel Mach	876,262		549	
	731	Machine Tools	30,135		19	
	742	Other Indus Mach & Parts	205,349		47	
	901	Gen Misc Commodity Nec	986		1	
				2,127,426		6,860
PAKISTAN	035	Dried Milk	154,364		1,146	
	103	Wheat	3,841		32	
	127	Veg & Prep Nec	30,090		50	
	190	Dis Spirits Liq & Wines	1,463		6	

APPENDIX B (*continued*)

Country	No.	Commodity*	Dollars	Total	Short tons	Total
	611	Metal Mfrs Nec	1,406		2	
	722	Construct & Rd Mach	13,264		8	
	742	Other Indus Mach & Part	8,534		3	
	787	Auto Truck & Access	16,091		3	
	901	Gen Misc Commodity Nec	5,015		8	
				234,068		1,259
NEPAL	109	Flour & Grain Prep Nec	6,904		97	
				6,904		97
CEYLON	035	Dried Milk	18,598		103	
				18,598		103
BURMA	035	Dried Milk	77,280		956	
				77,280		956
THAILAND	035	Dried Milk	2,250		124	
	742	Other Indus Mach & Parts	1,095		1	
				3,345		125
LAOS	035	Dried Milk	19,362		113	
				19,362		113
VIET NAM	035	Dried Milk	2,240		123	
	109	Flour & Grain Prep Nec	278,596		2,966	
				280,836		3,090
FEDERATION OF MALAYA	035	Dried Milk	750		42	
	787	Auto Truck & Access	902		1	
				1,652		43
SINGAPORE	035	Dried Milk	570		31	
				570		31
INDONESIA	035	Dried Milk	460,719		3,396	
	109	Flour & Grain Prep Nec	2,154		30	
	127	Veg & Prep Nec	13,160		28	
	901	Gen Misc Commodity Nec	10,030		17	
				486,063		3,470
PHILIPPINE REPUBLIC	103	Wheat	10,795		96	
	107	Wheat Flour Semolina	77,268		978	
	109	Flour & Grain Prep Nec	94,245		889	
	127	Veg & Prep Nec	96,056		341	
	722	Const & Rel Mach	3,728		2	

APPENDIX B (*continued*)

Country	No.	Commodity*	Dollars	Total	Short tons	Total
	742	Other Indus Mach & Part	6,403		10	
	781	Auto Trucks Exc Parts	1,595		2	
	787	Auto Truck & Access	15,912		17	
	901	Gen Misc Commodity Nec	48,900		80	
				354,902		2,415
MACAO	035	Dried Milk	15,312		90	
	109	Flour & Grain Prep Nec	3,216		43	
	127	Veg & Prep Nec	97,204		164	
				115,732		298
SOUTH KOREAN REPUBLIC	109	Flour & Grain Prep Nec	1,225,788		12,915	
	127	Veg & Prep Nec	81,455		232	
	810	Medic & Pharm Prep	2,013		2	
				1,309,256		13,149
HONG KONG	035	Dried Milk	42,978		322	
	039	Dairy Prod Nec	775		1	
	127	Veg & Prep Nec	129,400		218	
	555	Nonmet Min Nec	13,670		24	
	844	Chemical Spec Nec	508		1	
	901	Gen Misc Commodity Nec	2,242		1	
				189,573		567
TAIWAN	103	Wheat	18,351		213	
	107	Wheat Flour Semolina	129,177		1,574	
	127	Veg & Prep Nec	114,648		873	
	390	Textile Prod Nec	157,620		82	
	901	Gen Misc Commodity Nec	395			
				420,191		2,742
JAPAN	035	Dried Milk	251,716		2,783	
	039	Dairy Prod Nec	80,747		278	
	060	Hides & Skins Raw	57,092		256	
	107	Wheat Flour Semolina	75,040		1,408	
	390	Textile Prod Nec	2,250		1	
	413	Lumber & Shingles	15,300		43	
	526	Stone & Mfrs Nec	600		0.5	
	611	Metal Mfrs Nec	7,130		51	
	620	Copper Ore Conc Scrap	14,209		27	
	632	Copper-Base Alloy Semi	71,367		185	
	652	Nickel Ore Conc Scrap	50,896		292	
	701	Elec Mach & App	71,689		5	
	722	Construct & Rel Mach	34,937		29	
	731	Machine Tools	25,150		5	

APPENDIX B (*continued*)

Country	No.	Commodity*	Dollars	Total	Short tons	Total
	742	Other Indus Mach & Part	11,334		3	
	770	Agric Mach & Parts	963		1	
	828	Other Indus Chem	16,920		112	
	844	Chemical Spec Nec	40,867		54	
	901	Gen Misc Commodity Nec	24,038		13	
				852,245		5,547
NANSEI ISLANDS	731	Machine Tools	10,708		5	
				10,708		5
AUSTRALIA	127	Veg & Prep Nec	551		2	
	611	Metal Mfrs Nec	15,140		18	
	710	Engines Turb & Parts Nec	49,481		50	
	742	Other Indus Mach & Parts	148,494		60	
	770	Agric Mach & Parts	7,700		8	
	781	Auto Trucks & Parts	2,100		8	
	844	Chemical Spec Nec	1,861		8	
	901	Gen Misc Commodity Nec	5,104		9	
				230,431		162
MOROCCO	035	Dried Milk	52,656		296	
	127	Veg & Prep Nec	26,352		64	
	781	Auto Trucks Exc Parts	120,369		85	
				199,377		446
ALGERIA	035	Dried Milk	156,787		1,122	
	107	Wheat Flour Semolina	180,281		1,797	
	127	Veg & Prep Nec	16,420		32	
	390	Textile Prod Nec	74,274		39	
	901	Gen Misc Commodity Nec	14,234		9	
				441,996		2,999
TUNISIA	035	Dried Milk	53,786		319	
	109	Flour & Grain Prep Nec	32,560		444	
	127	Veg & Prep Nec	46,875		475	
				133,221		1,238
LIBYA	035	Dried Milk	16,443		91	
	297	Veg Prod Ined Nec	53,790		255	
				70,233		346
EGYPT	035	Dried Milk	73,444		315	
	107	Wheat Flour Semolina	389,994		3,914	
	109	Flour & Grain Prep Nec	161,489		2,068	
	127	Veg & Prep Nec	40,120		66	

APPENDIX B (*continued*)

Country	No.	Commodity*	Dollars	Total	Short tons	Total
	190	Dis Spirits Liq & Wine	1,009		4	
	722	Construct & Rel Mach	161,355		104	
	901	Gen Misc Commodity Nec	1,003		2	
				828,414		6,472
CAMEROONS	107	Wheat Flour Semolina	6,984		57	
				6,984		57
FRENCH EQUATORIAL AFRICA	035	Dried Milk	725	725	40	40
TOGO	035	Dried Milk	179,410		1,071	
	103	Wheat	768		10	
	107	Wheat Flour Semolina	14,677		207	
	109	Flour & Grain Prep Nec	130,969		1,870	
	127	Veg & Prep Nec	111,954		189	
	722	Construct & Rel Mach	468,591		327	
				906,369		3,674
GHANA	035	Dried Milk	92,937		533	
	109	Flour & Grain Prep Nec	22,235		303	
	127	Veg & Prep Nec	72,876		327	
	190	Dis Spirits Liq & Wines	582		3	
	742	Other Indus Mach & Parts	570			
				189,200		1,166
NIGERIA	035	Dried Milk	29,128		164	
	107	Wheat Flour Semolina	6,984		57	
	901	Gen Misc Commodity Nec	4,602		4	
				40,714		224
BRITISH WEST AFRICA	035	Dried Milk	77,880		450	
	109	Flour & Grain Prep Nec	12,000		100	
	127	Veg & Prep Nec	26,588		45	
	901	Gen Misc Commodity Nec	10,503		1	
				126,971		597
LIBERIA	035	Dried Milk	13,889		67	
	107	Wheat Flour Semolina	707		6	
	127	Veg & Prep Nec	42,784		53	
	710	Engines Turb & Parts Nec	21,504		5	
	722	Construct & Rel Mach	86,744		58	
	770	Agric Mach & Parts	52,973		19	
	844	Chemical Spec Nec	1,776		1	
				220,377		210

APPENDIX B (*continued*)

Country	No.	Commodity*	Dollars	Total	Short tons	Total
BELGIAN CONGO	035	Dried Milk	199,870		723	
	039	Dairy Prod Nec	27,538		48	
	103	Wheat	111,013		1,055	
	107	Wheat Flour Semolina	1,511,914		15,902	
	109	Flour & Grain Prep Nec	7,042		93	
	722	Construct & Rel Mach	18,469		11	
	742	Other Indus Mach & Parts	9,000		10	
	901	Gen Misc Commodity Nec	30,090		50	
				1,914,936		17,893
ETHIOPIA	035	Dried Milk	6,381		342	
	109	Flour & Grain Prep Nec	2,767		37	
	722	Construct & Rel Mach	61,654		38	
				70,802		417
SEYCHELLES	035	Dried Milk	1,200		66	
				1,200		66
MAURITIUS	035	Dried Milk	2,210		89	
				2,210		89
KENYA	035	Dried Milk	32,417		1,774	
				32,417		1,774
REPUBLIC SOUTH AFRICA	035	Dried Milk	6,141		337	
				6,141		337
		GRAND TOTAL		60,353,626		410,258

Source: Chicago Association of Commerce and Industry, Research and Statistics Division, *U.S. Great Lakes Ports Monthly Statistics for Overseas and Canadian Waterborne Traffic*, 1963, Monthly Data. Place names are given as in source.

Figures have been rounded.

*Commodities are classified according to schedule T. Wording of description of commodities differs slights from description in Tables 4-3 and 5-5 because of the difference in source.

†Not elsewhere classified.

‡Tonnage figures have been omitted where there was less than one ton.

APPENDIX C

EXPORTERS SURVEY QUESTIONNAIRE

1. Name and address of firm:—————————————————————
2. Goods or commodities exported:—————————————————————

3. Total annual exports: Value:—————————. Tonnage:—————————
4. Estimated per cent of exports shipped via Port of Milwaukee.—————%
5. Estimated per cent of exports shipped via Atlantic Ports.—————%
6. Estimated per cent of exports shipped via Gulf Ports.—————%
7. Estimated per cent of exports shipped via other Great Lakes Ports.
   (Please name Ports)—————————————————————————%
8. Other Ports (If over 10% please name Ports).—————————%

IF ANSWERS TO QUESTIONS 5 THROUGH 8 ARE OVER 10%, PLEASE COMPLETE
THE FOLLOWING QUESTIONS.

9. The primary reasons most often mentioned by Wisconsin Area exporters, who use Gulf and Atlantic Ports in lieu of the Port of Milwaukee, are listed below. With respect to your exports through the Gulf and Atlantic Ports, is it *principally* due to: (Please indicate reasons in order of importance by placing a 1, 2, 3, etc.)
   a. Greater frequency of sailings from the Gulf and
      Atlantic Ports?   Yes——No——
   b. Sailings from Gulf and Atlantic Ports to
      destinations not available from Milwaukee?   Yes——No——
   c. Rate differential?   Yes——No——
   d. Control of shipment by buyer, who specifies Port? Yes——No——
   e. Gulf or Atlantic forwarder?   Yes——No——
   f. Other (such as banking, export office in N.Y.,
      seasonal, costs, etc.) Please state——————————————

10. Please indicate where the head office of your forwarder is located.
    New York————— New Orleans————— Other (name)—————
11. Of your exports which go through the Gulf, Pacific, and Atlantic Ports, please indicate the estimated annual volume to each of the following shipping areas:
    Europe: Value:———. Tonnage:*———.
    Mediterranean: Value:———. Tonnage: ———.
    East Coast South America: Value:———. Tonnage: ———.

West Coast South America: Value:_____. Tonnage: _____.
Canada: Value:_____. Tonnage: _____.
Central America–Cuba–Mexico: Value:_____. Tonnage: _____.
Islands of the Atlantic: Value:_____. Tonnage: _____.
Far East: Value:_____. Tonnage: _____.
Indonesia: Value:_____. Tonnage: _____.
Red Sea–Persian Gulf: Value:_____. Tonnage: _____.
India–Pakistan–Burma: Value:_____. Tonnage: _____.
South & East Africa: Value:_____. Tonnage: _____.
West Africa: Value:_____. Tonnage: _____.
Australia: Value:_____. Tonnage: _____.
Islands of the Pacific: Value:_____. Tonnage: _____.
Other: Please state:

_____ Value:_____. Tonnage: _____.
_____ Value:_____. Tonnage: _____.

12. Other comments:

*indicate whether net or gross.

Yes, send me a copy of the final tabulation_____.

Return to:

Professor Eric Schenker   Furnished by_____
University of Wisconsin-Milwaukee
Department of Economics   Title _____
3203 North Downer Avenue
Milwaukee 11, Wisconsin   Date _____

APPENDIX D

TRANSIT TIME STUDY ON 207 VOYAGES
From the Port of Milwaukee to the first port of call overseas
Departures from April 18 to August 31, 1964

Vessel	Date sailed from Milwaukee	Date arrived overseas	First overseas port of call	Time in transit (days)
RANGE: *Continental Europe*				
Tindefjell	4/26	5/16	Le Havre	21
Transeuropa	4/18	5/17	Rotterdam	30
Braheholm	4/25	5/16	Le Havre	22
Svanefjell	5/4	5/22	Le Havre	19
Chicago	5/4	5/25	Rouen	22
Catherine Sartori	5/4	6/3	Rotterdam	31
Transcanada	5/6	5/27	Rotterdam	22
Learina	5/18	6/5	Rotterdam	19
Virgilia	5/7	5/31	Rotterdam	25
Transpacific	5/11	6/6	Hamburg	27
Torsholm	5/18	6/8	Le Havre	22
Prins Alexander	5/25	6/13	Le Havre	20
Yildun	5/22	6/11	Rotterdam	21
Hildergard Doerenkamp	5/25	6/15	Le Havre	22
Transquebec	5/27	6/22	Rotterdam	27
Cleveland	6/1	6/22	Le Havre	22
Transatlantic	6/2	6/28	Rotterdam	27
Christian Sartori	6/5	6/25	Rotterdam	21
Vibyholm	6/6	6/27	Le Havre	22
Prins Willem Van Oranje	6/8	6/26	Le Havre	19
Polaris	6/18	7/5	Hamburg	18
Congo	6/11	7/1	Le Havre	21
Leapaul	6/11	6/30	Rotterdam	20
Poseidon	6/12	7/5	Bremerhaven	24
Leada	6/26	7/14	Hamburg	19
Vaxholm	6/18	7/9	Le Havre	22
Transeuropa	6/28	7/20	Rotterdam	23
Tindefjell	6/29	7/20	Le Havre	22
Carlsholm	6/30	7/21	Le Havre	22
Salambria	7/1	7/16	Rotterdam	16
Catherine Sartori	7/2	7/29	Rotterdam	28
Clemens Sartori	7/2	7/23	Bremen	22
Virgilia	7/10	7/26	Rotterdam	17

TRANSIT TIME STUDY ON 207 VOYAGES (*continued*)

Vessel	*Date sailed from Milwaukee*	*Date arrived overseas*	*First overseas port of call*	*Time in transit (days)*
Chicago	7/10	7/31	Le Havre	22
Transpacific	7/12	8/11	Bremerhaven	31
Saldanha	7/12	7/28	Rotterdam	17
Belgien	7/14	8/7	Le Havre	25
Braheholm	7/16	8/6	Le Havre	22
Learina	7/16	8/2	Hamburg	18
Chatham	7/17	8/16	Rotterdam	31
Transcanada	7/20	8/16	Rotterdam	28
Yildun	7/22	8/12	Rotterdam	22
Alexander Sartori	7/22	8/19	Rotterdam	29
Prins Alexander	7/23	8/13	Le Havre	22
Lealott	7/29	8/17	Hamburg	20
Helga Schroeder	7/25	8/28	Antwerp	35
Neptun	7/26	8/16	Le Havre	22
Prins Johan Willem Friso	7/30	8/20	Le Havre	22
Transquebec	7/31	8/25	Bremerhaven	26
Prins Willem van Oranje	8/3	8/26	Le Havre	24
Christian Sartori	8/6	8/27	Hamburg	22
Transatlantic	8/14	9/2	Rotterdam	20
Cleveland	8/7	8/28	Le Havre	22
Wasaborg	8/10	8/25	Rotterdam	16
Torsholm	8/11	9/3	Antwerp	24
Leapaul	8/13	9/1	Rotterdam	20
Tidaholm	8/14	9/6	Antwerp	24
Harpefjell	8/15	9/5	Le Havre	22
Haukefjell	8/17	9/11	Le Havre	26
Polaris	8/20	9/8	Bremen	20
Transeuropa	8/25	9/23	Rotterdam	30
Leada	8/27	9/15	Rotterdam	20
Vibyholm	8/27	9/17	Le Havre	22
Salambria	8/28	9/12	Rotterdam	16
Tindefjell	8/29	9/18	Le Havre	21
Svanefjell	8/31	9/25	Le Havre	26

Number of voyages checked to Continental Europe: 66 vessels
Number of voyages 22 days or under: 44 vessels
Number of voyages 23 days or over: 22 vessels
Fastest transit time: 16 days
Slowest transit time: 35 days

RANGE: *United Kingdom*

Torr Head	4/20	5/15	Dublin	26
Ternefjell	5/1	5/24	London	24
Phrygia	4/25	5/16	Liverpool	22

TRANSIT TIME STUDY ON 207 VOYAGES (continued)

Vessel	Date sailed from Milwaukee	Date arrived overseas	First overseas port of call	Time in transit (days)
Nordia	4/30	5/25	London	26
Prins Frederik Hendrik	4/30	5/21	Glasgow	22
Birgit Ragne	5/4	5/27	Liverpool	24
Prins Willem IV	5/8	6/6	London	30
Manchester Renown	5/12	6/3	Manchester	23
Tautra	5/12	6/6	London	26
Norholt	5/14	6/5	Avonmouth	23
Maj Ragne	5/21	6/13	Liverpool	24
Carrigan Head	5/18	6/15	Dublin	29
Bernd Leonhardt	5/18	6/10	Avonmouth	24
Grindefjell	5/23	6/15	London	24
Lycia	5/21	6/12	Liverpool	23
Nardo	5/30	6/21	London	23
Prins Casimir	6/6	6/28	London	23
Silvaplana	6/4	7/7	London	34
Eva Jeanette	6/8	7/3	London	26
Fredrik Ragne	6/10	6/29	Liverpool	20
Fair Head	6/10	7/1	Dublin	22
Nordia	6/21	7/14	London	24
Bernhard Howaldt	6/22	7/14	Avonmouth	23
Ternefjell	6/28	7/18	London	21
Monica Smith	6/25	7/22	Liverpool	28
Roonagh Head	6/29	7/25	Belfast	27
Prins Frederik Willem	7/1	7/25	London	25
Phrygia	7/3	7/24	London	22
Tautra	7/6	7/31	London	26
Lycia	7/15	8/23	Liverpool	40
Nardo	7/17	8/15	London	30
Grindefjell	7/17	8/2	London	17
Birgit Ragne	7/18	8/6	Liverpool	20
Carrigan Head	7/23	8/18	Belfast	27
Manchester Faith	8/1	8/23	Manchester	23
Prins Casimir	8/1	8/23	London	23
Eva Jeanette	8/4	8/28	London	25
Fair Head	8/10	9/3	Belfast	25
Prins Willem V	8/12	9/7	London	27
Maj Ragne	8/12	9/2	Liverpool	22
Bysanz	8/16	9/7	London	23
Nordia	8/16	9/10	London	26
Phrygia	8/22	9/13	Liverpool	23
Manchester Commerce	8/22	9/13	Manchester	23
Ternefjell	8/23	9/15	London	24
City of Alma	8/24	9/19	Rotterdam	27
Fredrik Ragne	8/26	9/19	Liverpool	25

TRANSIT TIME STUDY ON 207 VOYAGES (*continued*)

Vessel	Date sailed from Milwaukee	Date arrived overseas	First overseas port of call	Time in transit (days)
Prins Frederik Willem	8/26	9/18	Glasgow	24
Tautra	8/28	9/25	London	29

Number of voyages checked to United Kingdom: 49 vessels
Number of voyages 22 days or under: 9 vessels
Number of voyages 23 days or over: 40 vessels
Fastest transit time: 17 days
Slowest transit time: 40 days
Note: 11 vessels made the voyage in 23 days

RANGE: *Mediterranean*

Vessel	Date sailed from Milwaukee	Date arrived overseas	First overseas port of call	Time in transit (days)
Hadar	4/18	5/16	Barcelona	29
La Hacienda	4/23	5/12	Casablanca	20
Borealis	4/24	5/16	Lisbon	23
Luka Botic	4/29	5/30	Genoa	32
Capo Noli	5/7	6/4	Valencia	29
Expeditor	5/10	5/29	Casablanca	20
Raki	5/11	6/3	Beirut	24
Marco Marulic	5/14	6/11	Naples	29
Fernspring	5/18	6/8	Genoa	22
Etrog	5/20	6/14	Cádiz	26
Prins Maurits	5/22	6/14	Casablanca	24
Natko Wodilo	6/5	7/2	Genoa	28
Utrecht	6/6	6/29	Malta	24
Sirefjell	6/8	7/3	Genoa	26
Dagan	6/15	7/8	Marseilles	24
Capo Mele	6/17	7/8	Casablanca	22
Vares	6/17	7/10	Genoa	24
Extavia	6/20	7/14	Tunis	25
Uranus	6/27	7/18	Bordeaux	22
Bengazi	6/26	7/19	Casablanca	24
Exiria	6/27	7/21	Tunis	25
Montcalm	7/5	7/25	Naples	21
Hadar	7/14	8/4	Barcelona	22
Borealis	7/15	8/5	Marseilles	22
Luka Botic	7/16	8/9	Lisbon	25
La Hacienda	7/20	8/10	Algiers	22
Expeditor	7/20	8/10	Casablanca	22
Bawean	7/22	8/17	Beirut	27
Zenica	7/25	8/31	Piraeus	38
Capo Noli	7/30	8/19	Valencia	21
Etrog	8/4	8/25	Barcelona	22
Prins Maurits	8/14	9/3	Casablanca	21
Marco Marulic	8/7	8/31	Savona	25

TRANSIT TIME STUDY ON 207 VOYAGES (*continued*)

Vessel	Date sailed from Milwaukee	Date arrived overseas	First overseas port of call	Time in transit (days)
Alberta	8/8	8/30	Oran	23
Orient Mariner	8/13	9/6	Alexandria	25
Sirefjell	8/17	9/20	Genoa	35
Natko Nodilo	8/17	9/14	Genoa	29
Extavia	8/19	9/5	Lisbon	18
Bengkalis	8/22	9/20	Beirut	30
Dagan	8/23	9/24	Barcelona	33
Capo Mele	8/23	9/15	Leixoes	24
Exiria	8/28	9/28	Derince	32

Number of vessels checked to Mediterranean: 42 vessels
Number of vessels 24 days or under: 23 vessels
Number of vessels 25 days or over: 19 vessels
Fastest transit time: 18 days
Slowest transit time: 38 days

RANGE: *Scandinavia*

Vessel	Date sailed	Date arrived	First port	Days
Topdalsfjord	4/27	5/20	Kristiansand S.	24
Maakefjell	5/8	5/31	Kristiansand S.	24
Lyngenfjord	5/21	6/13	Kristiansand S.	24
Byklefjell	6/6	6/28	Stavanger	23
Topdalsfjord	6/22	7/12	Bergen	21
Maakefjell	7/8	7/26	Kristiansand S.	19
Lyngenfjord	7/15	8/6	Kristiansand S.	23
Caroline Smith	7/15	8/4	Kristiansand S.	21
Byklefjell	8/2	8/23	Tou	22
Topdalsfjord	8/13	8/30	Kristiansand S.	18
Borgholm	8/18	9/11	Gothenburg	25

Number of voyages checked to Scandinavia: 11 vessels
Number of voyages 24 days or under: 10 vessels
Number of voyages 25 days or over: 1 vessel
Fastest transit time: 19 days
Slowest transit time: 25 days

RANGE: *Middle East*

Vessel	Date sailed	Date arrived	First port	Days
Jalagomati	5/19	6/20	Bombay	33
Ellen Kladtschke	6/1	7/21	Jedda	51
Morning Light	6/22	7/24	Assab	33
Orient Lakes	6/1	7/16	Jedda	46
Jalaganga	7/2	8/8	Bombay	38
Zenobia Martini	8/20	9/19	Jedda	31

Number of voyages checked to Middle East: 6 vessels
Average time in transit: 38.6 days

TRANSIT TIME STUDY ON 207 VOYAGES (*continued*)

Vessel	*Date sailed from Milwaukee*	*Date arrived overseas*	*First overseas port of call*	*Time in transit (days)*
RANGE: *Far East, Japan, Australia*				
Mikishima Maru	4/27	6/10	Yokohama	45
Leeds City	5/3	7/22	Nagoya	81
Manjusan Maru	5/15	6/30	Yokohama	47
Sefra	5/24	8/22	Yokohama	91
Tsuneshima Maru	6/5	7/18	Yokohama	44
Mayasan Maru	6/6	7/31	Yokohama	56
Masashima Maru	6/10	7/28	Yokohama	49
Bolivia Maru	6/14	8/3	Yokohama	51
Martin Thore	6/24	8/20	Brisbane	58
Kunikawa Maru	7/5	8/19	Yokohama	45
Kamikawa Maru	7/10	8/28	Yokohama	50
Mikagesan Maru	7/10	8/29	Yokohama	51
Surna	7/20	9/22	Nagoya	65
Texas Maru	7/27	9/8	Yokohama	44
Kasugasan Maru	7/28	9/16	Yokohama	51
Mogamisan Maru	8/12	9/30	Yokohama	50
Alcoa Marketer	8/20	10/16	Inchon	58
Makishima Maru	8/25	10/9	Yokohama	46
Fairport	8/26	10/12	Kobe	48
Orient Trader	8/26	10/29	Pusan	65
Spildra	8/31	10/25	Nagoya	56

Number of voyages checked to Far East,
Japan, and Australia: 21 vessels
Average time in transit: 54.8 days

RANGE: *Caribbean*				
Marionga Maris	6/5	6/22	Veracruz	18
Elisabeth Henriette Schulte	6/12	7/3	Bridgetown	22
Barbara	8/10	8/31	Santo Domingo	22
Johann Christian Schulte	7/3	7/24	Santo Domingo	22

Number of voyages checked to the Caribbean: 4 vessels
Average time in transit: 21 days

RANGE: *East Coast South America*				
Mormacdove	5/25	6/13	Belém	20
Mormacowl	6/18	7/20	Buenos Aires	33
Mormacpine	7/25	8/20	Recife	27
Mormacfir	8/12	8/31	Belém	20

Number of voyages checked to the East Coast of
South America: 4 vessels
Average time in transit: 25 days

TRANSIT TIME STUDY ON 207 VOYAGES (*continued*)

Vessel	Date sailed from Milwaukee	Date arrived overseas	First overseas port of call	Time in transit (days)
RANGE: *West Africa*				
African Crescent	6/1	6/24	Freetown	24
Fairwind	7/27	8/21	Lagos	26
Afram River	8/5	8/31	Port Etienne	27
African Rainbow	8/19	9/13	Freetown	26
Number of voyages checked to West Africa: 4 vessels				
Average time in transit:			25.7 days	

Source: Milwaukee, Board of Harbor Commissioners records, Office of the Traffic Division, 1965.

ADJUSTED AVERAGE TIME IN TRANSIT FROM MILWAUKEE TO SELECTED PORTS

First overseas port of call	Number of sailings	Average time in transit (days)	Range (days) Shortest	Range (days) Longest	Adjusted average (days)
London*	23	25.13	17	34	24.94
Le Havre*	26	22.08	19	26	21.95
Rotterdam*	25	23.04	16	31	22.88
Liverpool	11	24.64	20	40	23.44
Hamburg	6	20.67	18	27	19.75
Yokohama	14	51.50	44	91	48.83

Source: Milwaukee, Board of Harbor Commissioners, "Transit time study," 1964.
*More than one sailing dropped at each end of array.

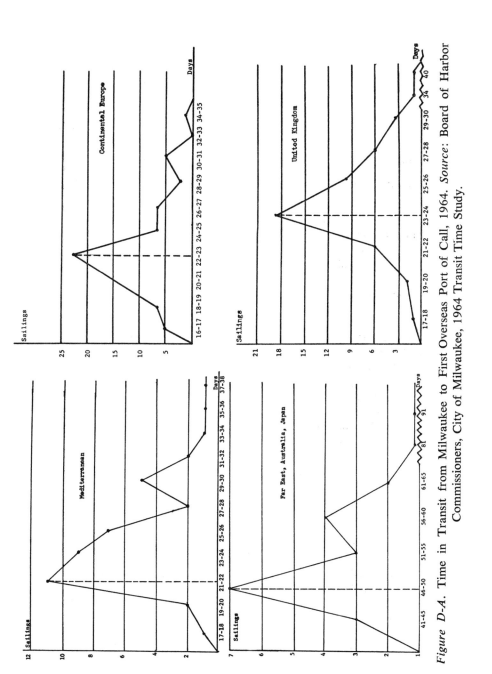

Figure D-A. Time in Transit from Milwaukee to First Overseas Port of Call, 1964. *Source:* Board of Harbor Commissioners, City of Milwaukee, 1964 Transit Time Study.

APPENDIX E

VESSEL DISBURSEMENTS SURVEY QUESTIONNAIRE

CODE #_____   DATE_____

CONFIDENTIAL—Information will not be divulged or disseminated except in consolidated form.

Vessel Disbursements at Port of Philadelphia

Trade (check)

Foreign_____ Inbound_____ Outbound_____
Intercoastal_____ Inbound_____ Outbound_____
Coastwise_____ Inbound_____ Outbound_____

Commodity (full description)_____
_____ Net Tons_____

Tanker_____ Bulk–(dry)_____ General_____
Days in Port: Loading_____Unloading_____ Other_____

Disbursements: (Total)_____

1. Pilotage _____
   Tugs _____
   Running Lines_____
   Dockage_____
2. Government expenses viz:_____
   Quarantine_____ Entrance/Clearance_____
   Fumigation_____ Customs–Overtime_____
   Immigration_____ Miscellaneous_____
   _____
3. Labor viz:_____
   Stevedoring_____
   Clerking–checking–watching, etc._____
   Cleaning–fitting–equipment rental_____
   Handling _____
4. Repairs _____
5. Supplies _____
   (including chandler, doctor, laundry, dunnage)
6. Bunkers viz:_____
   Coal   Oil   Water

Miscellaneous _____

(including reporting, launches, certificates, fees)

198

SURVEY QUESTIONNAIRE

VESSEL DISBURSEMENTS SURVEY

CARGO _____ TRADE _____

TOTAL DISBURSE-MENTS	TOTAL NET TONS	WORKING DAYS IN PORT	PORT & TERMINAL CHARGES	GOV'T CHARGES	LABOR	REPAIRS	SUPPLIES	BUNKERS	MISCELLANEOUS

APPENDIX F

THE REGIONAL MULTIPLIER

By Kenneth J. Schlager,[1] Chief Systems Engineer
Southeastern Wisconsin Regional Planning Commission

A dual approach to socio-economic forecasting has been attempted in the land use-transportation study of the Southeastern Wisconsin Regional Planning Commission. Traditional independent projections of population and employment (by industry) have been supplemented by an experimental economic simulation model that incorporates an input-output framework for simulating the growth of the regional economy.

This economic simulation model was described in detail in an earlier issue of the *Technical Record*,[2] and socio-economic forecasts for the land use-transportation study are being developed through the use of this simulation model. Model forecasts will be compared with traditional extrapolation forecasts, and both will then be evaluated to determine the final best estimates of population and employment at five-year intervals to the year 1990.

Neither of these two forecasting methodologies have directly involved the use of the economic base concept of a regional economy and its associated primary parameter, the regional multiplier. The economic base type of analysis makes a distinction between basic (primary) industries that export goods or services outside the region and service industries that provide goods and services to regional residents. The underlying premise for such a classification is that regions exist and grow primarily because of the goods and services that are exported and sold beyond the borders of the region. If such a concept is valid, regional economic analysis must distinguish between basic and service industries.

Early attempts at measuring the economic base stressed the basic-service employment ratio.[3] From this same employment data, a regional multiplier may be calculated. Such a multiplier relates the change in *total* employment to the change in *basic* employment.

1. Sources: SEWRPC, *Technical Record*, 2, No. 3 (Feb.–Mar., 1965), pp. 9–13.

2. See SEWRPC, *Technical Record*, Vol. 2, No. 1, October–November, 1964.

3. Walter Isard, *Methods of Regional Analysis: An Introduction to Regional Science*, John Wiley, New York, 1960.

$$\text{Multiplier} = r = \frac{\text{change in total employment}}{\text{change in basic employment}}$$

The term multiplier is appropriate since it is a measure of the multiplying effect of a change in basic employment on total (basic and service) employment.

A regional multiplier is useful for determining the gross effects of a change of exports on income and employment within the Region. Regions with large multipliers tend to be less stable economically since small changes in exports produce large swings in total regional income and employment. More stable regions are characterized by smaller multipliers. This relationship of the multiplier with economic stability makes it extremely useful as a guideline for stabilizing the regional economy through the introduction of industries tending to lower the multiplier. Moreover, many economic analyses and forecasts do not require the detail needed by the land use-transportation study and are greatly aided by the application of a regional multiplier. The data required to calculate the regional multiplier is a natural outgrowth of the economic data collection program of the land use-transportation study since some of the same data needed for the economic simulation model is directly applicable to multiplier analysis.

The multiplier has also been an important concept in the theory of national income determination. Although analysis in this area has been somewhat unrelated to regional economics, it is directly transferable to a regional economy if the importance of regional exports and imports are understood. Preliminary to such a comparison, some definition of regional income is appropriate.

Individuals and business enterprises receive income as a reward for services rendered from the following sources: (1) production of goods and services for regional residents (C); (2) local private and public investment in capital goods (I); (3) local public expenditures for current expenses (G); (4) exports of goods and services (X).

Not all of the gross production revenue of the above goods and services results in income to regional residents since some of it "leaks" out of the region to pay for goods and service imports from outside the region. Total regional income, Y, may be expressed in terms of the above sources:

$$Y = aC + bI + cG + gX$$

where a, b, c, g represent the regional income generated for each dollar of expenditure in each category.

Consumption in turn is a function of income:

$$C = kY$$

where k = propensity to consume regionally (i.e., the proportion of income that is saved or spent outside of the region).

If investment (I) and current government expenditures (G) are ignored for the moment, the equation for income may be rewritten:

$$Y = aC + gX$$

but since

$$C = kY$$

$$Y = akY + gX$$

and therefore

$$Y = \frac{gX}{(1 - ak)}.$$

The factor $1/(-ak)$ is the regional multiplier, and it is the result of the chain of spending that results from the injection of outside money into the regional economy. In the first round of spending resulting from the income gained from exports X, the recipients would spend akgX in the region, producing additional income. A second round of income will result in additional regional spending of $(ak)^2gX$. Successive rounds of spending will produce the following total income:

$$Y = gX (1 + ak + (ak)^2 + \cdots \cdots) .$$

The sum of the above infinite series is equivalent to $1/(1 - ak)$ if ak is less than one and therefore:

$$Y = \frac{gX}{(1 - ak)}$$

which is identical to the other expression above.

Public and private investment spending (and government spending) will also produce the same multiplier effect so that the complete relationship is:

$$Y = \frac{(bI + cG + gX)}{(1 - ak)}.$$

The above relationship is often designated as the short-term multiplier since, in the short run, investment and regional government spending depend on factors other than the local income level.[4] In the long run, however, local investment and government expenditures will be related to income, so that only exports will remain as an exogenous input to the system. Following a similar derivation as above:

$$Y = \frac{gX}{(1 - ak - bk' - ck'')}$$

where k' = propensity to invest
    k'' = propensity of regional government to spend.

4. Charles M. Tiebout, *The Community Economic Base Study,* Committee for Economic Development, New York, 1962.

The long-run multiplier then is equal to:

$$1/(1 - ak - bk' - ck'') .$$

In both the short-run and long-run multipliers above, constant parameters are assumed. In reality, these parameters vary somewhat with the level of income so that a marginal propensity to consume or invest would be a more accurate representation. As a first approximation, a linear multiplier is useful. Further refinement may be of questionable value because of the other inaccuracies resulting from aggregation of commodities, industries, and households. Disaggregation of these units would tend to evolve into an input-output matrix, such as is used in the regional economic simulation model.

The above multipliers are also static in that they assume that production, income, and spending (consumption and investment) occur simultaneously. Actually time lags do exist between production and income, income and spending, and spending and production. Attempts to account for these dynamic effects would result in a model similar in structure to the regional economic simulation model.

In essence, the static aggregated multiplier is really a simplified regional economic model. It provides a useful measure of the gross effect of changes in regional exports on the income, employment, and general economic activity of the region.

The employment multiplier described earlier in this report is really an approximation of the long-run multiplier described above inasmuch as exports in the form of basic employment provide the only exogenous variable. Such a long-run multiplier is most meaningful in regional planning because of the interest in long-term changes. For this reason, a long-term employment-based multiplier was calculated from the data originally collected and analyzed for the regional economic simulation model. Employment data was for 1962. Estimates of basic and nonbasic employment were based upon the ratio of export sales to total sales obtained from data collected in industrial surveys of sampled firms in each industry.

The multiplier computations are shown in the following table. It is of interest to note that the multiplier 2.43, which results from a basic employment/total employment ratio of 0.409, is directly related to the ratio of manufacturing to total employment in southeastern Wisconsin, which is about 42 per cent. Such a result seems logical. Although some manufacturing industries, such as food, provide a large share of nonbasic employment and some non-manufacturing industries, such as utilities, provide some basic employment, the overall average is close to the proportion of manufacturing employment. In some urban areas, this manufacturing/total employment ratio has been used for a first estimate of the multiplier. Such an approximation should be more accurate in a region such as southeastern Wisconsin because of the important role of manufacturing and the minor role of services in export earnings.

REGIONAL MULTIPLIER = (r)

Industry	S.I.C.	Sector	Nonbasic employment (1962)	Basic employment (1962)*	Total employment (1962)*
Agriculture	A	1	8,760 (60.0%)	5,840 (40.0%)	14,600
Mining	B	2	688(100.0%)	0	688
Construction	C	3	24,822(100.0%)	0	24,822
Food	20	4	6,730 (30.6%)	15,270 (69.4%)	22,000
Leather, apparel, textiles	22,23,31	5	278 (2.0%)	13,622 (98.0%)	13,900
Paper, lumber, furniture	24,25,26	6	2,718 (33.3%)	5,436 (67.7%)	8,154
Printing & publication	27	7	4,440 (26.9%)	12,045 (73.1%)	16,485
Chemical, petroleum, & rubber	28,29,30	8	531 (10.0%)	4,779 (90.0%)	5,310
Primary metal & glass	32,33	9	2,250 (10.9%)	18,449 (89.1%)	20,699
Fabricated metals	34	10	1,124 (6.0%)	17,610 (94.0%)	18,734
Machinery, engines, & turbines	351	11	357 (3.0%)	11,553 (97.0%)	11,910
Machinery, farms	352	12	70 (0.7%)	10,366 (99.3%)	10,436
Machinery, construction, & mining	353	13	270 (2.0%)	13,265 (98.0%)	13,535
Machinery, metalworking	354	14	236 (4.0%)	5,657 (96.0%)	5,893
Machinery, special	355,6,7,8,9	15	865 (5.0%)	16,436 (95.0%)	17,301
Elec. Mach. — transmission distribution & industrial	361,362	16	4,710 (21.6%)	17,088 (78.4%)	21,798
Electrical, medical	364, 369	17	60 (2.0%)	2,972 (98.0%)	3,032

REGIONAL MULTIPLIER = (r) (continued)

Industry	S.I.C.	Sector	Nonbasic employment (1962)	Basic employment (1962)*	Total employment (1962)*
Elec. mach., household appliances	363	18	56 (2.0%)	2,725 (98.0%)	2,781
Elec. mach., communications & comp.	365,366,367	19	531 (4.0%)	12,738 (96.0%)	13,269
Transportation equipment	37	20	652 (2.0%)	31,974 (98.0%)	32,626
Instruments	38	21	185 (5.0%)	3,513 (95.0%)	3,698
Miscellaneous manufacturing	39, 19, 21	22	138 (2.0%)	6,763 (98.0%)	6,901
Transportation	40,47	23	19,467 (81.0%)	4,566 (19.0%)	24,033
Communication	48	24	3,800 (58.0%)	2,731 (42.0%)	6,531
Utilities	49	25	5,192 (90.0%)	577 (10.0%)	5,769
Trade	50 to 59	26	123,075 (98.0%)	2,510 (2.0%)	125,585
Banking & insurance	60–67, not 65	27	16,946 (80.0%)	4,237 (20.0%)	21,183
Real estate	65	28	5,553 (98.0%)	114 (2.0%)	5,667
Services	70–89, not 80	29	64,625 (96.0%)	2,693 (4.0%)	67,318
Medical services	80	30	13,850 (78.0%)	3,838 (22.0%)	17,688
Subtotal			312,979	249,367	562,346
Government		31	50,566 (95.0%)	2,661 (5.0%)	53,227
TOTAL			363,545 (59.0%)	252,028 (41.0%)	615,573 (100%)

r = 1/(Basic Employment/Total Employment) = 2.44

*Employment associated with goods or services produced within the Region and marketed outside.

SELECTED REFERENCES

Alderson Associates, Inc. *The Economic Impact of the Delaware River Ports.* Philadelphia, 1959.

American Association of Port Authorities. *Annual Report of Committee II, Standardization and Special Research.* Long Beach, Calif., 1961.

Austin, H. Russell. *The Milwaukee Story.* Milwaukee: The Milwaukee Journal, 1946.

Bruce, William George. *History of Milwaukee City and County.* 3 vols. Chicago: S. J. Clarke Publishing Co., 1922.

Chicago Association of Commerce and Industry, Research and Statistics Division. *U.S. Great Lakes Ports Monthly Statistics for Overseas and Canadian Waterborne Traffic.* Chicago, 1962–64.

Clapham, J. H. *Economic Development of France and Germany, 1815 to 1914.* Cambridge: University Press, 1921.

Delaware River Port Authority. *The Economic Impact of the Delaware River Ports.* Philadelphia, 1959.

———. *Foreign Waterborne Commerce of the Delaware River Port,* Calendar Year 1960. Philadelphia, 1961.

———. *The Value of a Ton of Cargo to the Area's Economy.* Philadelphia, 1953.

Draine, Edwin H. *Import Traffic of Chicago and Its Hinterland.* Chicago: University of Chicago, Department of Geography, 1963.

Durr, Frederick R. E. "Economic Importance of the Port of Miami," *Miami Economic Research,* Vol. VIII, no. 4 (Oct., 1955). Coral Gables, Fla.: University of Miami.

Federal Reserve Bank of Philadelphia. "The Delaware Valley and the Big East Coast Ports," *Business Review* (May, 1965), pp. 3–11.

Great Lakes Commission. *Great Lakes Foreign Commerce.* Annual Reports, 1957–60. Ann Arbor, Mich.

———. *Great Lakes Overseas Commerce.* Annual Reports, 1955–56. Ann Arbor, Mich.

Gregory, J. G. *History of Milwaukee, Wisconsin.* 4 vols. Chicago: S. J. Clarke Publishing Co., 1931.

Hamming, Edward F. *The Port of Milwaukee.* (*University of Chicago Department of Geography Research Paper,* no. 26.) Chicago, 1952.

Hoch, Irving. "A Comparison of Alternative Inter-Industry Forecasts for the Chicago Region," *Papers and Proceedings of the Regional Science Association,* V (Philadelphia, 1959), 217–35.

Jenks, Leland Hamilton. "Railroads as an Economic Force in American Development," *Journal of Economic History*, IV (May, 1944), 1–20.

Journal of Commerce and Shipping Telegraph (Liverpool, England), August 27, 1965, pp. 6–7.

Kahn, Richard F. "The Relation of Home Investment to Unemployment," *Economic Journal*, XLI (June, 1931), 173–98.

Keynes, J. M. *The General Theory of Employment, Interest, and Money.* New York: Harcourt, Brace, 1936.

Krueger, Anne O. *The Impact of the St. Lawrence Seaway on the Upper Midwest.* Minneapolis: University of Minnesota, 1963.

Locklin, D. Philip. *Economics of Transportation.* 5th ed. Homewood, Ill.: Richard D. Irwin, 1960.

Marshall, Alfred. *Principles of Economics.* 8th ed. London: Macmillan, 1920.

Mayer, Harold M. *The Port of Chicago and the St. Lawrence Seaway.* (*University of Chicago Department of Geography Research Paper*, no. 49.) Chicago, 1957.

Milwaukee. Board of Harbor Commissioners. *Chairman's Annual Reports,* 1961–64.

———. *Annual Statistical Reports,* 1961–64.

———. *Impact of the Milwaukee Public Port Development on the Community Economy.* A Report to Hon. Henry W. Maier, Mayor. Milwaukee, 1962.

———. *Port of Milwaukee.* Milwaukee, 1957.

———. *Port of Milwaukee.* Milwaukee, 1962.

———. *Port of Milwaukee.* Milwaukee, 1965.

———. *Review of Municipal Harbor Leases.* A Report to a special committee of the Common Council. Milwaukee, 1965.

———. Statement of the Board of Harbor Commissioners before U.S. Corps of Engineers at Public Hearing, Milwaukee, Wisconsin, November 29, 1956.

Port of New York Authority. *Foreign Trade at the Port of New York.* Annual Reports, 1961–65.

———. *The Port and the Community.* New York, 1956.

Schenker, Eric. "Federal Expenditures and the St. Lawrence Seaway," *Public Utilities Fortnightly*, LXIII, no. 13 (June 18, 1959), 1–7.

———. *General Cargo Capacity at Wisconsin Lake Ports.* Madison: University of Wisconsin, Bureau of Business Research and Service, 1961.

———. "Public Investment in Navigation Projects: A Case Study," *Land Economics*, XXXVI (May, 1960), 212–16.

———. "Southern State Port Authorities and Florida," *Land Economics*, XXXV, no. 1 (Feb., 1959), 35–47.

Small Business Management Research Reports. *Opportunities and Problems for Small Business in Foreign Trade via the St. Lawrence Seaway.* Minneapolis: University of Minnesota, 1964.

Smith, Adam. *An Inquiry into the Nature and Cause of the Wealth of Nations.* Modern Library ed. New York, 1937.

Southeastern Wisconsin Regional Planning Commission (SEWRPC). "Land Use-Transportation Study," Planning Report No. 7, *Inventory Findings, 1963,* Vol. I.

————. *Regional Planning Systems Study.* Waukesha, Wis., December, 1962.

————. *Technical Record,* II, no. 3 (Feb.–Mar., 1965), 9–13.

Taff, Charles A. *Traffic Management, Principles and Practices.* Rev. ed. Homewood, Ill.: Richard D. Irwin, 1959.

Tontz, Robert L., and Angelidis, Alex D. "U.S. Agricultural Export Shares by Regions and States, Fiscal Year 1963–64," *Foreign Agricultural Trade of the United States* (Department of Agriculture, ERS-Foreign-106, Nov.– Dec., 1964).

Toro, Carlos E., and Dowd, Laurence P. *The St. Lawrence Seaway, Practical Aspects for Michigan Industry.* (Michigan Business Reports, no. 37, International Series.) Ann Arbor: University of Michigan, 1961.

United States. Army Corps of Engineers. *Annual Report of the Chief of Engineers.* Annual Reports before 1952. Washington: Government Printing Office.

————. ————. *Waterborne Commerce of the United States.* Annual Reports, 1951–64. Washington: Government Printing Office.

————. Army Engineer District. *Great Lakes Harbors Study, Interim Report on Milwaukee Harbor, Wisconsin.* Chicago, 1960.

————. Army Engineer Division, North Central Corps of Engineers. *Grain Traffic Analysis to Accompany Great Lakes Harbor Study.* Chicago, June, 1965.

————. Bureau of the Census. *County and City Data Book, 1962.* Washington: Department of Commerce, 1963.

————. ————. *Domestic Movements of Selected Commodities in United States Waterborne Foreign Trade.* Washington: Department of Commerce, 1959.

————. ————. *Statistical Abstract of the United States, 1965.* Washington: Department of Commerce, 1965.

————. ————. *Survey of the Origin of Exports of Manufactured Products, 1963.* Washington: Department of Commerce, June, 1965.

————. ————. *United States Census of Population, 1960, Final Report PC(1) — 51C; Wisconsin, General Social and Economic Characteristics.* Washington: Department of Commerce, 1962.

————. ————. *United States Foreign Waterborne Commerce.* Annual Reviews, 1951–63. Washington: Department of Commerce.

————. ————. *United States Foreign Waterborne Commerce, Great Lakes Area,* Annual Reports, 1951–63. Washington: Department of Commerce.

————. Bureau of Labor Statistics. *Domestic Employment Attributable to U.S. Exports, 1960.* Washington: Department of Labor, 1962.

————. Department of Agriculture. *Changing Shipping Patterns on the St. Lawrence Seaway.* (Marketing Research Report no. 621.) Washington, August, 1963.

————. Department of Commerce. "Export Origin Study, State of Wisconsin." Unpublished, 1962.

————. ————. *U.S. Income and Output.* Washington: Office of Business Economics, 1963.

————. ————. *Value of Exports of Manufactured Products with Estimates by Region and State, and by Major Product Group: 1960.* Washington: Office of Business Economics, Bureau of International Programs, 1962.

————. ————. *Value of Exports of Manufactured Products, with Estimates by Region and State, and by Major Product Group: 1963.* Washington: Office of Business Economics, Bureau of International Programs, 1965.

————. Department of Defense. *Surface Movement of Export Cargo (to Europe and Mediterranean Areas).* Washington: Office of the Assistant Secretary of Defense (Installations and Logistics), January, 1962.

————. House Committee on Harbor and River Improvement. *A Report Upon the Improvement of Rivers and Harbors in the Jacksonville, Florida, District.* Washington, 1947.

————. Interstate Commerce Commission. *Freight Revenue and Wholesale Value at Destination of Commodities Transported by Class 1 Line-Haul Railroads, 1959.* Washington, October, 1961.

————. ————. Motor Vehicles — Wayne & Wixom, Michigan to Milwaukee, Wisconsin, No. 33945, 1963.

————. Senate Special Subcommittee of the Committee on Commerce. *Great Lakes–St. Lawrence Seaway Transportation.* Washington, September 13, 1965.

University of Virginia Bureau of Population and Economic Research. *Measuring the Impact of the Waterborne Commerce of the Ports of Virginia on Employment, Wages, and Other Key Indices of the Virginia Economy, 1953–1963.* Charlottesville, Va., 1964.

Whitbeck, Ray H. *The Geography and Economic Development of Southeastern Wisconsin. (Wisconsin Geological and Natural History Survey Bulletin no. 58.)* Madison, Wis., 1921.

Wisconsin Business Research Council. *The Economic Significance of the St. Lawrence Seaway to Wisconsin.* Madison: University of Wisconsin, Bureau of Business Research and Service, 1959.

Wisconsin Department of Resource Development. *Wisconsin Manufacturers and Foreign Trade.* Madison, Wis., 1960.

Wisconsin Division of Industrial and Port Development. *Wisconsin Ports — Gateways to the Upper Midwest.* Madison, Wis., 1959.

INDEX

Administration of port facilities, public, 4

Alderson study, 131

Army-Air Force Exchange Service, 97

Assets: accumulated appraisal of Milwaukee Public Port, 117

Astor, John Jacob, 25

Auto traffic: cross-lake, 35, 109n, 133

Board of Harbor Commissioners, Milwaukee, Wisconsin, 4, 5, 35, 36, 72, 99, 100, 116, 123, 125, 132

Breakwater, 81

Brewing industry, 3n, 50

Building materials, 132

Canada: Milwaukee's trade with, 26, 44, 148

Canal Commission, 100

Cargo: relief, 50, 53, 84–95, 150, 151; base, 84, 92–94; U.S. Department of Defense, 95, 96, 98, 154

Cargo Preference Laws, 96, 153

Chesapeake and Ohio RR, 4 passim, 101 passim, 112 passim, 140

Chicago, Port of: 3, 19; hinterland, 55, 57

Chicago and Northwestern RR, 134

Commodity Credit Corp., 95

Costs: storage, 72; transport, 144, 145; industrial fuel, 145

Delaware River: Port Authority, 5; ports, 14

Dock cranes, 108, 109

Draine, Edwin H., 54–57

Dredging, 81, 82, 100, 117–20, 141

Duluth, Minnesota: hinterland, 55, 61, 62; overseas shipping, 57, 73

Employment: port's effect on, 138–47

Exports: bituminous coal, 9, 10, 11, 25, 26; general cargo, 9, 11–14, 15; value of Midwest manufactured, 14; Great Lakes share of Midwest, 14, 15; grain, 26; petroleum, 35, 36, 108, 131; iron and steel scrap, 40, 53; machine, 49, 53; equivalent share, 62; Wisconsin Agricultural, 64; Iowa, 64, 65; Illinois, 65; Minnesota, 65; growth, potential of, 68; Atlantic Coast and Gulf ports, 68; forwarders, 75; services, economies of scale, 75; Defense Department relief cargo, 84, 87, 95–98, 132; relief shipments, 94; manufactured, 143, 144; employment generated from, 143, 144; income generated from, 144; Great Lakes, 148

Exporters Survey Questionnaire, 65–78

Federal government: port development, 6 passim, 79–83, 120, 152; shipper, 84–98

Ferry: Milwaukee car, 28–35, 149; Ann Arbor railroad, 29n; general cargo, 33. See also Chesapeake and Ohio RR; Grand Trunk Western RR

Fishing industry, 141, 142

Fjell Line, 37, 73n, 104

Foreign shipping: 41–53; Atlantic and Gulf coasts, 24; growth of, 41–44, 53; diversification of, 44; buyer's control, 72; transit time, 76, 77

Fur trade, 25

Grand Trunk Western RR, 5, 29, 104, 140

Great Lakes conference of U.S. senators, 94

Green Bay, Wisconsin, 78

Harbor Commission, advisory, 101

"Harbor Escort," 112

Harding, H. McClellan, 101

"Highway 16," 35, 109, 133